Southern Biography Series
Bertram Wyatt-Brown, Editor

THE COLOR OF SILVER

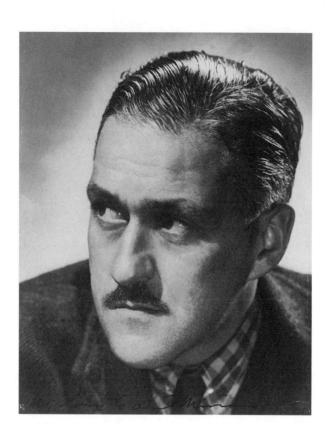

Taylor D. Littleton

THE COLOR OF SILVER

William Spratling

His Life and Art

Louisiana State University Press   *Baton Rouge*   ✠   MM

For Caroline Draughon —
given with affection and in
remembrance of many good Auburn
times /
                Taylor,
        May 21, 2000
                —

Designer: Barbara Neely Bourgoyne
Typeface: Sabon
Typesetter: Coghill Composition Co., Inc.
Printing and binder: Thomson-Shore, Inc.

Library of Congress Cataloging-in-Publication Data

Littleton, Taylor.
    The color of silver : William Spratling, his life and art / Taylor D. Littleton.
        p.   cm. — (Southern biography series)
    Includes bibliographical references and index.
    ISBN 0-8071-2533-4 (alk. paper)
        1. Spratling, William, 1900–1967. 2. Silversmiths—Mexico—Taxco de
Alarcân—Biography. 3. Silverwork—Mexico—History—20th century. 4. Decoration and
ornament—Mexico—Taxco de Alarcân—Art deco. I. Title. II. Series.

NK7198.S67 L58 2000
739.2'372—dc21   99-053775

The photograph of Dwight and Elizabeth Morrow is from *Dwight Morrow,* copyright
1935 and renewed 1962 by Harold Nicolson, reprinted by permission of Harcourt Brace
& Company and the Estate of Harold Nicolson.

Frontispiece: Spratling in about 1940. Photograph by Nickolas Muray, courtesy Spratling
family.

Opposite page 1: Spratling hallmark. Courtesy Alberto Ulrich, Sucesores de William
Spratling.

Para Lucy . . .
y para nuestra familia,
todos más puros que la plata
.980 de Spratling! . . .

Dowe and Elizabeth; George and Dorothy, Wells and Ben;
Franklin and Carole, Taylor and Lucas;
Mary Wood, Lucy and Anne, Edna and Keller

The true color of silver is white, the same color as extreme heat and extreme cold. It is also the same color as the first food received by an infant and it is the color of light. Its very malleability is an invitation to work it. It lends itself to the forming of objects in planes and in three dimensions of great desirability, objects to be done by hand in precious metals.

—William Spratling
Artes de Mexico

Contents

Illustrations

Lillian F. Marcus
Caroline Wogan Durieux
Spratling and Faulkner
Natalie Scott
Announcement for *Old Plantation Houses in Louisiana*
Woodlawn
Bel Air

following page 178

Guanajuato
The Shrine, Guadalupe
Cathedral, Vera Cruz
Dwight and Elizabeth Morrow
Diego Rivera
Panels from Rivera's *The History of Mexico (Cuernavaca and Morelos)*
Spratling, painted by David Siqueiros
Photographic chart depicting the organization of Spratling's silver workshop
Spratling, ca. 1932
Christmas card for the 1937–38 holiday season from the Taller de las Delicias
Spratling with Miguel Covarrubias and Gladys Steadham
Mary Anita Loos and Rosa Covarrubias
Pre-Columbian clay figurines
Spratling at the ranch, ca. 1948
Spratling with Lyndon and Lady Bird Johnson
Spratling at Auburn to receive honorary doctorate
Sketch of Spratling by Rene D'Harnoncourt
Spratling in his last year
Salt spoons
Maya motif bracelet
Brooch, silver and tortoiseshell
Cigarette box
Brooch and earrings
Duck sugar spoon
Child's place setting, silver

Acknowledgments

I wish to express my gratitude to a number of persons for their help and encouragement along the way:

To members of the Spratling family who made available to me letters, drawings, and documents from their personal collections: Kenneth Spratling Kirkwood and Miriam Ann Syler, grandchildren of Leckinsky W. Spratling, and Paula Wester, daughter of David Spratling; to Alberto Ulrich, owner of Sucesores de William Spratling, and his associates for their generosity in sharing the experience and archival holdings of Rancho Spratling at Taxco-el-Viejo, for commissioning the photographs taken by Jason Creagh, and for permission to reproduce photographs of Spratling designs taken by Gerardo Suter; to several of my Auburn University colleagues: Donathon Olliff, J. Hunter Peak, José Escarpanter, Bert Hitchcock, Glenn Anderson, Nicholas Davis, and the late Eugene Current-García; to my former students who from time to time became my research associates: Elizabeth Newton Lundey, Jennifer Johnston Colquitt, Julie Burch, Leigh Askins Smith, Blair Hobbs, Palmer Harris, Katie Plunk, and Allison Cahill; to Ann Waldron for undertaking several library searches on my behalf; to individuals who either through interviews or correspondence shared with me photographs or recollections of Spratling and his times: W. Kelly Mosley, Adriana Williams, C. W. Warner, the late Maltby Sykes, Ralph Hammond, Nathaniel Curtis, Jr., Katherine Hatch, John W. Scott, Howard Bahr, and Gillett Griffin; to Sandra Ramey and Mary Waters for their care and patience in preparation of the manuscript and of the index.

Additionally, I am grateful to Reeve Lindbergh and Smith College for permission to quote from the correspondence of Elizabeth Cutter Morrow in the Sophia Smith Collection at Smith College; to Amherst College for permission to quote from the Dwight Morrow Papers in Archives and Special Collections, Amherst College Library; to the Trustees of the

University of Pennsylvania for permission to quote from the Carl Zigrosser Papers, Annenberg Rare Book and Manuscript Library, University of Pennsylvania; to the Tulane University Library, Manuscript Division, for permission to quote from the Natalie Scott Papers and N. C. Curtis Papers and to reproduce certain photographs; to the New Orleans Historic Collection for permission to reproduce photographs from the Collection; to the National Autonomous University of Mexico for permission to reproduce photographs from *More Human than Divine,* © 1960; to Adriana Williams and the University of Texas Press for permission to publish a photograph from *Covarrubias,* © 1994; to Harcourt Brace and Company for permission to publish a photograph from *Dwight Morrow,* © 1935 and renewed 1962 by Harold Nicolson; to the Brooklyn Museum, the Birmingham, Alabama, Museum of Art, and the Library of Congress for various forms of assistance; to the staff of the Auburn University Archives; and to Sylvia Frank, to Bertram Wyatt-Brown, and to the editorial staff of the Louisiana State University Press. And as always, I am deeply appreciative of the generous financial support of the John and Mary Franklin Foundation of Atlanta, Georgia.

THE COLOR OF SILVER

Introduction

"Bill and his driver left the hacienda about 5:30 a.m. on Monday, 7 August, for Mexico City. It was his habit to visit Mexico every Monday (payroll purposes, I believe). It was not light; it had been storming, and a tree had fallen across the road between Taxco and Iguala. The driver swerved to avoid the tree, the car skidded and struck the embankment. . . .

"The following afternoon, Taxco's oldest church, Santa Prisca, was the scene of Bill's funeral. There were hundreds upon hundreds of people at the service, all following to the grave. The procession contained no vehicles. An entire block of people carrying huge floral wreaths was followed by the American Embassy representative, the President of the Council of Taxco and every business man in Taxco. The coffin was carried by many people, for it was nearly a mile to the cemetery. . . .

"Every house in Taxco was draped in black, every street, especially the Calle de Guillermo Spratling—had black bows attached. Even, I noticed, earth-moving trucks had small black bows attached to their front bumpers. . . .

"Bill was a great American."

This account of the funeral in 1967 of William Spratling was written by his brother David to one of their Alabama aunts,[1] and it is likely that few, if any, of the thousands in attendance would have disputed the one brother's claim about the life of the other. Certainly no confirmed resident of Taxco would have done so. The town had long ago designated Spratling as *hijo predilecto*, its favorite son, confirming the bond of affection and cultural integrity between this man and the little insulated

---

1. David Spratling to Maude Palmer, September 3, 1967. This letter and all other referenced correspondence within the Spratling family are from the collections of Kenneth Spratling Kirkwood, Gold Hill, Alabama; and of Miriam Ann Kirkwood Syler, Lanett, Alabama.

mountain village which began to flourish anew on his arrival some forty years earlier. Even before his permanent settlement there in 1930, his sensitive responses to the history, art, and contemporary spirit of Mexico, recorded in his journal publications of the late twenties, seem always to have made him more *amigo* than *gringo,* even sanctioning something of that native identity suggested in the portrait painted by his friend David Siqueiros in 1931. By then he had already set about his life's work of conserving, redeeming, and interpreting the ancient culture of his adopted country. And though it probably would not have occurred to anyone in the crowd of some twenty thousand on that hot August afternoon, the simple tributes of homage and grief, fastened even to the humble working vehicles of the town, ironically placed the life of William Spratling in an historical juxtaposition to that of an earlier foreigner— Hernando Cortéz—who arrived in the Taxco region and whose presence led to the plunder and suppression of the very artistic and spiritual life that Spratling sought to resurrect.

It is, in fact, this sense of recovering and what we would call today "recycling" the past that informs Spratling's finest writing and artistic work and that should be the most proper legacy of the life that ended shortly after the collision on the rain-swept Iguala road: his renderings or discussions, for example, of ante-bellum Louisiana architecture and old New Orleans ironwork; or, more significantly, his descriptions of the pre-Conquest Indian life, with its dark, violent, patient charm, which he called "little Mexico" and whose motifs he would incorporate into the elegant modernism of his revolutionary designs—the "Spratling style"—in silver, wood, tin, and other native materials. Indeed, his silver designs even by the end of the 1930s were already in the process of becoming the foremost influence on an entire generation of Mexican and American silversmiths, now routinely described as the "American School." His resurrection at Taxco in the 1930s of a moribund art form, together with his entrepreneurial genius, have been no less pervasive in their aesthetic influence than in their permanent effect on the economic life of Mexico. To be sure, that legacy is today very much alive among collectors who know the extraordinary value of the increasingly rare original Spratling hallmarks; and, to a lesser extent, among cultural historians aware of Spratling's critical role in illuminating for an international audience what he himself portrayed as "figures in a Mexican renaissance." And beyond his interpretive associations with Diego Rivera, Covarrubias, Siqueiros, and other Mexican artists, he is still visible too in the relatively minor but yet continuing intersections of his career with those lives more familiar to us: with Faulkner's, Sherwood Anderson's, and Hart Crane's, for example, and with the brief but rich density of the artistic life in New Orleans of the twenties.

Yet the diverse identity of this Spratling has been submerged in that of another, whose shape was confirmed within a week of his death in one of *Time*'s matter-of-fact obituaries, which remembered the "New York–born architect-artist" and "reviver" of the silver craft industry in Taxco who had spent most of his life "building the village into a major tourist attraction."[2] It is a remembrance he would have disliked, suggesting as it did a continuing cultivation of the tourist trade toward which he had felt an increasing ambivalence as his own reputation gradually began to rise, during the thirties and forties, as one of the best-known and most admired Americans in Mexico. At least he was spared in the obituary the "Silver Bill" title that he had hated ever since it appeared in a widely read magazine article just after the war, one of several popular notices connecting Spratling's presence with the quaint silver bracelets to be found in the shops of sunny, colonially picturesque Taxco, about which American schoolchildren had been reading for years. And it was immediately after the war that his popular reputation, which, obviously, followed him to his death, was reinforced by Hollywood itself, using for a special color film on his achievements in the Mexican silver industry a title he liked much better: *The Man from New Orleans*.[3]

He liked the title because it suggested what in fact was true, that his Louisiana years in the twenties had been an artistic and professional prelude to his creative flowering in Mexico, just as the same period had prefigured the greatest work of his young New Orleans roommate and collaborator, William Faulkner, whose worldwide distinction would begin to emerge in 1946, the year that *The Man from New Orleans* was filmed. For Spratling, however, the end of the war would conclude the period of his greatest commercial success, begun early at Taller de las Delicias, which subsequently became Spratling y Artesanos, when he

2. *Time*, August 18, 1967, p. 70.
3. Spratling wrote in November 1947 to the producer of the film, Luis Osorna Barona, that it was "understood that the tentative title, 'Silver Bill,' will be changed to one more adequate and less familiar." Auburn University Archives. The article was by J. P. McEvoy, "Silver Bill: Practical Good Neighbor," *Reader's Digest* 47 (September 1945): 19–22.

made at least one fortune in the manufacture and design of silver, shipping his tableware, jewelry, and occasional pieces from Taxco throughout the world.

Spratling may well have intuitively understood that the kind of commercial success he had worked so hard to achieve was not guaranteed to last, especially when the war's end opened up again the international gold and silver markets, the latter of which he had managed to dominate since the late thirties. In his private correspondence, as we shall see, there is considerable bitterness expressed at the disastrous decline of Spratling y Artesanos following World War II and at the fraudulent deceptions of his American partners in the process. However, by the time some twenty years later he was about to give a public account of the matter, he seems to have reconciled that significant turn in his career as another ironic example of the *Americano* exploitation of Mexico. It is probably no exaggeration to say that his departure then for a few miles south to Taxco-el-Viejo was a relief, and the last third of his life he was to spend there was properly marked by the distinctions and reputation for which the early entrepreneurial years and the gradual absorption during those years of the older culture had prepared him: the maturity of his art, then produced on a much smaller scale in the new workshops of "William Spratling, S.A."; the establishment of his reputation as one of the finest collectors in Mexico of pre-Columbian art; the compilation of his classic assessment of this civilization's ancient sculpture, *More Human than Divine*; and the widespread museum exhibitions in both Mexico and the United States of his lifetime achievements. Indeed, by then his career had assumed an almost legendary status, a status that encouraged the three men subsequently elected to the U.S. presidency in the 1960s decade, along with hundreds of others, to seek him out in his final home at Taxco-el-Viejo. The "Cellini of Taxco" was an American they wanted to see, one who had attained his extraordinary distinction in another country.

But long before his move to the ranch below Taxco, Spratling had also begun to perfect another dimension of his multiple persona. Not only was he already a man in whom his Mexican compatriots took pride and placed great trust, he was gradually becoming an American presence in Mexico that formed a visible and culturally attractive link between a steady stream of prominent American visitors—literary and political figures, artists, movie stars—and the country they wanted to see and experience. As early as 1931, for example, he was moving with great ease and confidence both in Mexico City and Taxco among the group of Guggenheim Fellows that included the painter Marsden Hartley and writers Katherine Anne Porter and Hart Crane. By then he was already at work on *Little Mexico,* which would be published in 1932, increasing his popular identity and confirming further friendships with Americans like Ambassador Dwight Morrow and Under Secretary of State Nelson Rockefeller, both of whom found in Spratling a talented and fully acclimated resident who shared their own commitment to strengthening political ties between their country and Mexico.

This side of the Spratling legend would continue to grow in the postwar years and up to the time of his death, although gradually he became less identified in the role of cultural agent, an important "man to know" in Mexico, becoming instead a prominent "personality"—irascible, generous, wary, "enigmatic," to use one of his own favorite words, yet sufficiently authoritative to be sought out in the environs of Taxco, the little town that through Spratling's artistic vision had been transformed into the "Florence of Mexico." But Spratling's personal reputation in this vein has faded also, existing now primarily in *File on Spratling,* the autobiography he developed in 1966 and which was posthumously published within a month of the letter written by his brother David describing the Taxco funeral.

The two fairly well known facts concerning Spratling's artistic and economic influence have given to his career an unquestioned significance. What we know about the man's life, however, is little indeed, especially if we set aside the anecdotal and somewhat romanticized accretions, some of them invented by Spratling himself, that are customarily repeated in cursory accounts of his career. Thus far, however, there has been no sustained attempt to integrate the career with the life which, arguably, can hold its own as one of the most interesting of all those of the American expatriates of the twenties and thirties. The portion of that life we know least about, what might be construed as his artistic apprenticeship, is contained in those experiences that preceded the emergence of the public persona that would be sustained and heightened even beyond his death. Spratling's youthful years in Alabama of family stress, frustrated anxiety, and artistic orientations toward drawing and sculpture were somehow preparatory for the liberation in New Orleans of his personal charm and social adaptability, together with his maturation as architectural artist and perceptive essayist. It was above all, however, the unexpected flowering of his powers of cultural absorption, first in the New Orleans scene and subsequently in that of the Mexican Renaissance, that gradually gave a focus to the sometimes innovative but often painfully disappointing opportunism that marked the period from 1922 to 1932. In that latter year, while barely surviving the Great Depression, he published *Little Mexico,* completed after a full-time residency of less than five years, and the volume testified, in the words of Mexico's greatest artist—and one of the greatest painters of our century—to this *norteamericano*'s exceptional identity: "because you love Mexico and because Mexico loves you—it is your right to make a portrait of that which you know so well."

Neither Rivera nor Spratling knew then that the book's simplicity of style and the precision of its "portrait" of a Mexico of intransigent memory and myth lying beneath the life of the nation still struggling to enter the twentieth century would be a significant verbal prelude to the brilliant experiment just beginning to take shape at the Las Delicias workshop in Taxco. There in the next five years Spratling's vision of a silvercraft of ancient lineage resurrected in designs that created "a Mexican style of our times" became triumphant, both in the economic history of Mexico and, of course, in the reputation of its creator.

The usual kinds of sources for a biographical investigation of the range of Spratling's life and career have previously been few. Of course there has always been his considerable legacy of essays and drawings, plus some sets of letters available in archival settings. And, too, there is the posthumously published autobiography, *File on Spratling,* curiously inaccurate though nevertheless, as we shall see, a valuable resource. But he kept little of his correspondence and some of that has been lost over the years in the high river waters periodically washing through Rancho Spratling. The opportunity for this study, however, to interpret what he drew and what he wrote within an epistolary chronology has been made possible by the generosity of members of the Spratling family and of Alberto Ulrich, owner of Sucesores de William Spratling. The good memory of the present owner of the Spratling family home at Gold Hill, Alabama, was especially valuable in this regard, recalling a collection of documents that had lain for at least twenty years in one of the plantation outbuildings; the principal yield from this was a series of over sixty highly personalized letters written by Spratling, mostly to his brother

David, during his high school and college years, providing original sources for this period where none were previously known to exist. Hearts of those interested in such matters must falter slightly at the knowledge that a similar collection was, for unknown reasons, destroyed by David on his retirement from military service, this one covering Spratling's early years in New Orleans when he and Faulkner were sharing the St. Peter Street apartment and Spratling was himself very much a participant in the important artistic ambience of that twenties epoch, whimsically recorded in the two young men's "mirror of our scene," *Sherwood Anderson and Other Famous Creoles.*

It is within this youthful correspondence that we must look first in our effort to find in William Spratling's life a shape and coherence beyond the sterile parameters of the *Time* obituary and to illuminate also the human identity of the public persona autobiographically created just before his death. That effort, continuing through an analysis of his ultimate artistic achievements, of the personal correspondence of his later years, and of the autobiography itself, will be, if successful, nothing more or less than a proper act of reclamation, of remembering a richly diverse American life whose unique aesthetic legacy is but part of its larger cultural achievement of profoundly influencing our attitudes toward a civilization different from our own. Given its history and conclusion, that life began in an unlikely place—in the small community of Sonyea, New York, although one's fancy might observe that the order and discipline of the Shaker buildings that the young Spratling would have seen there in his childhood years early in the century found their place in the designs he ultimately created in another country, a thousand miles to the south.

1

Alabama

"Things look pretty black without a college course. When I think of what life will be for me if I quit my education now, I shudder. In three or four years I would be getting $120 per mo. as a draughtsman—and there I'd be stuck.

"I've got to see Uncle Leck and convince him I'm worth a college education. You know I'm not 18 yet—it's too soon to give up."

This youthful assessment and declaration was written by "Billy" Spratling to his brother David in July of 1918, when he was working, following his first year of college, as a summer employee in Birmingham as an architectural draftsman. The year had been one of contradictory experiences, of personal achievement and loneliness, but it had also initiated what became a critical period—extending into the summer of 1919—in the development of the individual who would be created in his autobiography almost fifty years later. That autobiographical file would not, however, contain any notice of memories such as this one, or scores of others that the older brother would regularly share with the younger almost on a weekly basis during these formative years. In fact, the drama of the first third of Spratling's life is crowded into thirteen pages of a 230-page text, with five of those being devoted to a description of a European freighter passage he took with some college friends in the summer of 1921. He mentions his mother and father, but gives almost no suggestion of the sense of separation and longing for family bonding that he expresses over and over again in his letters to David.

Of course, the self created in *File on Spratling* would not allow such expression. It did not fit into the confident and fully liberated persona that seemed to have been born when Billy Spratling, just before turning twenty-two, settled into his new address in New Orleans. There is a hint or two, however, even in the autobiography, of the family stresses he cheerfully for the most part suppressed in the file. The one reference to his mother, for example, records that she "died from over-work sewing for former social friends." And he states that his own period of dislocation began shortly thereafter, when the "comfortable surroundings" of his childhood disappeared.

The emotional distance covered between Spratling's loss of an apparently stable, nurturing family structure and the critical episode of evaluation and commitment contained in the 1918 letter to his brother found its geographical parallel when he began in 1912 a long journey southward from New York, first to live with relatives in Atlanta and thence to Alabama to live with still others. He had been born in 1900 at Sonyea, New York, where his father, William Philip Spratling II, had since 1893 been superintendent of Craig Colony, a state institution for epilepsy treatment. He was named William Philip after his father and grandfather. He had two older sisters, Lucile and Wilhelmina; and David was born in 1903. Both sides of his family were dominated by medical doctors. Spratling's paternal grandfather, William Philip Spratling I, Civil War veteran and successful plantation owner in the Oak Bowery community of east Alabama, had provided three of his sons with medical training. His mother, Anna Gorton, a native of New York, was the daughter of Dr. David Allyn Gorton, a leading advocate of eugenics and founder of the Eugenics Society of America. His only maternal uncle, Eliot Gorton, was also a medical doctor and founder of Fair Oaks, an experimental psychiatric hospital in Summit, New Jersey.

Spratling's father had received his M.D. degree from the College of Physicians and Surgeons in Baltimore, Maryland, and subsequently worked for the Marine Hospital Service (forerunner of the United States Public Health Service) before joining the staff of the New Jersey Hospital for the Insane at Morris Plains. While working at Morris Plains, Dr. Spratling met and married Anna Gorton, whose brother Eliot was then also on the staff of the Morris Plains hospital. Following his appointment by the state of New York as director of the new epilepsy treatment center being established at Sonyea, the former Shaker community south of Rochester, Dr. Spratling developed pioneering principles of treatment that were widely dispersed in his scientific publications and the influential text *Epilepsy and Its Treatment* (1904), leading to his being generally recognized as the leading authority on the diagnosis and treatment of epilepsy in the first decade of the century.[1] Theodore Roosevelt highly complimented his work, and Mark Twain, whose daughter Jean may have been one of his patients, became a friend of the family. It was into this atmosphere of scientific energy and distinction contained within the neat symmetrical designs of Shaker buildings that Spratling was born and passed his early years. But by 1908 the social isolation of Anna, the lack of educational opportunities for the children, and the tuberculosis infection of both Anna and their daughter Wilhelmina led the father to resign his position at Craig Colony. After a period of convalescence in Bermuda, where Spratling remembers that Twain visited the family, the father returned to Baltimore and established a private practice, serving briefly on the faculty of the College of Physicians and Surgeons.

Dr. Spratling's own deteriorating medical condition and the diagnosis that Anna and Wilhelmina would not recover initiated the difficult period for the family that lies behind Spratling's slightly bitter reference in the autobiography to his mother's death. She had repaired with the children to the less frigid climate of Summit, New Jersey, to live with her brother Eliot and his wife Bertha; though the family was not to be permanently re-united after that, visits of the father seemed to hold out that possibility. "Dear papa," wrote Billy in July of 1909,

> Mama sezes to hurry and come to see us because we are lonesome without you. Chink [David] and I have a fine time out under the big willow tree. We go over to Ant Berthas three or four times a day.

and, again, in August:

> Dear Papa
> I recived your letter this morning and was glad to get it. Mama said she would be verry disappointed if you do not come to Azbearrie [Asbury Park?] and meet her.

Certain surviving letters indicate that marital discord may have caused the fragmentation of the family. A remarkable letter written from Berlin in 1936 to Spratling alludes to troubles. The letter is from the nurse of the three older children, who had lived with the family from 1889 to 1902. She and Spratling had miscommunicated about a visit following

---

1. For a valuable and extensive analysis of Dr. Spratling's career, see Edward J. Fine, Debra L. Fine, Lilli Sentz, "The Importance of Spratling," *Archives of Neurology* 51 (January 1994): 82–86.

his trip over on the *Hindenburg;* the letter is a tearful expression of regret as well as a remembrance of the family before its separation:

> Do you remember Sonyea? In one of her letters Mamma [Mrs. Spratling] wrote me: "Billie boy is still the dashing of our household and Oh! Elfriede, if you will come back to live with us, you will have two of the finest boys you ever saw." . . . Until Nov. 08 Mamma wrote me to come for she needed me so much. After I was married I knew that Mamma in spite of you all really was alone always. . . . Mamma was a complecated character and expected much from everybody. But I was to young at that time and did not know anything about men. Yesterday I laid all the letters from Mamma and all the pictures from Sonyea ready for you to look at.[2]

Virtual confirmation of marital discord appears in a letter from 1909. Worried about her husband's health and the uncertainty of the domestic future, Mrs. Spratling in her letter wondered about the arrangements he had made to work in Baltimore, where, she said, at least he would have the "advantage of being a big light among the lesser ones."

> My spirit is quite crushed. My heart is sad, and there is not a hope for the future that makes my life worth the living. . . . I have no heart for social things anymore. I feel now depressed in a society of people who had a natural and happy life. I think you ought to consider a little the welfare and future prospects of your children—it is hard for them to have to suffer for the failure of their parents to make their home a happy one.

Both mother and daughter died in 1910. And in 1911 Dr. Spratling suffered a physical and, apparently, emotional breakdown as well. The father's condition led him to move with the children to the home of his own father in Alabama, and shortly thereafter Spratling, his brother David, and older sister Lucile became wards of their paternal grandfather when Dr. Spratling, in his continuing convalescence, moved farther south to the home of Dr. D. C. Main, a Baltimore friend, near Welaka, Florida.

The highly compressed and somewhat inaccurate chronology recorded in the autobiography for the years 1912 to 1916 suggests that this difficult period in Spratling's life was one that, recalled fifty years later, he either did not wish to resurrect, or could not. The few months at the end of 1912 that the three children spent on the family plantation, called Roamer's Roost, near Gold Hill and Auburn, Alabama, are re-

2. Elfriede Glitzl to "My dear Billie boy," October 15, 1936.

membered in a few rather idyllic sentences, and the grandfather is surrounded with affectionate tall tales. But by the end of the year the
children were separated, each going to live with uncles or aunts: Lucile
to her Gorton relatives in New Jersey; David to a paternal uncle—a navy
career doctor, Leckinski Ware Spratling ("Uncle Leck"), in Pennsylvania;
and Billy to another paternal uncle, also a medical doctor, Edgar Johnson
Spratling, in Atlanta. Shortly before their grandfather's death in 1913,
he added a codicil to his will diverting to them their father's share of the
senior Spratling's estate and providing for their guardianship to pass to
Uncle Leck.

Although Spratling states in the file that his Uncle Edgar (who is called
"Uncle Johnny" in the brothers' correspondence) "did not think much
of this little northern nephew," there is nothing to indicate that the period he spent in Atlanta, where he began attending Georgia Tech High
School, was not one of growing stability or that he was not finding in
Uncle Johnny an image of male reassurance which had begun to disappear from the family with the illness of Dr. Spratling in 1908–1909. And
it was at this time that his artistic interests in drawing and sketching
found a wider correspondence when in the summer of 1915, invited to
the home of his maternal relatives the Gortons, he attended for several
weeks the Art Students League in New York City. But in the fall of that
year, the poor health of Uncle Johnny's wife led to yet another re-location, back to the family home in Alabama where David and his guardian's family were temporarily residing awaiting Uncle Leck's naval
reassignment. Three days before Christmas, Spratling's father died from
a hunting accident in Florida. Eight months later, in August of 1916,
Uncle Johnny was murdered in Atlanta by a deranged patient.

When Uncle Leck shortly after Dr. Spratling's death took David with
him to his new assignment at the Norfolk Naval Hospital, Billy was left
in east Alabama. He was fifteen years old and had experienced since he
was eight the continuing dislocation of his childhood family structure,
and the deaths of his mother, his grandfather, his father, and an uncle
with whom he had lived and whom he apparently admired. Moreover,
he was now placed in an essentially feminine familial environment of
aunts and cousins whom he did not know at all well. It is difficult to
surmise, of course, the effect of all this on the young Spratling. But the
death of his father, the circumstances of which had raised the possibility
of suicide, seemed quite troubling, for in December of 1916, the anniver-

sary month, he sent to his brother David a copy of the "poem that Papa had composed" during his incapacitated year of 1910. The poem, which Spratling said his father's sister Corinne had given to him, is a brooding reflection on the approach of death, and in its final line it rejects suicide as a means of ending one's life. "Always remember," the older brother wrote to the younger, "what it says and revere it."

How ambivalent he may have felt about the last years of his father's life and their impact on his mother and on his own situation, or in fact how much he carried over such feelings into his troubled relationship with Uncle Leck, his last legal guardian, we cannot know. But we can with some confidence propose that the Spratling who would in a few years leave Alabama and begin a life marked by a strong, even fierce, sense of independence and self-reliance and by an unwaveringly ironic view of experience was largely fashioned during this period. He would report to David in March that he "would be going up to Oakbowery soon & see how the ivey is doing on Papa's grave," that "it must look nice by now," and he included a sketch of the marble slab and urn that Aunt Clara has "put over Uncle John's grave." And on August 24, the first anniversary of Uncle Johnny's death, after writing to David in May that he was "worried" about the upcoming trial (of the accused murderer), and how "of course, the papers will be full of it," he wrote that "Aunt Jessie, Aunt Mamie and I took flowers to his grave." But references to the two senior Spratlings, who had provided for him a home and some measure of security, gradually disappear from the teenager's correspondence. They are replaced with continuing but futile attempts to secure a closer relationship with his brother David, whom he implored to think about joining him in Alabama, and to win approval from Uncle Leck, on whom he depended for financial allocations from his father's estate.

The crisis of identity which the young Spratling would begin to resolve only after the climactic confrontation with Uncle Leck is fully recorded in his letters to David during the two years between 1916, when he completed his senior year at Auburn High School, and 1918 when, during his first year at the college a few blocks away, then called Alabama Polytechnic Institute, he encountered an environment whose structure and encouraging response to his developing artistic capacities seemed gradually to counter the dysfunctional patterns of his own family life. And it is certainly revealing to see in the highly personalized references in these letters, references so notably absent in the autobiography, the stirrings of those qualities of self-discipline and achievement under personal stress that would not be released from the psychological file, although had they been, they would have rendered more credible the continuing success story that *File on Spratling* so nonchalantly records.

The complex mixture of feelings the young Spratling experienced and gradually assimilated during these two years fuses his continuing sense of loneliness and displacement with his rising satisfaction in his various artistic experiments. Even though in the autobiography he states that family pressure on him to prepare for a suitable profession prevented him from declaring early for a career in art and design, nothing in his letters to his brother substantiates this claim. He did, in fact, move quickly into the teenage society of the small college town. He was popular enough to be elected senior class president, and he designed the class ring, proudly sending to David a sketch of its configuration of letters. Early during his final high school year he began experimenting with plaster molds, which he hoped to sell for Christmas expenses ("I have asked Uncle Leck to send me Xmas money and I *hope* he will"), and later in the year he sent David a self-portrait. His letters during these months are full of news of cousinly outings and the social kindnesses of relatives and of Mrs. Thach, wife of the president of the college. And his letter of May 16, 1917, describing his high school graduation and the exchange of gifts with a girl, Gladys Steadham, who would remain a life-long friend, was a happy one: "Well Dave . . . I'm ready for college. I graduated with honors. Gladys gave me a box of candy she'd made—she has been mighty good to me—and I gave her a bouquet of sweet peas."[3]

Even, however, prior to this charming euphoric sense of having completed, finally, an important stage of his life, Billy Spratling as early as the winter of that year, as he reported in a letter to David on March 11, had unsuccessfully sounded out his older sister, Lucile, now pursuing a nursing career, about coming to live with her in New York. And within two weeks of the graduation letter, he found himself isolated once more, this time working for room and board on the east Alabama farm of his grandfather's widow. "I wish you were here," he wrote to David on May 31.

3. Gladys Steadham (later Stewart), would enroll in college with Spratling in 1917. They kept up an occasional correspondence for over forty years.

I don't have much of a time by myself—and, really, cousin Ella and Andrew are not entertaining associates. Whatever I do for pleasure, whether it's berry-picking, reading or grazing Dandy, the colt, I do it by myself. I drop peas, set out sweet potatoes and tomatoes, and replant corn and peas. Next week I will probably be chopping some late cotton. . . . Do you think there are any chances of your getting down this summer?

The summer was indeed difficult. By mid-July Billy had moved into the town of Opelika to live with another aunt, securing a job first at the local swimming pool and a few weeks later at the "picture-show," earning $20 a month and paying $16.00 for room and board. College lay ahead and somehow might help to resolve the restlessness and sense of alienation that are expressed repeatedly in his July and August letters:

I feel more and more that there's not room for me here. As much as I hate Atlanta I may have to go there for a job. You can imagine my position. [July 14]

David, I am more disconnected than ever now. On account of crowded conditions here at Aunt MW's, I am spending the nights at Aunt Mamie's and eating here. [July 17]

I'm supporting myself for the first time in my life. . . . I was offered a job at the picture show at $5.00 a week and took it. You don't know how independent I feel. You can just bet your boots I don't live on kinfolks and be pitied and despised next summer. [August 2]

Your letter and Uncle Leck's came. Uncle Leck didn't say much—he seems imprest with the idea that I have an overpowering sense of "hard luck." Fact is, I never felt better or more independent than now. Once in a while when I think of all our past troubles, etc., I get the blues. Then I'll write to you and tell you how lonely I feel. Consequently Uncle Leck thinks I brook on hard luck. At present I am happy over the prospect of a four year course at college—a degree. . . . I thought Uncle Leck would be pleased at my supporting myself, but he didn't mention it. [August 19]

The continuing failure, as he saw it, to win the approval of the last authoritative male Spratling in his immediate family would continue to haunt Billy during these critical transitional years of 1917–1919. And that failure was often charged with feelings of resentment at what he perceived as parsimonious treatment in the matter of his allowance. This resentment may well have lasted a lifetime, for the most absolute misrepresentation of fact in the entire autobiography seems to occur when

Spratling, in the brief passage describing his college years, states that he "received no money from home" but had been dexterous enough in his artwork commissions and waiting on tables to earn his "bed and board." Whatever his psychological reasons may have been for suppressing something he could not possibly have forgotten, the example is very much within the pattern of the casual remembrances of *File on Spratling*, which essentially reconstructs a life congenial to the final self-image of its author. Spratling may, however, have tried to recapture some of these feelings of resentment and anxiety over approval through the brief autobiographical allusion that he must in 1917 have seemed "inhibited" and "frequently depressed" because his "sensibility" was at odds with the atmosphere in a "college football town." His enthusiastic entrance into the pluralities of freshman experience, however, as described in his letters during this year subverts the accuracy of this interpretation. He *was* frequently depressed, he *did* at times get "the blues," but not because of his new collegiate environment. In fact, the strains of depression experienced by his mother and father seem not to have emerged in either Lucile or David; and, as we shall see, Spratling's creative life, even in its most disappointing periods, shows no comparable sign or influence. All of his financial unease and desire for some kind of authoritative endorsement, which many of his letters to David indirectly request, did not erode his sense of family pride and loyalty, which likewise does not appear in the autobiographical file but would nevertheless be held for the rest of his life, as his correspondence from New Orleans and Mexico confirms. Even in the August 19 "hard luck" letter, for example, he asked if Uncle Leck passed his examinations for promotion to medical director, "I hope well, because I am very proud of him."

In *File on Spratling* Uncle Leck is mentioned only once in passing, and the long-distance drama of youthful maturation and male authority is acted out entirely in the brotherly correspondence. Uncle Leck, himself firmly committed to the regimented life of a naval doctor, was undoubtedly a stern and exacting guardian, certainly not given to the kind of praise his young Alabama nephew needed. He required Billy to send him regular statements of his expenses and to make specific petitions for additional money. But there is some evidence to suggest that he had a sincere desire to save as much of his deceased brother's estate as possible until the three Spratling children would reach their majority. Even during this difficult period for Billy, some of his resentment toward his guardian moderated, and ten years later he would write affectionate inscriptions to him and to his wife, Aunt Miriam, on copies of his early publications in *Architectural Forum*—inscriptions that were sincere beyond question but were also doubtless a kind of quiet affirmation that his achievements were beginning to triumph over what as a college freshman he had perceived was Uncle Leck's low opinion of his future possibilities:

> Your letter [David] gives me a great deal of sympathy and almost satisfaction. I haven't been able to understand Uncle Leck's attitude toward me for a long time and I mentioned in my last letter to him his lack of encouragement. He seems to take it for granted that I will never be more than a ditch-digger and that there is no hope for me. Well—I'll show him.

Written on May 11, 1918, toward the end of Billy's first year at Auburn, this letter and the attitude it expresses led directly to the mid-summer confrontation with Uncle Leck anticipated by Billy's statement of resolution with which this chapter begins.

During the war year of 1917–1918, scores of college freshmen at Auburn and elsewhere no doubt were worried about their financial support. Billy was clever in using his talents for drawing and painting as a means to supplement his income, but even so his letters are notably marked by almost a week-to-week anxiety about money for supplies, clothes, and some costly dental work he required preparatory to enrollment. More often than not, the shortage of funds was intertwined with his sense of family. For example, he had not seen his sister Lucile since she went north in 1913, and her infrequent letters were shared by the two younger brothers. He had been unable to send her anything for the Christmas of 1917, and when he learned in February that she would soon be going to France as an army nurse, he bought sugar with money he had earned painting signs, persuaded "Cousin Leila" to make candy, and sent it off. But Lucile had already sailed. When the candy, "hard as a rock," was returned by the postal service, the dispirited Billy could only lament to David in a March 11 letter the great "waste" of 50 cents for the sugar and 35 cents postage and close with almost the inevitable query, "Aren't any of the family coming down to the plantation this spring?"

That first college Christmas holiday, which was also the second anniversary of his father's death, had been especially lonely. Uncle Leck had briefly visited Gold Hill in early December, and a month earlier Billy had written to David how a visit to the plantation property, especially seeing the "Bungalo" house, where he and David had apparently lived for a period with their father, made him homesick. As the holidays approached, he expressed to David the most melancholy and poignant feelings recorded in the entire multi-year correspondence: "I'm going to Atlanta to see Aunt Clara, but there is nothing for me there. I suppose I'll visit the Palmers and Cousin Ella too, and anybody else who'd invite me" (December 9). And toward the end of that academic year, he was still wistfully expressing his sense of isolation:

Dear Dave:—

Heard from you today about your debate, etc. Do you know Cousin Ella told me that Aunt Belle told her, that Aunt Emma told her that Cousin Carrie Wright told her that Uncle Leck was very busy. I believe that's the way the news reached me. Can't you tell me if any of the family expect to be down this summer? [May 27]

But as we seek to know better the celebrated but rather distant figure of Taxco's William Spratling through examining his early life, we should observe further that during his first college year he seemed gradually to be working free of his pervasive sense of displacement. Just before the fall term began, he had written to David that he had earned the money for a birthday present that he had sent to Uncle Leck and that before the summer ended he had "wanted to see him particularly so I could talk to him." This August expression implying a need to interpret himself to his guardian, together with other letters that month about being "pitied and despised" by kinfolks, about Uncle Leck's adverse judgments, and his resolution the following July to confront Uncle Leck about his future—these epistolary moments "frame" this critical year of 1917–1918 in the life of Billy Spratling.

Even a cursory reading of his first college letter to his brother (September 26) suggests in its eight closely written pages a genuine excitement in his encounters with new faces and experiences. Uncle Leck had not responded in over a month to his request for money for architectural supplies and had not acknowledged either receiving "Mr. Britling," the birthday gift, which was apparently a copy of H. G. Wells's *Mr. Britling Sees It Through*, the wartime novel which had been published in 1916 and whose purchase, given Bill's financial straits, must have represented a genuine sacrifice. But "you asked me to write about college—There isn't a better life going," he states, and goes on to describe with considerable good humor such matters as the customary hazing by upper-classmen and his induction into the newly instituted Reserve Officers Training Corps, which immediately issued him an 1844-model rifle—"it reminds one of a blunder buss—the devil to clean." This letter, in fact, with its blend of a new life with the old, sets the tone for this period of Spratling's withdrawal from the self-absorption and occasional touches of self-pity that, however understandable, Uncle Leck had accurately diagnosed in the "hard luck" letter. This is not to say that he ever lost completely his sense of loneliness, expressed so poignantly as we have already seen as he faced his first college Christmas. But as he entered a new environment, he seemed to realize that his Auburn and Gold Hill relatives were indeed caring and supportive. He was now living at his Cousin Leila Terrell's boardinghouse, and he records that her "great big 4 layer cake" helped to make his eighteenth birthday a happy one: "Bless her. She certainly is sweet to me." And he had begun to hear more from his sister Lucile, then getting ready for France. With the developing ironic sense of self that he would nurture for the rest of his life, he could obliquely refer to his perennial lack of funds by describing Lucile's birthday gift as "a beautiful, valuable, significant, useless pocketbook," while in the next paragraph he could sound his familiar note of family dispossession by stating "I am rather apprehensive lest we see her again."

He occasionally alludes to the fruitless twice-a-day trips to the post office that every college freshman has made, hoping for letters from home, and to the monotony of cold winter days in a small college town. But in the main, these letters are happy ones, describing social and intellectual dimensions previously unknown. And the letters, too, as we read them eighty years later, evoke a kind of curious nostalgia, as we witness, in a sense, the almost artless patriotism with which a college community integrated its life with the nation's hurried preparations for entering the Great War: "Last night Gladys and I went to the Websterian lit. society to a mock trial. . . . a very fat rat for violation of the food conservation regulations as laid down by Hoover, and was very good" (October 7).

Spratling's impressionable though sensitive immersion into college life and the new identity he was gradually discovering there would no doubt sooner or later have led to some kind of expression to his guardian of confidence in his own self-worth. That expression was hastened, however, by the entrance into his world of a new figure of male authority, not one who would in any sense displace the ties of emotional history that ran beyond Uncle Leck to Uncle Johnny and to the distinguished physician-father Spratling, but one who would help the young Spratling resolve that history and usher him toward the first stage in his adult life. His name—the only one mentioned in the autobiography specifically connected to Spratling's college years—was Frederic Biggin, and he was head professor of architecture. He appears briefly in *File on Spratling* as "a nervous little man with a genius for teaching" and who "impressed in my mind principles of design and architecture as a sort of religion. I flatter myself I was his star pupil that year." This is one of the few elements chosen from the autobiographical file that in no way appears to have been re-interpreted. "I like architecture better every day," he wrote to David on November 15 early in the fall term, "and prof. Biggin seems to take a special interest in developing my free-hand drawing. . . . I have drawing every afternoon from 2–4 or 5. . . . I have no class on Saturday. Instead I *draw*."

And draw he did, as he recalls in the autobiography, everything from banners for football rallies to lettering menus on shop windows to artwork for the college yearbook. Little in these early efforts could be called a style, but perhaps in the imaginative discipline of the yearbook drawings for 1918 and succeeding years, which he carefully retained in a scrapbook for the rest of his life, appear the beginnings of the ultimate Spratling expression that would eventually be influenced by his architectural study and practice and by his response to an ancient and sophisticated native culture far beyond Alabama. The range of his experimental work, however, during his freshman year also included more serious work and must have served as a private counterpoint to the occasional remembrance of what he described to David of "all our past troubles."[4] He entered the design competition for medals to be given as student prizes in architecture and engineering; each winner would receive a prize of ten dollars and, as he noted to David whom he exhorted to "pray for me," "maybe . . . the designer's initials will be on the medals for 20 or 30 years to come." A small, somewhat melancholy oil landscape, exe-

---

4. For an extensive discussion of connections between mental depression and artistic creativity, with references to the considerable literature on the subject, see Kay Redfield Jamison, *Touched with Fire: Manic-Depressive Illness and the Artistic Temperament* (New York: Free Press, 1993).

cuted during the period and sent to Uncle Leck and Aunt Miriam, shows in its precise brushwork a carefully controlled integration of deep browns and greens. He was also working with plaster molds that were finished in bronze, including busts of General John Pershing that were praised by college president Charles Thach and several members of the faculty. He sold the pieces for a dollar each, and as usual, he wanted his brother to have one—but it was too heavy for Aunt Mae Willie to carry on her trip to Virginia, so he sent David a dollar instead, promising later a parcel post delivery. The academic highlight of the year came when he received the highest grade in architecture in the design of a bronze memorial tablet. "Understand," he wrote to David, on January 25, "it was in competition with the whole four classes in the department, regardless of your class. How do you like that?"

But while freshman Spratling was beginning to find his future through exemplary work in such subjects as elements of architecture, freehand drawing, and descriptive geometry, his grades in first semester chemistry and algebra were poor. The strong reprimand that came from his guardian was justified, Bill admitted to David, but he resented the accusation of Uncle Leck, who "says I piddle," and went on to sound his customary complaint that his uncle would not answer his questions, particularly those about his sister Lucile and whether or not any of the family would be coming south in the summer. This resentment continued when his uncle seemed to show no interest in Bill's securing a summer job as draftsman with a Birmingham manufacturing firm at the rate of sixty dollars a month; he would stay at the YMCA, he wrote, and though his salary would barely cover his expenses, he would gain the kind of practical experience Professor Biggin was asking his architecture students to secure.

The confrontation toward which all this was leading took place in mid-summer and was clearly hastened by Bill's recognition during the long hot days at the drawing board in Birmingham just how dreary such a permanent future as that would be for him. Letter writing, private confessions to his younger brother, would no longer do; he had somehow to be able to say directly to his guardian that the legacy of financial support for his education was not being misspent. In what was perhaps the most assertive act of his young life, he made plans to go to Uncle Leck's Coast Guard station in Virginia, pawning his father's watch to get the money for passage. We cannot know how things went in the meeting between uncle and nephew, but Bill apparently returned to his summer job at least partially reassured that some faith in his possibilities still lay in his father's representative.

This is not to say that his feelings of ambivalence in this direction would entirely disappear (he and Uncle Leck would later exchange stinging letters once the watch-pawning action was discovered), or that his chronic financial plight would immediately lessen. But his letters for the rest of the summer are rather happy and optimistic ones even though by the end of August he was reduced to spending, beyond his room and board costs, only five cents all week, hoarding it for a copy of his favorite *Saturday Evening Post.* And so we find him, as this first year of new experience draws to a close, looking ahead to a second college September, working during the day, studying his trigonometry at night. Though, he wrote, he would have "to hobo" back to Auburn, he had somehow managed to secure the $16.50 necessary to redeem his father's watch, and he could no doubt still remember the statement he had communicated to David soon after his Virginia quest for reassurance, that "Dave, Uncle Leck gives awful good advice—one profits by it almost unconsciously."

From this detailed review of William Spratling's year of 1917–1918, one cannot say that he was remarkably precocious and that he had already begun to exhibit that combination of intellectual discipline and assimilative power that would eventually lead to his being described almost casually as a "genius" by the authoritative biographer of William Faulkner. In fact, one might observe that Faulkner himself, three years older than Spratling, was also during this particular year in a small college town in the adjoining state exhibiting possibly even less momentum toward his own future eminence. As Spratling would do later for his college yearbook, Faulkner was from 1916 to 1920 drawing illustrations for the *Ole Miss* and, as Spratling's would be, they were the best ones in the publication.[5] And the rough analogy holds further in that Faulkner, though appearing to his family somewhat aimless in pursuing any kind of specific prospect for success, was, like Spratling, moving through an important period of personal and artistic apprenticeship that must have included considerable self-doubt. For him, this would lead in the summer

5. See Joseph Blotner, *Faulkner: A Biography* (New York: Vintage Books, 1991), 77. The allusion to Spratling as a man of talent and genius is on p. 133.

of that year, about the time Spratling was preparing for his Virginia pil-
grimage, to the exhilarating and perhaps even liberating encounter with
military service in the RAF, which he would shortly be using for fictional
purposes. In 1918 Spratling had no need, as Faulkner may have had, to
project a future for himself that would make almost necessary a romantic
involvement with the idea of war and heroic death, and he would not, of
course, in his art reach back into his inherited and personal past as Faulkner would always do. Spratling's personal past may have been dysfunctional, but his creative life would never be marked—even in its appraisal
of ante-bellum architecture and its cultural setting—by the sense of mor-
bidity and "conflicted relationship" with both community and region
that were the complex inheritance of many southern intellectuals.[6] What
he had, rather, begun to do during this year, although he did not seem to
realize it at the time, was to disengage himself from the past. He carried
no badge, or even burden, of family identity in his college town as Faulkner carried in his, and he had no desire to escape, even temporarily, the
environment that was dimly promising a future which would confirm
further the self-awareness and longing for independence he had expressed throughout the year to his brother.

In three more years Spratling would himself be ready for the next stage
in his life, but his return to college at the end of what seems to have been
a summer of significant personal assessment and commitment was clearly
a relief. The academic year of 1918–1919 was no less significant in the
advancement of his self-confidence. His letters to his brother are not as
frequent and focus much less on his own perceived problems of alienation and adjustment. Instead, they often adopt almost a paternal air as
he advises David—and undoubtedly himself—on this or that aspect of
behavior, encouraging him especially to be assertive. "What you need,
Dave," he wrote on April 21, "is backbone, sportsmanship, etc.—I'm
afraid you are too precise. A true gentleman must be polite, polished and
well educated but as a foundation he must have the firmness of manhood. Don't want to preach, but Auburn will make a man of you." If
this somewhat pontifical advice seems properly sophomoric, it was at

    6. For a recent analysis of this larger topic, see Bertram Wyatt-Brown, "The Desperate
Imagination: Writers and Melancholy in the Modern American South," in *Southern Writ-
ers and Their Worlds*, ed. Christopher Morris and Steven G. Reinhardt (College Station:
Texas A&M University Press, 1996), 73.

least balanced by the more humble qualities of manhood the older brother held out in his response to David's feeling that he was peculiar: "Look here David, everybody is peculiar, . . ." but "Dave, if you can come to summer school, it will do you more good than you can imagine. If it wouldn't ruin your moral character, I wish you'd learn to smoke, cuss, and hobo!" And he advised his brother, too, on his choice of profession, perhaps revealing in the process a feeling of satisfaction in his own separation from the professional heritage of the three senior Spratlings who had been most influential on his early life: "By the way, Dave—I'd ten times rather see you in the diplomatic service than a doctor."

When Spratling returned to college in the fall of 1918, he had already begun to find in the achievements of his freshman year a capacity for the artistic rendering of both human and natural subjects that does not always accompany architectural skill in design. And in the development of his professional future, the new year's studies would offer him further the early opportunity to respond intellectually and perhaps emotionally to the architectural monuments of other cultures, but only as contained in textbooks, since it would be three more years before he could get to Europe. Professor Biggin, continuing his encouragement and support of his promising young student, appointed Spratling as a part-time instructor to lecture nine hours a week to freshman classes. He had just turned eighteen and was now required to criticize the work of students only slightly younger than he and to illustrate before them in blackboard sessions issues, however elementary, of scale, perspective, and structure. This new opportunity to develop his talent further was augmented by the happy arrival in Auburn of Sarah Spratling, Uncle Leck and Aunt Miriam's daughter, who enrolled as one of the dozen or so women in the college population of about 1,300. Bill's correspondence throughout the year reflects an active social life in which Sarah figures prominently ("It makes me very glad to be cousin to her") along with his longtime friend and classmate Gladys.

During the fall, however, the college was transformed as a result of the United States in the previous April entering the First World War. The college had passed under the quasi-military control of the federal government. On October 1 most of the male students at Auburn joined some 140,000 others at over 500 colleges and universities throughout the country in simultaneously staged induction services for the Student Army

Training Corps (SATC).[7] Swept along on a tide of patriotism, Bill responded warmly to this new opportunity to belong to and participate in a larger community endeavor. But the opportunity was a brief one, for the November armistice led to the termination of the SATC program by the end of 1918.

Although Bill's army service had lasted only three months—shorter than Faulkner's six months in the RAF—its impact had been significant, particularly in a practical economic sense. The room, board, tuition, and thirty dollars a month must have seemed a godsend—no need to rely on Uncle Leck, or to put a further drain on the estate, the money from which Bill may even then have been anticipating. Moreover, the loss of faculty to military service had been partly responsible for his teaching appointment. The federal takeover, however, also had a negative side for Bill in that it threatened to destroy for him the island of stability and order upon which he had based the next three years. Not only did he face the prospect of being transferred to regular army service, probably in France, within a year, but equally important for Bill, the military takeover produced a reorganization of the college curriculum that eliminated the architectural program as nonessential to the war effort. The architecture department was abolished and its faculty and students were transferred to other engineering departments, and Spratling found himself lecturing before civil engineering as well as architecture students.

But the winter and spring terms of 1919 were the best yet. The war was over; he received from Lucile the news that she had married a medical doctor with whom she had worked in France; and, most important of all, the architecture curriculum was re-established with Professor Biggin as department head. The letter conveying this last-mentioned bit of news was written on December 30, the second letter to David he wrote on that day, with the first thanking David for his Christmas gift and his letter, which had come, with Lucile's, on Christmas Day. The tone of these expressions, together with his allusion to his own "quiet, uneventful" holiday and his hope that a "good, jolly Xmas" prevailed at Uncle Leck's, is self-possessed and responsive—and how different from the mournful lonely voice of only a year earlier. "Believe me, I'm overjoyed,"

7. For a history of the SATC, see Carol S. Gruber, *Mars and Minerva: World War I and the Uses of Higher Learning in America* (Baton Rouge: Louisiana State University Press, 1975), 215–52.

he writes in the second letter, to describe how he himself was partly responsible for the restoration of architecture in that he had that very morning engaged the college president in a two-hour conversation about the matter—an undergraduate could actually do this in 1919—with the outcome being "the best piece of news in the world."

The termination of the SATC program with its financial advantages led to the re-appearance of Bill's dependency on the monthly allocations from his guardian and, for the rest of the school year, a reprise of the tension between them which had been partly ameliorated by the confrontation of the previous summer. Uncle Leck, for example, had turned down his nephew's request (who had complained to David in June that his feet were blistered from having to wear still his heavy army boots) for twenty to thirty dollars for the purchase of clothes which he needed for another teaching appointment in the college, this time in the summer session instructing public school teachers in mechanical and freehand drawing, arts and graphics, and assisting the faculty in descriptive geometry. Moreover, the uncle had, to Bill's perception, showed his usual lack of interest in what was obviously yet another mark of his nephew's progress and maturation. But this tension also passed, leading Bill not as in the previous summer to further introspective analysis, but to a point of what might best be described as a withdrawal from reliance on family and a cultivation of a future lying somehow outward, resting on himself and what he now seemed to perceive he was capable of accomplishing. In all fairness to Uncle Leck, it was a development they both had long awaited.

The immediate impetus for this second critical instant in the movement of young Spratling into the persona of "the man from New Orleans" was the offer in June of a full year's appointment as assistant instructor at $250 with the opportunity to continue a regular course of study. On June 26, he wrote to David: "When Prof. Biggin called me in last night he scared me when he started off by saying that he had been watching my teaching, but he said that I was giving a very 'intelligent' course . . . and told someone else that I was a 'splendid instructor.' " Bill had been chosen over senior and post-graduate candidates; but there was yet more. He had been specifically instructed by Professor Biggin, in a letter dated June 28, that before he began the new position, "you manage to take somewhere expert instruction in charcoal drawing, water color painting (architectural), pen and ink rendering, and perhaps also clay modeling." Suddenly, the prospects "outward" were coming into focus. The next day, Bill quickly got off another letter to David in Virginia, enclosing Biggin's professional requirements and his further suggestion that an outlay of $150 against Bill's forthcoming salary would be adequate for study of some seven or eight weeks, perhaps at the Beaux Arts School for Architects in New York. But "how am I going to get it?" he carefully concluded.

This letter of June 29, 1919, is in its own way a masterpiece, and in its tone of contrition and persuasion would bear comparison with all those indirect but successful pleas for money that thousands of undergraduates have written home. But beyond that, it is critical in our story as one of the two most illuminating letters in the long brotherly correspondence, revealing and defining as it does that point of withdrawal and departure that seemed to occur midway in Spratling's college experience. Bill clearly meant for Uncle Leck either to see or be told its contents, hoping that they would resolve favorably the long-standing difficulty that had existed ever since it had been revealed that Bill had pawned his father's watch the previous summer in order to finance the trip to Portsmouth, and would thus also remove any possible opposition Uncle Leck might have to the $150 allocation. The watch business, of course, was one of those family matters that had become a disproportionately tense subject. It is not clear whether Uncle Leck became angry over Bill's not having told him about it or whether the act itself—a commercial transaction with his dead brother's personal possession—had assumed some kind of immoral symbolic meaning. He himself had the watch now, Bill having sent it to him for safe keeping following his induction into army barracks.

While Bill's rhetorical approach to the delicate situation was clever, there is no reason to believe he was not sincere in what he said. He was tired of the festering issue, especially now that it might deter his hopes. "I did not remember ever telling Uncle Leck about the watch. That was an experience so serious & such a bitter lesson that I thought it best not to share it with anyone." And though he briefly chastises David's possible lack of trust, as he earlier had cousin Sarah's, both of whom he had eventually confided in, it no longer mattered who had told on him; the point was that *he* had not told.

> Of course I am not going to ask for it [the watch] again. I have *been* perfectly satisfied as to its safety in Uncle Leck's hands, & as Uncle Leck thinks it is right I am not going to mention it again. . . .

> I believe I realize as much as anyone that my resources are limited. That is why I am so glad at the prospect of this assistantship, and you should be too, because it may mean that during my Sr. year I may become a full instructor and be able to take a Post—with no drain on the estate at all.
>
> And so, Dave, I'll ask you to beg Uncle Leck's pardon humbly for me. I feel too mean to do it myself. I have already asked his pardon but now that I see there was such an immense misunderstanding & realize what I've done, I feel very badly about it.

And with this statement of confession and remorse, fused as it is with the persuasive rationale about the economic advantage to all of them of the assistantship, he turns at the close of the letter, almost as an afterthought ("By the way . . .") to the implied request of the $150 allocation.

The results couldn't have come more quickly in a "long sweet letter" from "the dearest brother in the world." Uncle Leck had relented, and Bill wrote that he would sail from Savannah for New York on July 15 to meet Lucile and her new husband, with whom he would live during this new period in his life. His letter was written on July 4, Independence Day.

Whatever skepticism Bill may have felt about his guardian's fairness in his treatment of the three young Spratlings seems to have dissipated as he became acquainted almost anew with Lucile after a separation of almost eight years. In the July 4 letter as he himself was moving outward, he expressed to his brother a concern that Uncle Leck's household environment may not have offered David a full share of "the highest essential of life, which is love, congeniality, and companionship," and closed the letter with a curious P.S., asking "Are you formally adopted?" Whatever wistful anxiety this may have expressed about the enclosure of David within a separate family and Lucile now married into a new life with another we cannot know, but the euphoria of the New York prospect together with the independence both it and his approaching majority held out seemed touched, if only slightly, with an understandable apprehension.

His first letter to David from New York, on July 18, was written on the letterhead stationery of his father, "Dr. W. P. Spratling, 1110 N. Charles St., Baltimore, Md." which either he or Lucile had kept since 1910. Perhaps the connection meant something to him because the issue of the condition of the senior Spratling's estate continued on his mind; he writes that he is "counting on needing not more than $200 from the estate this year," and he praises "small, dear & spunky Lucile. . . . *she does not squander money.*" He has been reassured also by his sister that Uncle Leck has been a proper steward and "is doing all he can for Lucile." And it is obvious that the warmth and conviviality of his sister's household were more than he could have expected. Moreover, "Dave, we have a splendid brother-in-law . . . very fine in every way."

The immediacy of this supportive family bond, which Bill had not experienced since he left Atlanta for Alabama in 1912, was latent in the series of affectionate letters written by Lucile to David, often on stationery "my dear young brother Billy sent me" during her tenure as a settlement house and hospital nurse in New York and later on war duty in France. For example, just after her unit's mobilization on Ellis Island, in early February 1917, she wrote to David that she had taken out insurance policies in the amount of $4,500 each, with the two boys as beneficiaries. This big-sisterly protective gesture is followed by an expression of sadness that she has not seen her paternal family in so many years, and this by the astounding news about which the brothers would wonder and speculate for the next year, "I am engaged to marry one of the doctors in the unit—Goodbye."

This flair for the dramatic and unexpected—it was nine months before she remembered to tell the boys their future brother-in-law's name—along with her gently authoritative manner suggests that Lucile was by far the most mercurial and self-assured of the three children. And her letters to David from France, in which she constantly assures him that she wants the two separated brothers to visit her in the home her forthcoming marriage will make, throw into a certain relief once more that the central drama of young William Spratling's life, to which he could but briefly refer in the autobiographical file, was his dislocation from a family environment of worth and nurture and his successful quest toward a new orientation. From the evidence we have, it seems a most happy irony that at the very time he was finding that orientation, he would be re-united for a few weeks with something of what had disappeared with the deaths of his parents and the sibling separations that followed. "It has all been very stirring," he concluded in the July 18 letter to David, "and I am very, very, happy."

It is also possible to observe a certain stylistic affinity—both in manner and word—between Lucile and Bill. He had not yet developed the almost reflexive mode of self-deprecation blended with praise that he would perfect later in life; nor had he discovered his gift for creating the kind of evocative prose that would mark his descriptive essays from New Orleans and Mexico. But something of this is present in Lucile. For example, in a September 1918 letter to David from her base hospital in Monpont, Dordogne, she writes on the one hand of her daily engagement with the wounded, "men who have had their jaws shot away or lost their eyes," and on the other of her stabilizing relationship with her future husband, who

> is here with me and we manage to spend our evenings together: we walk, have supper picnics, journey down town to dinner, I sew while he plays the mandolin, or we sit on the edge of the river bank with the moon shining through the tall Lombardy poplars and watch the ripples on the water.... So often we wonder what you all at home are doing. Here everything is so peaceful and serene that if it were not for the convoys of wounded men coming in, we might begin to doubt the existence of a war.

And continuing what must have been for her youngest brother a dazzling letter, she notes from what Billy has written to her that David is

> easily shocked—which remark caused me to wonder what sort of things Billy had been saying to you. I am afraid that I would shock you most dreadfully: for instance I wear my hair bobbed, indulge in silk stockings, expensive french perfumerys and face power, beautiful lingerie which I make all by hand, flirtations whenever anyone appeals to me and I read naughty novels and enjoy them. I say and do all kinds of wild things until Eddie wonders what his future life when wedded to me is going to be like. Of-course I never go to church as I have yet to find a religion which I can believe in. And yet despite all these horrible traits, most people find me more or less interesting, or clever I think they call me. Some of my evil traits are offset by the fact that I have two very attractive and desirable brothers.

Reflective, then witty, self-confident in her worldly experience—and somehow vaguely maternal—this was the sister into whose encouraging household Bill moved in July of 1919. His new brother-in-law, Dr. Edward Bleir, wrote to David shortly thereafter, on July 22, that he and Bill have "hit it up pretty well," and there are in the family correspondence of this month and August several glimpses of domestic vignettes, Lucile cooking the family meal at the end of the day, Eddie and Bill taking turns at getting breakfast and washing the dishes. "Billy is all right," Eddie wrote on August 4. "He's got plenty of plunk and he is taking his work seriously. . . . I believe that he will have sketched all of N.Y. before he goes home." And Bill was no less restrained in his description to David of the unfolding experience of meeting at its very center the wider artistic life of America, certainly finding there many young people like himself who were also just beginning in a serious way their aesthetic indentures. He wrote on August 4: "I am taking 4 hrs a day sculpture at the 'Beaux Art' & 3 hrs a day water-color rendering, charcoal, etc. at Columbia—the Beaux Arts is free—Columbia will cost $12. I am very lucky in being able to qualify for the life class in sculpture. . . . very busy at the League and the Metropolitan Museum—spend all my time sketching and rarely go to a show. . . . I'm enjoying it all immensely & am chock full of ideas."

These were almost, but not quite, the last words Bill would write in a letter to his brother before leaving to return home. In a P.S. he asked, with hardly a trace, one feels, of the anxiety he would have felt two years earlier, "What does Uncle Leck think of my trip?" It was a question to which, no doubt, he felt he already knew the affirmative answer. And perhaps it didn't then make much difference anyway. It had been, after all, a triumphant summer. He was returning to his junior year instructorship at a wage that would make him less dependent financially than he had ever been and, as he had pointed out to David, would not significantly erode the legacy from his father's estate he would receive in two years. This critical stretch of experience, contained only in the family correspondence, is completely omitted from the autobiography and thus from the chronological addendum an unknown hand posthumously constructed for it. The omission is consistent, as we have seen, with Spratling keeping closely in the file of memory almost every nuance of personal feeling, essentially drawing a curtain between the enigmatic genius and the child and young man who together were his parents.

Reading that young man's letters some eighty years later allows us to push back the curtain, at least partway. And, of course, there is no reason to assume that what was important to Spratling in the summer and fall of 1919 should not become increasingly unmemorable to him during the next forty-five years. Such may be the case for any life. Still, one would hope to find autobiographical connections between the earlier and later Spratling, connections that would make the whole life hang together. Though omitting, or suppressing, much about his teenage years, he can record over four pages of precise detail in the autobiography the account of the voyage he and five college friends took in the summer of 1921, working their passage to Europe on the SS *Oskaloosa,* a freighter bound for Antwerp. In the midst of various difficulties with the ship's balky progress, the boys engaged in some racial give-and-take with the black stewards on board. In reconstructing the tale, Spratling goes to some trouble to satirize the cavalier prejudice that "we white, very southern fraternity brothers" felt about the stewards' exaggerated accounts of their sexual prowess with various white women in the port towns. All ends in friendship, but Spratling concludes the account with his observation that for forty years he has "lived in a country where there is not the slightest racial bias and where there exists no distinction based on color."

While this shipboard episode seems to have been filtered through Spratling's Mexican sensibility, it is one of the very few episodes of any kind that he places into the autobiographical file of his last two college years. And while the description there is shaped in the form of youthful hijinks, its very presence substantiates that however Spratling wanted to recall it for publication, his first trip to Europe was a critically memorable experience. The extensive scrapbook contents of the European voyage are comparable in their detail only to Spratling's descriptions of the New York residence with Lucile. Each scrapbook memento from the European trip is numbered, often with an identifying phrase. He noted of the cathedral at Antwerp both its height and the name of its architect; and on the photo of the great square in Brussels surrounded by enormous buildings of mixed periods, he wrote: "The most interesting place, architecturally, I've ever seen." For each of the five friends, Spratling hand-lettered a complete log of the trip.[8] The photographs of the several friends on shipboard and on the streets of Brussels and Antwerp, together with postcard pictures and numerous architectural sketches of urban and museum scenes both there and in New York were obviously to Spratling a record of significant liberating experiences during his maturing years. And it was during this period, actually in the spring of 1921, that he conceived the plan of what must have been for him a highly personalized act both of liberation and of family loyalty: the casting of a bust of his father as a presentation to the Department of Archives and History in Montgomery. He did not execute the piece, but had sent a

8. Letter to the author from one of them, C. W. Warner of Valdosta, Ga., December 17, 1992.

model of a bust of President Thach as a sample of his work, and the response of the director must have been gratifying in its recognition of him both as a young artist of promise and as the son of a distinguished medical scientist:

> Permit me to express my profound appreciation of the talent you have shown in modeling this work. There is a feeling amongst sculptors and critics that America is now beginning to manifest an art consciousness and it is particularly gratifying to find a young Alabamian, the son of an eminent Alabamian, in the good company of young Americans who are revealing genius in this form.
>
> Confirming my verbal request this morning I wish again to say that this Department will very gratefully accept a bust of your father, Dr. Wm. P. Spratling, who at the time of his death was regarded as the greatest authority in America on the treatment of epilepsy.[9]

Of course, nothing in the correspondence with his family even hints at the slightly flamboyant portrait he paints of himself in such autobiographical allusions as his description of a bawdy joke related by a madam in the red-light district of Montgomery—perhaps recalled in part for the purpose of confirming his youthful masculinity—or his devotion to that southern version of bathtub gin, "white lightning," which he says became for him a "demobilization" from the pressure of his heavy teaching schedule and his own classroom-studio assignments. His description of his life as "a renewal of exciting doings, hectic and full of anxieties" are words that will do as well as any in catching something of the rush and exhilaration of Prohibition and the twenties, which had not failed to reach Alabama. And there is adequate testimony from Spratling's classmates that his figure with its slightly bohemian appearance was well recognized and fully integrated into the congenial structures of disorder that then and still characterize undergraduate life.

If Bill Spratling had grown up, however, he was also restless. Relatively unfettered now from the claims of what for years had been an absentee authority, he was, seemingly to his own satisfaction, showing what he could do. He would still readily accept a commission to paint an image of the college's tiger mascot high on the town water tank, but the diversity of his teaching assignments in his part-time student appoint-

---

9. Marie Bankhead Owen to W.S., June 1, 1921, Archives, Rancho Spratling, Taxco-el-Viejo (hereinafter ARS).

ment and the range of his architectural renderings had about reached the limit of his academic environment. As a draftsman he would be good enough early in 1922 to receive an assignment to render an elaborate master plan for the college campus, showing the new buildings that the college hoped would be built as a result of a capital funds campaign; and during the previous years he was commissioned to prepare a new design for the official institutional seal which, with minor alterations, is still in use today. But he was now in his fifth year of undergraduate residency, having failed because of his instructorship responsibilities—and, as he put it in the autobiography, the "adverse element" of mathematics requirements—to complete his degree in four years. The paternal legacy he had received following his twenty-first birthday in September of 1921 had alleviated the usual financial stress, and there is some evidence that, on receiving it, he was not reluctant in transferring it to proper excessive uses. During the spring he accepted, perhaps impulsively, a full-time position with an architectural firm in Birmingham, but in doing so he actually faced the very drab future at which he earlier had "shuddered" in the pivotal letter of July 1918, the letter which had immediately preceded, as we have seen, a series of liberating experiences.

Within a few weeks, however, the life of William Spratling would once more turn southward. Partly through the good offices of his longtime mentor, Professor Biggin, he was offered a teaching position at Tulane University in New Orleans. And thus in September of 1922, with his new title "Instructor, College of Engineering" assured, he made preparations, although this time most willingly, to become once more a stranger in a new place, this time in a city which beckoned, as his new friend Faulkner would write in his earliest fiction two and one-half years later, like "a courtesan . . . to whose charm the young must respond."[10]

Before he departed, however, he had completed his most ambitious artistic project thus far: a bronze bas-relief portrait of Dr. Charles Coleman Thach, who had been president of the college from 1902 into the 1920 school year. Mrs. Thach had been Billy's church school teacher during his freshman year, Dr. Thach had praised his early work in plaster

10. From "New Orleans," published in January-February 1925, in the *Times-Picayune*; collected in *New Orleans Sketches*, ed. Carvel Collins (London: Sidgwick and Jackson, 1959), 49. Spratling's appointment was effective September 18, 1922. The unsigned notation, William Spratling File, Manuscripts Department, Tulane University Library.

casting, and Spratling believed that his long conversation with the president in the weeks after the war was over had been important in the restoration of the architecture curriculum. When the portrait was cast and finished, Bill donated it to the class of 1921 as a memorial gift to be presented to the institution. Newspaper accounts of the gift to the college and, later, of a plaster copy of the original bronze donated to the archives "as a free will offering by the young sculptor," emphasized Spratling's youth, and his training in architecture and in the curricula at the Beaux Arts School and the Art Students League. "That Mr. Spratling has a future before him was the consensus of opinion of persons in the capitol who knew Dr. Thach and who believe that the young sculptor has caught a likeness."[11] Even with this first, unexpected public recognition, Spratling at the time may nevertheless have regarded the gift as a gesture of appreciation to the little college town where in his ten years' residency he had discovered and developed further a dimension of himself he had not known when he arrived and which he would never know he had recorded for us. He certainly carried the gesture in his memory for the rest of his life, keeping the clippings in his scrapbook, and when he returned to Auburn forty years later to receive his alma mater's tributes, it was one of the first things he wanted to see. Perhaps by then it had become a conveniently symbolic event, marking off one part of his life from another part, which in the fall of 1922 began to take shape as he set out on the second leg of his journey down the long continent.

11. "Auburn Seniors to Present Portrait"; "Thach Portrait Is Added to Archives," *Montgomery Advertiser*, January 30, June 22, 1921.

2

New Orleans, 1922–1925: New Friends, First Publications, and Travels with Faulkner

> From the hotel window, the dull chocolate and slate-lilac city with its high roofs and narrow windows, in the dim, damp light of March, and, beyond it, the muddy river Maidenhair ferns in front yards and wisteria vines . . . delicately fronded and foliated like the wrought-iron designs of the balconies. . . . In the streets of the old French Quarter, that toasted smoky smell. . . . Some unidentifiable, invisible person whistling . . . more softly, more melodiously, more roundly, than one ever hears it in the North.
> —Edmund Wilson, "New Orleans, March 1926,"
> *The Twenties*

> New Orleans is not like other cities.
> —Tennessee Williams, *A Streetcar Named Desire*

Although William Spratling's knowledge of cities was limited at the time of his arrival in New Orleans, he knew immediately that he had entered a world of sensation and languid beauty unlike anything he had experienced before. Not characteristically given to understatement, he yet compresses into the autobiographical memory what must have been a culture shock of tremendous proportions, remembering only that it was "lively and colorful" and "presented broad horizons to a young man fresh from Auburn." It would be one of the two cities giving shape to his artistic career: this, where he would stay for almost seven years, the other in Mexico, where he would spend the rest of his life. In fact, the two lay in a certain orderly sequence, for in New Orleans his architectural and verbal confrontation with its multicultural past would prepare him for the more profound encounter in Taxco with an order of expression less visible and lying much further beneath the encroachments of intervening centuries.

New Orleans in the twenties, as Taxco would appear to him in the thirties, had, perhaps without much effort, managed to retain an historic presence. At least part of the city had, and it was for Spratling a happy choice that in the fall of 1922—against, he says, the advice of some of the older faculty at Tulane—he settled in a small apartment in the original "old square," the Vieux Carré. It probably was his only choice, for his chronic financial predicament had followed him from Alabama, and the living there in the French Quarter was relatively inexpensive, the area not yet having discovered even its slightest possibility for peddling to an enormous tourist trade what Walker Percy would describe some forty years later as "lewdness" on the one hand and "Old World charm" on the other. But Percy would also describe the elusive, almost ineffable quality of New Orleans life to which almost every writer on the subject has testified. Its "peculiar virtue"

> ... may be that of the Little Way, a talent for every day life rather than the heroic deed. If in its two hundred and fifty years of history it has produced no giants, no Lincolns, no Lees, no Faulkners, no Thoreaus, it has nurtured a great many people who live tolerably, like to talk and eat, laugh a good deal, manage generally to be civil and at the same time mind their own business.[1]

As the young Spratling walked from south to north across the civic but also symbolic parameter of Canal Street, he would soon have discovered too the sense of enclosure and leisurely intermingled strains of conversation, habit, and custom emanating from the complex fusion in the Vieux Carré of Creole, Anglo-Saxon, and West Indian cultures. Writing of his own first visit to the Quarter only six months before Spratling arrived, Sherwood Anderson described how "in the evening soft voices, speaking strange tongues, come drifting up to you out of the street." And Lyle Saxon, one of the most indigenous and typical interpreters of the place would, a year later, in his introduction to one of Spratling's first publications, reaffirm the same note that Lafcadio Hearn had sounded over and over in the late nineteenth century, in *Creole Sketches* and other works, that the strangeness and contradictory charm of the French Quarter stood in quiet opposition to the progressive industry of the larger city

---

1. Walker Percy, "New Orleans Mon Amour," *Harper's Magazine* (September 1968): 86, 88.

as it sought to overcome the economic losses and deprivation suffered during Reconstruction. Even in its "dying splendor," wrote Saxon, the old Creole city still held its bizarre romantic fascination, especially at night, "when the kind darkness blurs out the modern world."[2] New Orleans was then, as still, the most foreign, the most European of all American cities, and inevitably Parisian in its comparisons. For Hamilton Basso, the French Quarter during the years of the middle twenties became "a sort of Creole version of the Left Bank," and he for one didn't need to make the expatriate journey: "I had Paris in my own back yard."[3]

Spratling may have arrived during a critical transitional period in the life of the Vieux Carré, whose heart, the *Times-Picayune* had dramatically announced, "stopped beating" when in December of 1919 the French Opera House at the corner of Bourbon and Toulouse burned to the ground.[4] Though the mid-nineteenth-century building had indeed been the social and cultural center of the district, there is some indication that in the early twenties a growing awareness of the unique personality of the Quarter may have arrested its potential swift decline into a slum. In fact, an article called "The Renaissance of the Vieux Carré" appeared in 1922 in the *Double Dealer,* which, since its first publication in the previous year, had begun to attract many literary "new men" to its pages and had already become a kind of cultural lightning rod for the Quarter. Directed primarily toward the new journal's non-residential readership, the piece was in part a walking tour of the district, with historical commentary, and emphasized how, in "our Paris of America . . . as interesting furniture for our drawing rooms is being brought down from the attics of our forefathers, so too, has this almost submerged and recently bedraggled group of early buildings been lately rescued by the curators of

2. Sherwood Anderson, "New Orleans, The Double Dealer, and the Modern Movement in America," *Double Dealer* 3 (March 1922): 125; Lyle Saxon, introduction to *Picturesque New Orleans: Ten Drawings of the French Quarter,* by William Spratling (New Orleans: Tulane University Press, 1923): 2.

3. Hamilton Basso, "William Faulkner, Man and Writer," *Saturday Review,* July 28, 1962, 11. See also the essays in *Literary New Orleans,* ed. Richard S. Kennedy (Baton Rouge: Louisiana State University Press, 1992), especially those by Hephzibah Roskelly on Hearn, W. Kenneth Holditch on Faulkner and Tennessee Williams, and Lewis P. Simpson on "New Orleans as a Literary Center."

4. *Times-Picayune,* quoted by Lyle Saxon, *Fabulous New Orleans* (New York: Appleton-Century, 1928), 281.

the State Museum." Some of the buildings named and described were those that would soon be drawn by Spratling for *Picturesque New Orleans* (1923), including the one into which he moved six months after the article was published. And he himself, before he left the city in 1929, would also become infected with the pervasive nostalgic absorptions of the history of the re-discovered Quarter, which, as the *Double Dealer* walking tour continued, was described as having had a Parisian quality when New York was an undeveloped colonial town and "before Chicago or San Francisco were thought of."[5]

But to a young architect whose visual experience with urban forms had thus far been limited, the severe scale and self-contained character of the Vieux Carré patterns must have been arresting. New Orleans across Canal Street to the northwest was rapidly developing the wide thoroughfares and skyscraper profiles that Spratling had seen and sketched during his early residences in Baltimore, Atlanta, and New York, and during his brief visit to Brussels during his undergraduate summer of 1921. The outward movement of the city, thrusting up here and there at irregular intervals, was in sharp contrast to the coherence in the old section, which the narrow streets, narrower-still alleyways, and banquettes, connecting street and building or opening to interior walled courts, helped to convey. Many of the two- or three-tiered eighteenth- and nineteenth-century buildings, whose Spanish or French architectural styles spoke to the city's history, had been both business and residential; the upper galleries, with their intricate iron grillwork masking the high-ceilinged interior living quarters and overlooking the cramped brickways below, contributed to the pervasive sense of verticality, where angles of vision seemed always up and down rather than horizontal. Architecturally, the facades of the buildings seemed at first glance to be plain, but as Spratling observed, "Attention should be called to the extraordinary refinements practiced in the proportioning of openings and the disposition of story heights."[6]

As the decade continued, thousands of Vieux Carré street scenes would be sketched and painted by numerous artists. Spratling's renderings in *Picturesque New Orleans,* however, of historically important

5. T. P. Thompson, "The Renaissance of the Vieux Carré," *Double Dealer* 3 (February 1922): 85–87, 89.

6. William Spratling, "The Architectural Heritage of New Orleans," *Architectural Forum* 46 (May 1927): 409.

buildings were among the first to capture in published form the combination in many of these structures of perpendicular grace and seedy elegance, these with their cracked plaster and unkempt facades standing in sharp contrast to one or two others already showing the early work of preservationists: for example, in the best of the ten sketches, that of St. Louis Cathedral, which had been restored in 1918. Spratling was certainly not the only one to define pictorially the transitional evocation in the early twenties of the French Quarter's physical appearance, but he would continue throughout his residence there to be attracted by such contrasts, including that between the two architectural worlds that lay on either side of Canal Street, as expressed in his *Vieux Carré Rooftops* (1924) and *Canyons of Commerce* (c. 1925).

We cannot, unfortunately, secure a sense of Spratling in New Orleans from the kind of regular epistolary voice that was available to mark his teenage and college years in Alabama. Instead we must rely on the less personal chronicle of his recorded accomplishments and associations, and on the highly selective autobiographical file. Clearly, however, he was, at the age of twenty-two, at last in an enviable position for his talents and ambition to seek their proper place. He no doubt owed a debt of gratitude for his instructorship appointment at Tulane to Nathaniel C. Curtis, a senior professor in architecture who had himself come to New Orleans from Auburn, where he had helped to organize the architecture program, serving from 1907 to 1912 as head professor. Curtis was an influential figure in both academic and professional architecture, serving as head professor at both Tulane and Illinois before returning to New Orleans in 1920 to join the firm of Goldstein, Parham and Labouisse and to serve as part-time professor at Tulane. It was from the Goldstein firm that Spratling would receive most of his part-time employment in New Orleans. Having probably received a complimentary assessment of Spratling from Professor Biggin, Curtis wrote in August of 1922 to the Tulane academic dean: "I understand that Mr. Spratling has received the appointment as Instructor in Architecture and I am glad to know this as I believe him to be exceptionally well qualified . . . besides being a young man of enthusiasm."[7] Curtis became an early mentor to Spratling, joining him in publication projects and introducing him to the membership and activity of the Arts and Crafts Club, which occupied its newly reno-

7. Curtis to Dean Douglas Anderson, Nathaniel Cortlandt Curtis Papers, Manuscripts Department, Tulane University Library.

vated quarters on Royal Street a month after Spratling's arrival. The younger man's genuine admiration for the older is indicated in the treatment of Curtis in *Sherwood Anderson and Other Famous Creoles,* which Spratling and Faulkner would publish four years later and which contained in its array of thirty-four caricatures, some with descriptive, often satiric, captions, essentially the full population of writers and artists who helped to make the Vieux Carré in the twenties a vital and extraordinarily creative community. Placed second in the collection only to Anderson himself and shown with a watering can, Curtis is described as "Irrigator of the Sahara of the Bozart," a caption suggesting not only his distinctive reputation within that community but also a recognition that the Vieux Carré environment hardly warranted inclusion within the derogatory depiction of the South contained in H. L. Mencken's famous phrase.[8]

In the autobiography the section on New Orleans, with its confused chronology typical of Spratling's remembrances, actually contains very little about the personal and professional life he lived there, although there is a good deal about his early years in Mexico. But the demonstrable level and range of his activity between 1922 and 1928, when he resigned his teaching appointment at Tulane, are sufficient to show that he was indeed "a young man of enthusiasm." His instructional schedule, as recorded in the university *Register,* was heavy, to say the least: for the academic year of 1922–1923, he was responsible each week for ten courses in architecture, some of them probably taught in studio combinations, ranging from beginning drawing and graphics to clay modeling to human figure rendering to the history of ancient and medieval architecture. He commuted each day from the Quarter down St. Charles Avenue to the university in the company of his two closest academic friends, Oliver La Farge and Frans Blom, both of whom had completed their advanced work in archaeology at Harvard and were then involved in Tulane's research program on Middle America.

Spratling's first apartment was in Orleans Alley, a narrow one-block street connecting Jackson Square with Royal; it was on an upper floor,

8. The book was subtitled *A Gallery of Contemporary New Orleans* and was published by the Pelican Bookshop in December 1926, with a total printing of four hundred copies. The "Sahara of the Bozart" phrase appeared as the title of an essay in *Prejudices: Second Series* (New York: Alfred A. Knopf, 1920).

overlooking the St. Louis Cathedral garden, and in close proximity to several of the structures he would soon be sketching for *Picturesque New Orleans*. The apartment was owned by Natalie Scott, one of the three women whom Spratling met in New Orleans who subsequently became important influences on his personal development and artistic career. By the time he arrived in the city, she had long been fully integrated into the highly reciprocal artistic society of the Quarter—not anything like a "school," which has a commonality of assumption and purpose, but a group, as Basso would later recall, which made the French Quarter "a sort of Creole version of the Left Bank," held together by "mutual friendliness and good will."[9] Natalie Scott lived in one of the tall four-story houses in St. Anthony's alley and, along with the Jack McClures—he being one of the *Double Dealer* editors—was identified in the Vieux Carré walking tour already mentioned as one of "a group of regulars— Bohemians who liked the atmosphere sufficiently to pay it the compliment of residing there in the shadow of the Cathedral." Like a few other members of the Quarter society, she was a working journalist, writing a weekly social column for the *Times-Picayune* under the name of "Peggy Passe Partout." But unlike most of the others, she had been a longtime resident of New Orleans, graduating from Sophie Newcomb College in 1909. Gregarious and active in a number of social causes, she was some eleven years older than Spratling, but their fast compatibility, together with her genuine interest in Louisiana history, would lead to their collaboration in 1925–1926 on *Old Plantation Houses in Louisiana*. And, at the end of the decade, as Elizabeth Anderson would do also, Natalie would carry the New Orleans friendship with Spratling to Taxco, the three of them living there for the rest of their lives, creating new and distinctive careers unexpected during their French Quarter time.

His heavy teaching schedule with its long afternoons in studio classes kept Spratling at the university all day. But it was not long before he began to participate in the activity of the Arts and Crafts Club, teaching cast and clay-modeling classes at night and helping to design the club's extravagant entertainments. He secured part-time employment with New Orleans architectural firms and eventually organized evening sessions for the instruction of draftsmen working on city projects. It is not clear if, during his first two years or so in New Orleans, Spratling envi-

9. Basso, "William Faulkner, Man and Writer," 11.

sioned any future for himself beyond an academic career, supplementing that with the professional opportunities afforded by the metropolis and with the rich bohemian life of the Vieux Carré. His absorption in drawing, and the subsequent study of its ordered forms in the architecture curriculum, had been for him, perhaps, an imaginative reconstruction linking his cloistered and uncertain life in the small college town of Auburn with a reality beyond that existence. And, as we have seen, his correspondence with his brother during those years both explicated and helped to resolve his sense of restlessness and growing self-confidence. During his later life, even when the international style of his silver designs was being exhibited in elegant shops on three continents, Spratling insisted that he had always considered himself, first, as a writer. In 1922–1923 he had begun to exhibit his drawings at the Arts and Crafts Club and with the New Orleans Art League. But he had not yet brought together what would eventually become one of his most characteristic expressions: architectural renderings accompanied by a text written by himself that would place the buildings within their cultural context. In fact, it was his work as what might be called an architectural artist rather than any special accomplishments as a designer of buildings that marked his artistic transition from the New Orleans experience to his creative life in Mexico.

Although one of Spratling's first teaching assignments at Tulane was in architectural history and although he had also taught the subject briefly as an undergraduate instructor, he had thus far had no firsthand experience in appraising buildings as cultural icons. His first trip to Europe, in which he and his college friends in 1921 had worked their passage over and back, was more in the nature of an undergraduate lark than a calculated cultural experience, and though they took weekend pictures of each other on the wide avenues of Brussels, all of them were rather closely confined during the week to their shipboard duties while docked at Antwerp. Spratling did some sketching in the Azores and some watercolors in Belgium, but these, as one of the group related, were stolen by a crew member, and thus the trip was pictorially recorded only in the several photographs and pencil sketches in Brussels that Spratling retained in his personal scrapbook.[10] It was to be quite different during the summer of 1923 when Spratling, having saved sufficient funds from

10. C. W. Warner, letter to author, December 17, 1992.

his meager salary during his first year in New Orleans, took a sketching excursion to France and Normandy. The results were part of his first publication, *Pencil Drawing,* which appeared in the fall of 1923 under the imprint of the Penguin Book Shop.

Part of the rationale for the book was no doubt economic, with Spratling hoping that his students would buy it and thus help him recover some of his expenses for the trip. But that its forty pages of text and ten illustrations meant more to him than that is indicated by his recollection of it some twenty years later in a letter to Aunt Miriam describing his publication as "a casual but awful serious little thing." Designed in the style of traditional drawing manuals he would have seen in the Tulane library holdings, with his own renderings illustrating such topics as "the line" and "composition," the text is elementary in nature and written with a clear, mildly authoritarian tone. The illustrations themselves, ranging from cathedral and chateau towers and doorways in Paris, Blois, and Versailles to old houses at Evreux and Rouen, seem much in the manner of the drawing masters and painters of the Norwich School in England, especially the work of John Sell Cotman, selections from whose early-nineteenth-century *Architectural Antiquities of Normandy* would have been reproduced in the slides used in architecture history courses such as those Spratling had been teaching.[11] But however the little book might have reflected the academic background of a young instructor of twenty-three, it also seems equally as much a statement to himself as one intended for others of the importance of the medium he would refine throughout his career. For what he described in the book as the qualities of "rare delicacy, sensitiveness and subtle suggestion that may be put in a mere pencil line" would soon be illustrated in the evocative composition of St. Louis Cathedral in *Picturesque New Orleans,* in the sensitive portraits of the Sherwood Andersons he would draw in the next year, and years later in his numerous unpublished silver designs. Perhaps, also, the book was "awful serious" because it was the first time he had profes-

11. W.S. to Mrs. L. W. Spratling, November 29, 1941. The *Antiquities,* whose scores of drawings, etchings, and paintings contain subjects such as those drawn by Spratling a century later, was published in 1822, based on Cotman's three tours of France, 1817 to 1820; for commentary on his use of pencil drawing and his architectural sensitivity to composition, see Adele M. Holcomb, *John Sell Cotman* (London: British Museum Publications, 1978); and Miklós Rajnai, ed., *John Sell Cotman, 1782–1842* (Ithaca: Cornell University Press, 1982).

sionally seen his work in print for an unknown audience, and, too, because it sent a modest message of gratitude and vindication back to Alabama: to Professor Biggin, to whom the book is dedicated, and, of course, to Uncle Leck, who received one of the first copies. The inscription on the latter was warm but avoided the familial "Billy" of their correspondence: "To Dr. L. W. Spratling—with affection—from his nephew—The Author, Oct. 3rd 1923."

As we have seen, "The Author" had that fall almost simultaneously with *Pencil Drawing* published ten impressions of the French Quarter under the title *Picturesque New Orleans,* this by the more prestigious Tulane University Press. Throughout his stay in the city Spratling exhibited a remarkable ability to get his work published, and newspaper notices of each of the two books not only helped to identify the energetic creativity of the young teacher-artist but also, much no doubt to Spratling's delight, indirectly recommended them to the buying public. Before ten of the European sketches appeared in *Pencil Drawing,* Spratling informally exhibited thirty or so of them in his Orleans Alley studio, and, as described by Lyle Saxon in an October review, "each evening last week groups of artists and art students from the neighborhood have climbed the studio stairs to look at these sketches. . . . The book will be off the press, ready for sale, by the time this issue of the paper is on the street—and it is safe to say that the book will command wide attention among artists and those interested in the arts." Shortly thereafter, *Picturesque New Orleans* was issued in a first printing of a thousand copies, just in time, as the reviewer observed, to make for Christmas "a distinctive and original gift—and a present which one may be sure will not be duplicated. Mr. Spratling's pencil drawings are full of charm, and it seems to me that the artist has caught something of the real feeling of the old quarter. . . . Perhaps the most interesting of all is a drawing of the St. Louis Cathedral, in the mist . . . an atmospheric effect which is most unusual. The drawings are all away from the stereotyped pictures of the old section." It was publicity such as this, together with his leadership in organizing the evening classes in architectural theory and practical applications for city employees and, also, his friendship with N. C. Curtis, that helped to introduce Spratling's name to the publishing activity of the American Institute of Architects, which led eventually to his contracts for articles on Mexican and European architecture. Relative to this later international work, where his pencil renderings would come to maturity, was his continuing interest in the architecture of New Orleans itself, whose history and unique place in American culture he was carefully studying. And it was during the latter months of this year that he began an extended series of drawings focused on the ornamental ironwork of the French Quarter, which he hoped would be his next publication success.[12]

As the academic year of 1923–1924 drew to a close, Spratling must have felt that his second year in New Orleans had been a good one: the publication of two books, positive reviews of his early exhibitions, and an enlarging social life with a group of interesting and influential friends. But it had been a strenuous year too and his dismal financial condition did not seem likely to improve despite his pursuit of whatever extramural activity would yield further income. He seemed determined, however, if not to replicate the pattern of the year just past, at least to continue his own professional and artistic self-education which he had initiated in the sketching tour of France during the previous summer. Thus toward the end of May he wrote to the President of Tulane asking for a loan of four hundred dollars against his salary for the forthcoming year,

> to enable me to carry out my plans for the summer, i.e., to spend two months on a sketching and study trip thru Italy. . . . It means a great deal to me to be able to get away from New Orleans for the summer. Work has been rather strenuous the past year and I don't feel that my health would stand up under the office work which my stay in New Orleans would necessitate.

In a manner reminiscent of a time when university fiscal affairs were less opaque and more personalized, he offered as a business proposition to put up as collateral two thousand copies of a second printing of *Picturesque New Orleans* with a "retail value," he wrote, "of $2200. . . . This, of course, could not be done at a bank."[13]

12. Lyle Saxon, "The Artists Come Home," *New Orleans Times-Picayune Sunday Magazine,* quoted in "Former Auburnite Gains Fame in Art," *Montgomery Advertiser,* October 25, 1924; unsigned review, *New Orleans Times-Picayune,* n.d. (*c.* December 15, 1924); Ethel M. Halsey, "Architectural Atelier Opens at Arts and Crafts Club with Large Class in Attendance," *New Orleans Item,* n.d., Artists Files, Historic New Orleans Collection (hereinafter HNOC).

13. W.S. to A. B. Dinwiddie, May 29, 1924; William Spratling File, Manuscripts Department, Tulane University Library.

The success of his proposal supported a tour that actually lasted three months, taking him to Italy, Spain, Greece, and Egypt. The return of "that enterprising young Tulane professor, Bill Spratling, [who] has brought back some treasures of sketches" was recorded by his friend Natalie Scott in her "Peggy Passe Partout's Letter" column of September 14, and documented in more detail a few days later in the *Times-Picayune*, which, in noting that Spratling managed the whole trip for $325, indirectly confirmed that his loan proposal was a pretty good estimate. Although he did not publish in a separate collection the drawings and paintings from this tour as he had done with those of the earlier trip in *Pencil Drawing*, Spratling exhibited them throughout that fall and during the next year to high praise, and it is clear from the *Times-Picayune* story about his return that his identity in the New Orleans cultural community was, first, that of an "artist," who "is also an architect and an instructor at Tulane." Reviews of the Italian work began in October with his inclusion of three pieces in the opening exhibition by member artists of the Arts and Crafts Club; in November, additional line drawings of buildings and bridges in Rome and Venice were added "that show so well his delicacy of treatment that loses nothing in the handling of masses."[14]

The letter to President A. B. Dinwiddie, however, about his financial stress had been no exaggeration, and here at the beginning of the new term he had already borrowed against his annual salary. He had hoped to sell to one of the popular architectural magazines an essay, with sketches, he had executed before leaving for Europe about the restoration of Roamer's Roost, the family home at Gold Hill: "The Evolution of a Pioneer Farmhouse in Alabama." But his summer's absence probably prevented its publication in *House Beautiful,* which had expressed initial interest but had filled its future issues by the time Spratling in the fall could assemble and communicate additional requested photographs.[15] During Spratling's first two years in New Orleans, living costs in the French Quarter had become more expensive than those he would later describe in the autobiography as prevalent when he first arrived. Then he had been able to hire a woman to fix his meals and do all the daily

14. The Papers of Natalie Vivian Scott, Manuscripts Department, Tulane University Library; William Spratling, Artists Files, HNOC; reviews appeared in the *Times-Picayune*: October 6 and November 16, 1924.

15. E. S. Allen to W.S., July 29 and September 19, 1924, January 3, 1925, Collection of Miriam Ann Kirkwood Syler.

housework; but shortly after his return from Europe, he wrote back to
Alabama that he "had let Elnora go, except for the Saturday cleaning."
And, three months later, he wrote that "I have practically no funds" and
reiterated an earlier request that Uncle Leck share with him expenses
of some nine dollars relating to "that Opelika telephone charge." The
telephone call was related to the procedure whereby Uncle Leck, who
had retired from the navy in 1921 and subsequently moved to the family
home in Gold Hill, had proposed to purchase from the three children
their interests, inherited from their grandfather, in the acreage and house,
which had been renovated and restored. After some hesitation, Lucile
had agreed to sign the deed, as had Spratling, who obviously needed the
money. But the brief correspondence is more than a commentary on his
dismal financial condition. It suggests further the continuing ambivalence
in Spratling toward his family past, an attitude encouraged both by affection and pride. At the time he is severing all legal connections with the
family property, which he will not re-visit for almost forty years, he is
grateful to Aunt Miriam for sending "the box of eats," especially the
fruitcake, and states his hope that they will both come down for a visit.
And while assuring Uncle Leck, as he had done so often in his youthful
letters, that he is "really trying to economize" and, moreover (though
there is plenty of evidence to the contrary), that he rarely entertains his
friends, he clearly wants them to understand that he had achieved a certain social status in the big city:

> I gave a real party the other night in honor of my own return. Sherwood
> Anderson and all the local literary and artistic satellites were there. Will
> send you an account of it if it appears in the paper Sunday. It's the only
> party I've ever given except having ones and twos to dinner.[16]

The Andersons, not many months married, had arrived in New Orleans in July, taking an apartment in one of the refurbished Pontalba
Buildings, only a short distance across Jackson Square and down Orleans
Alley to Spratling's upper-floor rooms. Within two weeks of his return
there, as the same letter to Alabama, written in September, makes clear,
he had begun with the Andersons a social acquaintance. His close friendship with Elizabeth Prall Anderson would not develop until both he and

16. W.S. to Dr. L. W. Spratling, September 24, 1924; W.S. to Dr. and Mrs. L. W.
Spratling, January 14, 1925.

she had settled in Taxco, but for the two years before the Andersons left New Orleans in 1926, the three of them were intimate members of the congenial Vieux Carré fellowship, who typically and often came together at just such an affair at Spratling's described in the *Times-Picayune* social column of November 17 ("the unique kind which only the French Quarter at its best can produce"), a column Spratling, had he thought about it, would have preferred Uncle Leck and Aunt Miriam not to see.

Elizabeth Anderson recalled that they had met Spratling through Caroline Wogan Durieux, who for some time had shown a special interest in him, taking him around to museum exhibitions, "instructing him in what was good and what was bad." Durieux, the only artist of wide reputation to emerge from the old Creole New Orleans world, influenced Spratling's artistic growth perhaps more than any of his associates at the Arts and Crafts Club, where she had been prominent and had exhibited following her return in 1919 to the city from her studies at the Philadelphia Academy. Her enthusiasm for the European and Oriental modernists, whose works were only then beginning to appear at the Delgado Museum, must have been communicated to the younger artist, and her own economic and inferential painting style may have helped Spratling to confirm these tendencies in his own work. They apparently shared, too, the qualities of temperament necessary for caricature and satire, which would appear only occasionally in his work but would characterize hers. She and her husband lived in Cuba and in Mexico City during the twenties, but she returned occasionally to New Orleans for extended visits. As Spratling in 1929–1930 was getting established in Mexico and she was turning to the lithographic form that would establish her reputation, they both exhibited at the same Mexico City gallery, and would remain friends throughout his Taxco years, she visiting Natalie Scott there and giving informal showings of her increasingly popular work.[17]

By the spring of 1925—the middle of his New Orleans experience— Spratling had indeed been fortunate in the influential opportunities available to him. If Caroline Durieux had helped to widen his aesthetic boundaries, others, such as N. C. Curtis and Lyle Saxon, had in imperceptible ways encouraged him toward the achievement by that time of

17. Caroline Wogan Durieux, Artists Files; Natalie Scott Papers; Richard Cox, *Caroline Durieux: Lithographs of the Thirties and Forties* (Baton Rouge: Louisiana State University Press, 1977).

an impressive level of artistic composition, which was essentially a strong creative response to the forms of "oldness" and cultural history in the New Orleans scene and, less so, in such European settings as Normandy and Venice. Elizabeth Anderson remembered the New Orleans Spratling "looking as slight and dark as a Mexican, with his jutting jaw and eyes that squinted half-defiantly at the world."[18] Half-defiant, no doubt. He would never cease to challenge the latent threat of displacement that the Alabama years had taught him to suppress and assimilate. Every allusion to him, however, during his New Orleans period seems to emphasize his energy, the diverse range of his activity, his self-confidence, and his ready accommodation to the possibilities of new experience. Perhaps the natural and genuine familial courtesy and the close student relationships in Auburn that may have seemed cloying at times had helped to underwrite the flair for verbal and social reciprocity that marked his personal identity in the Vieux Carré. And his capacity for easy friendship found its artistic counterpart again and again in the quick but perceptive renderings of the Quarter's permanent or transient social and intellectual membership, some probably professionally contracted, such as that for the poster advertisement for a November 20, 1926, concert by New Orleans pianist-composer Genevieve Pitot, and that of Elizabeth Anderson. Others, perhaps privately drawn, sometimes found their way into the local press: those, for example, of John Dos Passos, which appeared in the *Times-Picayune* in March 1924 during his two-month working vacation in the city; and of Sherwood Anderson ("by the notable French Quarter artist, William Spratling"), which was included with a review in early December 1924, of *A Story Teller's Story*.

In March of 1925, a new friend—one who would be among his closest companions for the next two years—walked unexpectedly into the Orleans Alley apartment, asking and receiving permission to take up residence there. William Faulkner had been in New Orleans for several weeks earlier in the new year, staying in the Anderson apartment as the guest of Elizabeth, who had been Faulkner's employer in New York, prior to her marriage to Sherwood, at the Doubleday bookshop. By early March, when he returned to the city from a brief Mississippi visit and,

18. Elizabeth Anderson and Gerald R. Kelly, *Miss Elizabeth: A Memoir* (Boston: Little, Brown, 1969), 83–84.

following a suggestion by the Andersons, moved in with Spratling, Faulkner had essentially completed a transitional emphasis in his writing from poetry and criticism to prose fiction; he had already in February placed in the *Times-Picayune* the first of a series of impressionistic sketches of New Orleans life, and was seriously at work on the novel that would become *Soldier's Pay*. Whatever rent he was able to pay for the first-floor spaces he shared with another roomer was a welcome addition to the diminished budget of the busy artist-architect in the upstairs studio. In that month, Spratling, in the midst of his regular and night-school teaching, his occasional contract work, and his annual involvement in helping to plan and design the post-Lenten Bal d'Artistes at the Arts and Crafts Club, was completing arrangements for the extensive showing that month at the Delgado Museum of his previous summer's work, some of which he doubtless hoped to sell. He was also now beginning to plan with Natalie Scott the research and travel they would initiate in the late spring for their collaboration on what would be Spratling's most ambitious project thus far, the book to be called *Old Plantation Houses in Louisiana*.

The availability of an elaborate personal and literary chronology of Faulkner's life in New Orleans does not significantly illuminate the nature of the Spratling-Faulkner friendship. Nor does Spratling's 1966 recollection of it, as recorded in "Chronicle of a Friendship," which he transported almost verbatim into the autobiography. A number of details from the latter, however, despite Spratling's usual collapsed chronology and uncertain memory, have found their way into the Faulkner story. But we may safely infer that here, during an important formative period for their subsequent years, they hit it off pretty well. Not necessarily alike at all in temperament, they seemed properly complementary in their work habits and level of energy. While the plural distribution of that energy on Spratling's part began early in the day with the long trip out St. Charles Avenue to the university, he remembered something of the focused intensity of Faulkner, who would habitually be up even earlier, already "tapping away on his portable." Faulkner would spend many afternoons talking with Anderson, walking often by the river. But Harold Levy, one of Faulkner's closer friends in the Quarter and to whom he dedicated one of his poems, remembered that Faulkner and Spratling were also often together, dropping around here and there especially in the evenings to visit and socialize.[19]

The two were certainly alike in the creative immediacy with which they utilized available subjects, and within a short time their companionship and occasional neighborhood walks together began to appear in the short fiction that Faulkner once more was placing regularly in the Sunday editions of the *Times-Picayune*. For example, the initial scene for "Out of Nazareth," which was printed on Easter, April 12, is set in Jackson Park, and opens with a brief conversation about what may have been one of their habitual subjects. The narrator, Faulkner, observes, as his companion begins a "discursive" response to his own remark about the art of Cezanne, that the hand of Spratling "has been shaped to a brush as mine has (alas!) not." Then both, the writer and the artist, are immediately arrested by the pictorial beauty and unaffected demeanor of a young man, David, whom they see standing in the park gazing at the cathedral. Spratling asks him questions about his interest in pictures and poetry, wishes to hire him as a model, and Faulkner, who gives him a dollar, is struck by the boy's gift to him of a written narrative of his travels, which is artless, simple and "blundering" but charged by "some impulse which caused him to want to write it out on paper." The reflective and symbolic little story is important, as scholars have established is true of almost all of the "New Orleans" sketches, for prefiguring significant themes and episodes in Faulkner's later fiction. But for our purposes it suggests the sense of easy reciprocity between painting and writing that the two young men probably shared and may well have discussed from time to time in the Orleans Alley apartment, where the story was written, or in their walks, where, as in the story, they strolled "between ancient softly greenish gates" into the great Cathedral square.

Spratling also appears by name in the half-hour-or-so scene of "Episode," which was published in August. Here, the writer and the artist, as in "Out of Nazareth," focus on an unexpected subject, an old woman whom Faulkner daily had seen passing below the Orleans Alley apartment balcony with her blind beggar husband on the way to the cathedral

19. The discussion of the Spratling-Faulkner relationship in the pages below is greatly indebted to the authoritative treatment of Faulkner's life by Joseph Blotner in *Faulkner: A Biography* (New York: Random House, 1974). All biographical facts related to the chronology of Faulkner's New Orleans years are taken from the one-volume edition (New York: Vintage Books, 1991), chapters 15–24, pp. 126–208.

square. As Spratling calls from above and arranges for them to pose, Faulkner seems to see her cheerfully ugly face transformed briefly into a Mona Lisa–like image of eternal feminine mystery. After Spratling has professionally paid his "models" with fifteen cents borrowed from Faulkner and the old pair have moved away down the alley, the two young men stare curiously at the finished picture with the writer seeing that what he intuitively had inferred the artist had drawn and made visible.

Each of the sixteen experimental stories Faulkner published during 1925 in the Sunday editions of the *Times-Picayune* no doubt drew to some extent on his immediate observations of the New Orleans scene, and several of them utilize a first-person narrator. "Out of Nazareth" and "Episode," however, as well as the unpublished "Peter," which the paper apparently chose not to purchase because of its prostitution setting and the naive involvement of a young mulatto boy in the hard dialogue of the brothel where his mother works—these are the only ones of the series wherein a member of the Vieux Carré group of writers and artists to which Spratling and Faulkner both belonged specifically appears by name and character. The view of Spratling in each of the three stories is clearly that of an artist whose search for creative material on the passing French Quarter stage is compatible with that of Faulkner, or at least with that of the authorial "I" of the narrator. And in the general absence of verbal messages sent forward by Spratling during this period in his life, the symbiotic relationship recorded in these stories, not by him but by another, suggests that he was then living at fairly close and familiar quarters with a friend whose disciplined determination to learn his craft through conscientious experimentation matched those attributes in his own character. Faulkner's education during his New Orleans period in the concept of modernism, in both art and fiction, would have been furthered by his associations with several of the circle within which he and Spratling moved—the Sherwood Andersons and Caroline Durieux, for example; and one recent estimate identifies Spratling "himself an architect and artist as a formidable influence."[20] To both Faulkner and Spratling, of course, well beyond their New Orleans days, "modernism" would come to mean a re-creation in new forms of a specific "history."

20. Panthea Reid Broughton, "Faulkner's Cubist Novels," in *A Cosmos of My Own: Faulkner and Yoknapatawpha,* ed. Doreen Fowler and Ann J. Abadie (Jackson: University Press of Mississippi, 1981), 75.

There is even a further suggestion, and that is all it can be, that the emerging impressionist style of Faulkner's writing in these three stories, as well as in some of the others in the series, is not unlike some of the qualities beginning to appear in Spratling's own work. In each of the three stories in which Spratling appears as a character, the central figures of David, the old woman, and Peter are bold enough in outline, but each under the writer's reflective eye or the artist's transforming pencil is diffused into a momentary abstraction of a wider identity: that of the ageless feminine enigma, for example, as of the old woman, "there was something in her face that was not her face." This sudden capturing of a fleeting impression also appears—almost in a painterly mode—in "Peter," where the interior passage of the Negro brothel, which with its "ineffable azure" walls obscures the paved reality of the outside street, frames a tableau of haste and passion, and as Spratling in the filtered sunlight sketches the wise and innocent figure of the boy, "art and vice" seem fused and the eyes of Peter's mother reflect "all the despair of a subject race." An actual comparison of the two young men's artistic work during this year of the middle twenties cannot be exact, of course, no matter how closely the fictional Spratling may with his pencil's eye have captured what his writer companion had seen and verbally expressed. But the anticipatory style of imprecise suggestion and abstracted meaning in these early Faulkner stories finds something of a parallel in a review of Spratling's painting that went on exhibit in November of that year, of work he had completed in Europe during the previous summer before meeting Faulkner.

Earlier reviews of Spratling's work, especially his pencil drawings of local and continental architectural settings, had emphasized his delicacy of line and his disciplined restraint in light and shadow composition. The new pictures, as judged by reviewers that fall, displayed an increased boldness and more loosely done treatment. "Spratling, long known to his critics as a master of line, has in this exhibit burst the bonds of line and done some remarkable color work," achieving a tonal quality and impressionistic feeling not as visible before. The sketches and paintings, set mostly in Florence, Venice, Genoa, and Rome, emphasized to one reviewer a quality not unlike Faulkner's verbal touch in the early experimental story just described: Spratling's "visioning" ability, his capacity to see beyond "the complicated masses of buildings and bridges and harbor-scenes, the essential lines, and eliminating every touch not necessary to set the impression he seeks." Spratling's emancipation from the "bonds of line" and his "broad, bold" style, especially in his pastels, seemed full of promise for further advancements, and the whole show itself, in which Spratling was equally represented with two other artists, was judged to be "the greatest exhibition the Arts and Crafts Club has ever offered New Orleans."[21]

For a young man of twenty-five, even one who might have been able to place such civic adulation in a proper perspective, praise like this would have to have been gratifying. And it must have been clear to him, if he thought about it at all, that his own artistic career, being developed in the context of a full-time academic position at Tulane, was at least keeping pace with that of his writer-companion on the lower floor. By the time these reviews appeared, however, Faulkner had completed the series of stories for the *Times-Picayune* and seemed to have assimilated Spratling, not by name this time, from the shadows of his imagination into one of the characters in the novel he had sent off, with an endorsement by Anderson, in June. And Spratling had by then seen the publication of an important collaboration with Curtis entitled *The Wrought Iron Work of Old New Orleans*.

Almost from the time of his arrival in the city Spratling had been very much in support of the preservationist movement led by Lyle Saxon, William Ratcliffe Irby, Elizabeth Werlein, and others to prevent what he described in a later *Architectural Forum* article as the phenomenon of how annually "these crumbling remains of an old world heritage continue to disappear with alarming rapidity before the commercial demands of a city growing in importance."[22] One expression of these themes was the joint publication with Curtis, brought out separately in a soft-cover edition by the American Institute of Architects. Curtis's essay, illustrated with his own fine renderings plus some photographs of Garden District houses, is an extensive comment on the dominant French character of residential architecture in 1840–1860 New Orleans and the relative absence of this important heritage in contemporary design. Spratling's contribution, though much shorter, complements the other by focusing on

21. *New Orleans States,* November 26, 1925. The other artists were the young Virginia Parker, who had just returned to New Orleans after studies in Europe and at the Philadelphia Academy; and Will H. Stevens, professor of art at Newcomb College.

22. Spratling, "The Architectural Heritage of New Orleans," 409.

ornamental ironwork, especially that in the Quarter, and how its distinctive character is also a unique historical resource for contemporary architecture practice. But of especial interest are Spratling's drawings, fifty-eight in number, of the seemingly endless variety of wrought- and cast-iron designs in such implements as balcony rails, grills, knockers, hinges, and catches. Many of the drawings are relatively undistinguished, but some are first-rate, such as an Empire bronze newel from a Barracks Street residence and a wrought gate and post detail from the old Exchange Bank on Royal. Yet all of them, with their intricate configurations of curved lines and angles and drawn as they were from closely observed authentic examples of a design style not indigenous to America, prefigure to some extent the design work Spratling in a few years would be creating in his Taxco shops. Similar to his illustrations in *Wrought Iron* was a page of twelve drawings, without text, published in the August, 1925 number of *Architecture,* entitled "Wrought Iron Crosses from the Old Jesuit Cemetery, Grand Coteau, Louisiana." Some of the sketches from Spratling's period of study in the summer of 1919 at the Beaux Arts School in New York, which he retained in his personal scrapbook, focus on museum examples of ornamental ironwork.[23]

During the busy spring months that ended the academic year of 1924–1925, Spratling was completing the drawings and text for the wrought-iron publication and planning the exhibitions of his previous summer's work. His daily life then, of course, had been much more regulated than Faulkner's. Although they were often together, each also went his separate way within the loose confederacy of Vieux Carré residents, who themselves led a reasonably disciplined existence, tied together in part by such linkages as the *Double Dealer* and the *Times-Picayune*, but also much enlivened by the pervasive presence of Prohibition liquor. Spratling's friend, painter and editorial cartoonist Keith Temple, recalled that "the big thing that bound all those artistic people together was alcohol," and confirmed Spratling's account in the autobiography that members of the group made their own, in five-gallon cans often literally located in a bathtub, using as a base Cuban alcohol discreetly secured along the waterfront. Gin was cheapest and easiest to make. "Was it good?" asked

23. N. C. Curtis and W. P. Spratling, *The Wrought Iron Work of Old New Orleans* (New York: Press of the American Institute of Architects, 1925).

Temple rhetorically. "Indeed it was . . . tasted fine, and we certainly drank a very great deal of it."[24]

Though Faulkner from time to time would disappear for a few days from the Orleans Alley apartment, Spratling remembered his presence there as "quiet and unobtrusive." The two of them shared cooking expenses with Oliver La Farge, and each seemed to have been sufficiently prudent with the money earned from his commercial sales and commissions, in fiction and architectural design, respectively, to support a trip to Europe together that summer. Although Spratling recorded that Faulkner decided to come along "at the last minute," Faulkner had originally come to New Orleans in January, hoping to earn enough for what would be his first trip over, and, one assumes, a crucially important one in his developing imaginative life. For Spratling, the passage would be his fourth, the last two having been enormously significant in expanding his pictorial vocabulary. In his enterprising manner he had arranged one, and possibly two, commissions to help with his living expenses and his five-dollar-a-day passage on the freighter *West Ivis*. With one of his slight but characteristic failures of memory, he records in "Chronicle of a Friendship" and subsequently in the autobiography that *Architectural Forum* had asked him to do some drawings-with-text on the Romanesque buildings of northern Italy. He remembered the commission correctly but not the journal, the work eventually being published in *Architecture*. The slip is insignificant in itself, but Spratling may have been recalling another commission that *Architectural Forum* might in fact have offered: to prepare a similar article—which he did—on the architecture of Savannah, where the ship was scheduled to dock and lie over for a few days before the Atlantic crossing and passage through the Mediterranean to Genoa.

The highest praise for his drawings and paintings was yet to come in the fall exhibits, but before sailing Spratling must have known that his strictly professional career was about to assume a new and truly impressive dimension: the forthcoming publication by the American Institute of Architects on New Orleans architecture and ironwork with the widely known and influential N. C. Curtis; a highly complimentary commission

24. Keith Temple, quoted in Stella Pitts, "The Quarter in the Twenties," *New Orleans Times-Picayune, Dixie,* November 26, 1972, 44.

for the piece on classic Italian buildings from *Architecture,* a journal which was published in New York by Scribner's and issued its numbers in England as well as America; and in all likelihood the contract for the Savannah piece, which would initiate for Spratling a multi-year relationship with the prestigious *Architectural Forum.*

The two friends were to sail on July 7, and, on the day before, Faulkner wrote to his mother that July was not the storm month, and in high humor:

> We expect to have a good crossing. . . . Bill and I have been given by kind friends a hundred addresses of nice people in Europe who will feed us. . . . Quite a gang are coming down to see us off. Hope they'll have sence enough to bring a band with 'em. I always have wanted to go some where to the sound of poorly played cornets and drums.[25]

One wishes, of course, that Spratling's account of the voyage and trip to Italy and France were more complete, although it does supply a few anecdotes of interest to the Faulkner story, such as Spratling witnessing—between New Orleans and Savannah—his companion one morning casually throwing overboard into the Gulf waters a lengthy manuscript he had apparently written during the months in Orleans Alley. The short stay in Savannah is not mentioned, although Faulkner's biographer records from a letter home that Faulkner spent some time examining tombstone inscriptions in the Colonial Cemetery there, perhaps having become momentarily interested in Spratling's tombstone drawings, which he would have seen in the upstairs studio. Spratling, meanwhile, was busy walking and sketching, gathering impressions for the short article on the city's architectural styles, which he probably completed after his return to New Orleans in September and sent off to meet the journal's deadline for the November issue, in which it was published.[26]

The article contains four substantial renderings, one of them full-page, and though its content is slight, only about six hundred words, it exhibits Spratling's increasing ability to fuse precise architectural observations with those that create a brief sense of ambience. In harmony with his

25. Faulkner to Mrs. M. C. Falkner, July 6, 1925, *Thinking of Home: William Faulkner's Letters to His Mother and Father 1918–1925,* ed. James G. Watson (New York: Norton, 1992), 213.

26. William Spratling, "Savannah's Architectural Background," *Architectural Forum* 43 (November 1925): 273–76.

quick pencil, his text captures the English character of the city, with its Georgian fronts, raised porches, open spaces, and smaller structures subtly half-hidden in the shadows of the masses of foliage that soften the transition between old and new buildings, a transition very different from the abrupt urban junctures of New Orleans. There is an almost unexpected ease of allusion in his linking the architectural feeling of Savannah with the English tradition in other old seaboard cities such as Charleston and Norfolk, which he appears to have visited once only briefly in his undergraduate journey north from Alabama to have it out with Uncle Leck. And though he may have gone over with Lucile and Eddie to see New Haven during his New York visit with them, his reference to its "snug little architectural mannerisms" may have owed something to Faulkner's remembrance of his own visits there in 1918. But as we try to assess, principally from what he wrote for publication and drew or painted during these years, Spratling's gradual passage toward his final place of residence where the nature of his art would be altered and would secure for him an audience immeasurably beyond the local or professional, the little piece on Savannah is further suggestive. It concludes with Spratling adapting the "travel" persona of the visitor-narrator he would so frequently utilize during the next few years. And almost in the manner of a late-Victorian Howells or Henry James contemplating the ambience of a Venice, he observes as "one who loves the beauty of old things" that the architecture of Savannah with its charm of gentility and simplicity has attained a quietly ironic triumph—ironic because the city lacks the commercial energy that produces modern modes of building bereft of these qualities. But if Savannah "may have missed her opportunity for a business boom . . . we must confess that we are rather glad of it, for in missing much, she has in one way gained more," preserving a quality that "would otherwise have been demolished and trampled underfoot in the frenzied rush of modern business life." This is the antiquarian voice of a young New Orleans preservationist, of course, but a voice also predictive, for it anticipates what he would in fact eventually accomplish for his adopted town of Taxco—though there he would remove the irony, initiating a commercial energy for the community that "progress" had overlooked, and yet as much as any one person, he would assure that its historical style of architecture would be maintained.

There was no doubt in Spratling's memory as to the central episode that occurred during the short stay in Genoa before he and Faulkner took the train north: hijinks in a local cafe with a lot of drinking and dancing, with Spratling, unbeknownst to Faulkner and other shipboard companions, being hustled off to jail after offending a prostitute and her agent. He spent the night there with an assortment of "piratical comrades" and was assured by one of them that he seemed destined for a future career of rock-breaking, which caused him to devise a plan to get a note out to the American consul. But unexpectedly he was released through the offices of Faulkner and the ship's purser and told by the magistrate that the charges of insulting the royal family of Italy were being dropped. (Spratling as a joke had tossed some coins on the cabaret floor to see the girl scramble for them.) There is no reason to doubt the colorful authenticity of the episode, and Spratling remembered that Faulkner had remarked he wished it had all happened to him. But when Spratling first recalled it forty years later in "Chronicle of a Friendship," he apparently did not know that Faulkner characteristically had long since assimilated the story into his fiction, and, indeed, as his biographer records, even made himself the hero as he re-told the story the following week in a letter home to Mississippi.

Spratling wrote that "our itinerary in Italy was vague," but he apparently knew already, perhaps from his side-trips from Venice during the previous summer or possibly also from his academic teaching in architectural history, the places he wished to see first for his drawings: Vincenza and the Romeo-and-Juliet town of Verona to the east and, in Lombardy, the ancient companion towns of Mantua, Cremona, and Pavia. After he and Faulkner separated on arrival in Genoa, he gradually sketched his way northward, making drawings in Verona and Mantua that would appear in the *Architecture* article. And, as he began in early August to work seriously at his assignment, he was incidentally completing also another portion of his artistic education in yet another cultural setting he had not entered before. In Cremona, for example, where the young Virgil had studied, he would have seen the Romanesque style at its height in the magnificent cathedral, and in many other churches and public buildings its transitional confrontation and merging with the new Gothic modes. The scale of this architectural chronology was no less pronounced in Pavia, and it was here that for a brief period the creative expression of both Spratling and Faulkner became unconsciously interwoven.

On his own journey northward to reconnoiter with Spratling, Faulk-

ner's romantic imagination was particularly touched by the medieval ambience of the town. The documentary record shows that two of the group
of sonnets he had been composing for months were dated "Pavia—
August, 1925," and though it is not clear from that record, at least one
of Spratling's recollections indicates that the two stayed there at the same
time. Of the seven drawings Spratling published from the sketching tour,
four were of buildings in Pavia, and it was possibly during his two or
three days of drawing there, more than in their later travels in Stresa and
the lake country north of Milan, that he remembered Faulkner's "pleasant humor," and, as in the previous spring in New Orleans, their pencil
companionship of writing and sketching:

> He wrote and wandered and meditated wherever I went. His medita-
> tions were usually out loud and rambling and it was difficult for one to
> draw and at the same time listen to Bill. While I would be drawing a bridge
> in Pavia, he would be discoursing to the effect that for him there were
> "only two basic compulsions on earth, i.e., love and death."[27]

Spratling's forty-year recollections, eclectic and usually discursive, seem
here curiously authentic, recalling, unconsciously it would seem, the the-
matic "love and death" vocabulary of the closing section of the completed manuscript his companion had left behind and whose fate may
well have been on his mind. And, somehow appropriately, it was a letter
from Spratling, then returned to New Orleans, that three weeks later
communicated to Faulkner in Paris the news that Boni and Liveright had
indeed accepted his first novel for publication.

For Spratling, Pavia also exhibited that quality to which his own romantic imagination was drawn throughout his life: "that sense of leisure-
liness which we of the New World find so enviably foreign," but which
to him New Orleans and Savannah had cultivated and retained. He had
gradually abandoned any emphasis his original assignment may have
been to record the "Romanesque," drawing instead buildings that
seemed of interest to him, especially those—like some he had drawn in
Normandy two summers earlier—whose rounded domes or towers rising
above ornamented octagonal or strictly rectangular bases were particularly challenging for the free-hand pencil. "Pavia is not classic," he

---

27. William Spratling, *File on Spratling* (Boston: Little, Brown, 1967), 33. The detail
of the Pavia bridge does not occur in the "Chronicle of a Friendship" account.

wrote, and even though "possibly the spirit of the place" still was imbued with a Romanesque and twelfth-century feeling, he chose to draw structures that illustrated the architectural history of Lombardy: "the manner in which the buildings have been allowed to grow up, their masses fitting amiably one into the other." His artist's eye caught the "curious and dramatic things" adorning Sant Michele, one of the most distinctive of all Lombardy-Romanesque churches, but he could not have shown in a small drawing the elaborate figurative vision of the medieval world carved there on its sandstone facade. He sketched instead the building which "quietly dominates the town," the great Renaissance duomo, begun in the fifteenth century on a site where early Romanesque cathedrals had stood, and whose vast tower and dome his perspective showed rising above and behind a cluster of secular shapes in the street below. As indicated in the autobiographical memory as well as the published drawing, he drew the red-tiled covered bridge with its sturdy graceful arches which spans the Ticino, showing, as one looks across it toward the town, the shapes of buildings and even the pathway by the shallow river still visible today, seventy years later. And he made the five-mile journey, perhaps with Faulkner, to Visconti Castle, where Leonardo had visited and worked, to see and sketch within its enormous park the Certosa, perhaps the most elaborate example of all Pavian composite architecture: its Gothic splendor made him feel "hopeless," and in one of his customary but still unexpected reflections on the human history of old buildings, this gregarious man ruminated "on the perfection of monastic life of the sixteenth century."[28]

By the second week in August Spratling had moved farther north, through Milan, with whose crowds of noisy tourists he contrasted the "genialness" of street life in the smaller towns, reaching Stresa on the western shore of the great lake that stretches across the border into Switzerland. There, he wrote, he and Faulkner had made plans, but in vain, to meet with Anita Loos, whom they had both known and admired in New Orleans. Despite his recollection in "Chronicle" that the Stresa weather was cold and depressing, his immediate impressions as recorded in the "Sketching in Northern Italy" piece were of the lake's "ineffable blue" water and the quaintness and charm of the small houses surround-

28. William Spratling, "Sketching in Northern Italy," *Architecture* (August 1926): 236–39.

ing it. Faulkner, of course, was writing all the time, identifying two additional poems in the sonnet sequence as written at "Lago Maggiore—August—1925"; and, just as usual, Spratling's sketch pad was always out, one drawing of which from this site—of the kind of old house with its crumbling brickwork and tall ungainly dignity he had sketched many times in New Orleans—he selected for publication under the title *Lago Maggiore, Isola Bella*. Spratling curiously does not record, as does his companion's biographer, their short but apparently expensive sojourn in Switzerland, where they saw Mont Blanc and visited Montreux and Geneva. But in the closing words of the brief descriptive essay he probably completed a few weeks later, he did express, in the architectural artist's vocabulary, his obvious affinity for what he had felt and tried to capture in the small Italian towns—the "warm earthiness of tone quality" that in fact always seemed to draw his own career southward—and the gradual disappearance of this elusive element as he and Faulkner took the train into France, toward "the pale monumental grays of Paris and the north."

Spratling wrote that the two of them took a small pension near the Luxembourg Gardens and together "frequented" such artistically allusive settings as the Deux Magots and Saint Germaine des Prés. Although his longterm retrospections called up the memory of their visit to Shakespeare and Company and their failure to meet any of the famous expatriates, there is no indication that in 1925 he was especially aware of the extraordinary vitality of the Parisian literary scene, the kinds of meetings and connections being made there. When they arrived in mid-August, for example, the most prominent couple in Paris, the Scott Fitzgeralds, had just departed the heat of the city for Antibes, still aglow from the enthusiastic reception of *The Great Gatsby*'s publication in April and new congratulatory acquaintanceships with a wide range of established and rising American writers then living there, from Edith Wharton and Gertrude Stein to Ernest Hemingway. It was Faulkner's first visit to the city, and he settled in for an extensive stay. Spratling had been there before, in the summer of 1923, publishing that fall in *Pencil Drawing* studies of the tower of St. Germain D'Auxerrois and of the orangery gate at Versailles. Now, he would be able to remain only two weeks or so before returning to his teaching duties in New Orleans. He apparently did no sketching this time, probably seeing no publication possibilities for more drawings of classic French structures; and to picture Left Bank building scenes would to some extent replicate what he had done so thoroughly in the Vieux Carré. Faulkner wandered repeatedly through museums and galleries, and Spratling may have gone along once or twice, seeing again the old masters at the Louvre and for the second or perhaps the first time, the work of the older Impressionists and of the Post-Impressionists, whose influence had not yet found its way to the Delgado in New Orleans. But for Spratling, there was another exhibit he had the possibility of seeing in the Paris of 1925 that was far more important to his future career than any scene connected with writers or painters: the "Exposition des Arts Decoratifs et Industriels Modernes." This elaborate show, from which the term "Art Deco" emerged, would have given him a firsthand view of the most advanced principles and illustrations of contemporary design. It would be another half-dozen years before he would begin to use these in a new creative life of his own. But the bold forms with their streamlined discipline may well have slipped into his consciousness, merging there with the curved images from architectural styles of other cultures, including those Gothic ones he had just admired in Lombardy.

If the summer's travels through Italy, Switzerland, and France had incidentally allowed Spratling to store up impressions and observations he would use in future years, as Faulkner certainly had done, there was no good reason for him to linger in Paris. He still had to refine the northern Italy sketches and accompanying text, but professionally he had essentially completed that contract. And there was plenty of work awaiting him in New Orleans. With his usual enterprising manner, he had secured—probably before sailing for Europe—an illustration contract with one of the South's oldest and most widely circulated professional-trade journals, the Atlanta-based *Southern Architect and Building News.* The contract, for six covers of the twelve monthly issues for 1926, probably was assisted by a reprint in its January 1925 number of Lyle Saxon's earlier review of *Picturesque New Orleans,* but it also is another example of Spratling's ability to promote his growing reputation as an architectural artist and also to re-cycle his work in differing commercial contexts. The covers for June, September, and October, for example, were "old" drawings from that 1923 book, the one for May a 1922 sketch of a hillside residence made during his months as a draftsman in Birmingham. The others, for the first three issues of the year, were new, all of classic doorway entrances to eighteenth- or nineteenth-century well-known houses in Savannah, Charleston, and Stafford County, Virginia; the frontispiece for June was an additional drawing, a study of Shirley, one of the colonial mansions along the James River. The subject location and necessary two-month lead-time for early 1926 publication of the new drawings suggest Spratling's itinerary following his voyage home. He sailed for New York, staying at the Lambs Club on West Forty-fourth Street for several days following September 15;[29] it was then that he would have sought out Horace Liveright and was thus able to communicate to Paris the good news that Faulkner's novel was to be published. It seems likely that he made his initial sketches of the Virginia and Charleston houses—he probably had the Savannah one left over from July—on his way back to New Orleans, refining them there in order to meet the submission deadlines.

Spratling and Faulkner apparently agreed to take an apartment together following the European trip, and either before they left or, more probably after Spratling's return, he engaged an apartment, at the attic level, only a block around the corner of Cabildo Alley on St. Peter Street, in the large building owned by his friends Marc and Lucile Antony. Faulkner would move in the following February, and presumably the new quarters would be more economical with two sharing the rent. Spratling may not have moved until the Christmas holiday at the university. In addition to the usual heavy instructional load, his occasional but steady illustration contracts, and his architectural associate work with city firms, which he described in the autobiography as extending his workday long into the night, he was especially busy during October in helping to mount two exhibits of his work for the following month at the Arts and Crafts Club.

During the second half of November 1925, he showed, as we have seen, to highly complimentary reviews, a wide selection of paintings and sketches from his 1924 summer in Venice and Rome and perhaps a few pieces from the summer just completed. For the new show he seemed, as always, to have reached back into his storehouse of material accumulated from each sketching excursion, refining or re-casting this or that initial study. His most original offering from the 1924 summer's work appeared to have been a watercolor of the interior of a ship's engine room, which had been complimented in the fall show by the influential academic artist Ellsworth Woodward of Newcomb College. Now, for the second exhibit, he included a colored drawing of the subject, with Art

29. Artists' Files, HNOC.

Deco suggestions, in which he captured a kind of hard metallic modernity through what the *New Orleans Item* described, under a two-column photograph, as "the dull, clean shine of propeller shaft and the smooth bulk of turbines." Illustrative as all this was of the growing elasticity of Spratling's art, the two-week exhibit that preceded it represented his most sustained effort on a single project, and would inform one of the most important publications of his early architectural artist years in New Orleans.

3

New Orleans, 1926–1928: Antebellum Sketching and "A Mirror of Our Scene"

Over a period of at least two years Spratling had traveled throughout the state with Natalie Scott, preparing over one hundred drawings for a publication to be called *Old Plantation Houses in Louisiana,* which would have a descriptive text by Scott. It was a large selection of these drawings that were exhibited in the November 1925 Arts and Crafts Club show, which also included some oil paintings of similar subjects by Alberta Kinsey. Lyle Saxon devoted his Sunday column in the *Times-Picayune* of October 25 to the forthcoming show, writing that it was "Spratling's most ambitious work" and that he and Scott by early that summer had visited and recorded some seventy-five plantation houses. Saxon's article appeared under a three-column reproduction of Spratling's drawing of Oak Alley, and the exhibit itself was coordinated with distributions of the New York publisher's descriptive brochure, which featured a drawing of Waverly, in St. Francisville, "announcing the intended publication for the spring of 1926." The book did not, in fact, appear until the fall of 1927, probably due to the length of time required for completion of the text, which Spratling recalled in the autobiography "caused Natalie, the gadabout, three years of suffering."

The book may originally have been projected as more comprehensive in its illustrations than it turned out to be, for although all of the seventy-five houses are discussed, some more than others, only thirty-four house drawings were printed. What Saxon called Scott's "sprightly style and sure approach" are consistently evident in her informative pictorial descriptions of the factual and anecdotal history of each house, its garden environs, its most distinctive architectural details, and its current state of repair—sometimes sadly declining. The drawings are not consistently of the finest quality among Spratling's work as an architectural artist, and some of the heavier pencil lines do not reproduce well, with the dark surrounding foliage in the black and white reproductions sometimes obscuring the house structure itself. But a few show a given house in an impressive perspective, such as those of Woodlawn and Oakley, and there is occasionally a fine line of clear column and ornamentation detail, such as that of Belle Grove. All of the illustrations, however, suggest a certain gloomy elegance, which to a mind less sympathetic and romantic than Miss Scott's, could even be construed as "somber and dead-looking," as Edmund Wilson described his first view of The Shadows at New Iberia—one of the finest of all the old Louisiana homes—on a windy March day in 1926, a few months after Spratling had drawn it: the "great gray skull of a plantation house against the gray stormy sky and the gray waters of the Teche, stripped of its columns and unpainted." But by the time the book was published, those columns had been re-built and shone white under a fresh coat of paint, and the text praised the restoration efforts of its owner, Weeks Hall, as well as those of several New Orleans architects whose work in that direction was helping to salvage a portion of multicultural history important to the country. To Saxon, the whole book could be seen as part of the preservationist movement in which "Mr. Spratling and Miss Scott are tremendously interested"; and N. C. Curtis, who furnished a brief preface, lauded the volume for its "sincerity" and the truthful impressions it conveyed of an historic and highly distinctive group of buildings in an early state of decay; it was "the first real book on Louisiana Architecture."[1]

The book was handsomely produced, with each copy containing a sepia-tinted frontispiece of Bel Air, a river mansion close to Baton Rouge that had, in fact, been washed away by the surging Mississippi between the time of Spratling's drawing and its publication. Spratling seemed justly proud of his work and sent to his brother David an original print of the frontispiece, which he signed, lettered, and tinted in a soft green. The print was one of several items he selected and made into a string-tied paperbound scrapbook, lettering on the beige water-colored cover, "William P. Spratling/W.P.S./621 St. Peter Street." The little book was apparently gotten together and mailed late in 1926, and its contents re-

1. Edmund Wilson, *The Twenties*, ed. Leon Edel (Farrar, Straus and Giroux, 1975), 259–60; Lyle Saxon, "What's Doing," *New Orleans Times-Picayune*, October 25, 1925; N. C. Curtis, preface to *Old Plantation Houses in Louisiana*, by William P. Spratling and Natalie Scott (New York: William Helburn, 1927), ix.

cord at least a goodly portion of Spratling's professional and personal activity during this important year in his career.[2] There was a series of card designs: a two-page paste-up of ten postcards under the advertisement "The Quarter, illustrated by Spratling" and published by Louis Clary of 318 Royal Street, with seven of the Vieux Carré scenes dated 1926; a double-fold postcard with interior colored sketches of the Green Shutter Tearoom on Royal; and three Christmas card designs, one cleverly styled "Greetings from Natalie Vivian Scott," and a curious but striking red and gold block print of a reclining nude (entitled *Heliodora*) done in a mildly Art Nouveau manner, printed with "Christmas Greetings" and signed "Affec'ly Bill"—hardly a card appropriate for Uncle Leck and Aunt Miriam. Extramural commissions of a more strictly professional nature are illustrated by his inclusion of two pictorial and layout renderings executed during 1925–1926: one of a new fifteen-story office building for the Union Indemnity Company in uptown New Orleans, the other of a large waterfront luxury hotel at Pass Christian, Mississippi, designed by Moise Goldstein.

As if to illustrate his wider audience, he included an offprint from the November *Architectural Forum* which reproduced the pencil drawing of Oakley prepared for *Old Plantation Houses*; plus a feature article from the *New York Times Magazine* of August 8, 1926, entitled "Negro's Art Lives in His Wrought Iron." This well-researched 2,500-word essay was illustrated by five Spratling drawings, one a three-column centerpiece, selected from the AIA booklet on New Orleans ironwork that he and N. C. Curtis had published in the previous year. While placing his work before the largest audience of his career, the article also developed in its central thesis a point Spratling had made in his own brief essay, that the early-nineteenth-century wrought ironwork of the Vieux Carré had been the work of black craftsmen. This had been, the *Times* piece emphasized, the first Afro-American art in America, with the indigenous capacity of black artisans finding full expression within the social and economic conditions of the forty-year period when the "old town" was being built after the disastrous fire of 1788. But the essay's further discussion, passages of which Spratling marked with marginal lines or ink rosettes, must have been for another reason satisfying to his own perception, especially

2. The scrapbook was sent to the author by Paula Wester, daughter of David Spratling; now in the Auburn University Archives.

in view of his sketching travels among the classic architectural styles of Europe: that this very ironwork he had drawn so extensively had achieved its striking originality through a kind of naive though powerful assimilation of the curves, spirals, and junctures of decorative motifs from past cultures. One of his own illustrations, for example, a corner railing on Chartres Street, was described as having a "strangely haunting Gothic quality." And, finally, in addition to suggesting how after a break of centuries ancient art forms had reappeared in the new designs of Vieux Carré ironwork, the essay described further the creative relationship between artist and craftsman that probably prevailed in early New Orleans. Spratling noted the passage marginally, although then he could not have known just why; yet it was this relationship that he himself would encourage and employ in a few years at his first silvershop in Taxco, on the Calle de las Delicias.

We shall return later, of course, to the nature of this relationship, but linking its suggestiveness about the future to the direction that Spratling's career was already beginning to take is the first item contained in the handmade collection he sent to David: a *Times-Picayune* reproduction of a drawing of the Nuevo Sagrario Cathedral in Mexico City. He had made his first visit to Mexico in the summer of that year and the drawing was the first of an extensive series he would eventually publish, commemorating not only the work completed then but also, as it turned out, his discovery of a new and permanent source of creative energy.

But there was much to do yet in New Orleans, especially during the fall and early spring of the final trips with Natalie Scott for completion of the *Old Plantation Houses* manuscript. And it is likely that during this period he made a sketching trip also to Natchez, Mississippi, storing away the drawings and notes for what would be his last work on antebellum architecture. The resulting article, "Natchez, Mississippi," is a geographical extension into the adjoining state of the *Old Plantation Houses* style, the sketches having heavy black pen-and-ink lines and dark foliage outlining the buildings and slightly distorting the composition. However, although the four drawings in artistic quality seem well below those of the first Mexican summer, the publication is important to mention in connection with the evolution of Spratling's work. And it should be considered along with what appears to be a companion piece, "Cane River Portraits," which he published in *Scribner's* five months after

"Natchez, Mississippi" appeared in the November 1927 number of *Architectural Forum*.

The text of "Natchez" was apparently being prepared during the same weeks as that for what would be published in two parts as "Some Impressions of Mexico," which gave Spratling three placements, with seventeen drawings, in the same journal over a period of five months. Some of the sketches from Mexico he was then refining were of structures already some two hundred years older than the oldest in Natchez and were a century old by Plymouth Rock time, such as the Altamarino "House of Cannons" in Mexico City, whose cornerstone had allegedly been laid in the 1520s by Cortez himself with a huge block bearing the image of a plumed serpent from Montezuma's Palace of the Sun. But to Spratling the buildings of Natchez and its environs, such as Richmond Plantation with its late-eighteenth-century Spanish style augmented by those of Greek Revival and a later ante-bellum addition, spoke to a part of the city's history much in the manner of the domed Colonial churches in Mexico he had drawn in such profusion. He found Natchez's pleasantly dormant atmosphere of departed prosperity and the relative absence of abortive attempts at urban renewal attractive, just as he had done in Savannah and as he would later do in Taxco.

In the one thousand words of the essay, with prose as restrained and suggestive as his drawing pencil, he compresses the city's two hundred years, especially its nineteenth-century experience, from its enormous mid-century wealth to the encampment there of Grant in 1863 to the barren post-war period. The tensions of these latter years were suggested to Spratling in the contents of an 1880s pamphlet which, though attempting bravely to assert that public affairs had finally been "restored to the intelligent people" without bloodshed, seemed hardly to mask the racial intensity and uneasy political settlements of Reconstruction. The article on Natchez, in fact, even though the accompanying drawings are not among his best, contains some of his most effective descriptive writing thus far, especially in its selection of suggestive details critical to the impression of a short essay. Where he found the old pamphlet, for example—perhaps in the dusty files of the chamber of commerce he said he visited—is less important than his perception that it silently expressed a futile attempt to reverse the sense of faded glory that still lay over the city even in 1927. And the piece illustrates also a kind of occasional visionary ability he would not have learned in the architectural studio, of seeing a physical setting in time as well as space: how, for example, a view of the magnificent site of Natchez could still evoke the feeling of vastness and wilderness that Bienville and the earliest settlers must have shared; and how, with its construction on the wooded bluffs high above the wide rushing river "and the brown and green haze of Louisiana beyond . . . the pioneer background of the great middle west almost completes itself."[3]

It is evident that since his first publication in 1923 on Vieux Carré structures, Spratling had affirmed a romantic fondness in his writing and drawing for subjects—like Natchez—whose traditional buildings express with a certain persistence in the face of the modern world definable historic moments. However, his first important journal publication outside of architectural periodicals themselves departed from this pattern. "Cane River Portraits" appeared in the April 1928 issue of *Scribner's Magazine* and prefigured, more than any other work he had done or would complete in the decade, the style and content of *Little Mexico*. The subject of the essay and its two pages of drawings—a black and mulatto community in northern Louisiana—was slightly unusual for *Scribner's,* and it may have been accepted in part because it was about "curious folk," as the descriptive cut-line stated. But for Spratling it was characteristically attractive and, seen in the context of the other work he was doing during these months, seems properly transitional, since it was the last non-Mexico subject he would address.

He visited the Isle Brevelle community on the banks of the Cane River, not far from Natchitoches, in the early spring of 1927, probably during the spring recess at Tulane and perhaps with Natalie Scott, whose old Buick would have taken all day to make the three-hundred-mile trip from New Orleans. He stayed several days in one of the great plantation houses, where thousands of acres had remained intact since ante-bellum days, sketching and making notes of his conversations with black workers in field and kitchen, paddling in a pirogue among their houses on the wide river-lake. There is no focus at all on architecture, but on human subjects entirely, and for the first time for publication he was drawing faces different from those of his "Creole" friends in New Orleans. The lined, intent, almost benign expressions that emerged from Spratling's

3. William Spratling, "Natchez, Mississippi," *Architectural Forum* 47 (November 1927): 425.

pencil individualized his brief description in the text of the unchanging pastoralism of the community's daily life, and it all—both the words and the drawings—must have communicated to much of the *Scribner's* readership a sense of "curious" remoteness.

What seemed, however, most quietly relevant to Spratling and what linked this visit to those of the Mexican scene he was just beginning to assimilate was the mulatto population, now close to poverty circumstances but who had been prosperous, free, and independent before the Civil War and whose French ancestors had come over from Paris to settle the Isle Brevelle in the early 1700s. Their five generations were less ancient surely than those of the "indigenous race" in Mexico, but there was a comparable consistency of integrity about their existence that seemed to him poignant and "epic." These qualities were personalized in the oldest member of the community: in her "good French" and in her pride in the distinctive history and traditions of the families there, symbolized by the huge elegant portrait of her grandfather; by her quilt collection ("such as would astonish any antiquary"), whose fusion of classic sophisticated designs and gay childlike colors must have reminded him of the Indian textile arts which he had praised in "Some Impressions of Mexico"; and by the cotton morning dress that she brought out to show him, made of a print bought by her mother in Natchitoches eighty years earlier. "There seemed some sort of curious connection," he wrote,

> . . . between the lives of these people and the soft white material with which their existence had been so closely interwoven—as though their very circumstances had partaken of the same quality. What it had done to them—this thing that was once the strength of the country and was now so powerless to bring prosperity! The effect was of something a little faded in pattern but infinitely vital. Here was Madame Aubert-Rocque in person, detached from the rush of life and still completely concerned with things of the soil which we have almost forgotten existed.[4]

Something faded but infinitely vital! The detail of the cotton morning dress seemed no less suggestive than the old pamphlet in Natchez, this time enclosing a panoramic era of prosperity and decline symbolically ended by the bullet hole and slashes in Madame Aubert-Rocque's cher-

---

4. William Spratling, "Cane River Portraits," *Scribner's Magazine* 83 (April 1928): 417–18.

ished portrait that had been inflicted by General Nathaniel Banks's raid-
ers in 1861. There were no buildings here to draw and describe, but
to Spratling a persistent "history" worth re-capturing. Perhaps such re-
capturings were especially important for this writer-artist, whose work
in this mode was coming to maturity but whose own twenty-seven-year
memory was made up of continual arrivals and departures on his long
journeys south. It might all be regarded as somewhat preliminary to his
permanent settlement within three years in Taxco. There he would find
not only a remote permanence and sense of faded glory but, as in the Isle
Breville, a highly creative population with long memories whose racial
identity had also been marked by an invasion from Europe. And of
course he would find there too a substance in the earth that would mark
his own future identity, a substance whose color was as white as the
cotton fields of Alabama.

During the highly productive period of late 1926 and early 1927,
however, the idea of moving his permanent home hundreds of miles to
the south was certainly less clear in Spratling's mind than the possibility
of a similar re-location may have been emerging in the consciousness of
his fellow tenant. Faulkner had moved into the attic apartment in February, making intermittent trips to Mississippi, including one for most of
the summer while Spratling was in Mexico. For those months in 1926
and a few in 1927 the two, as before, moved forward with their drawing,
painting, or writing, each at his own pace, the skylight and small side
windows always open in the New Orleans heat. The nature of the place
where they lived, worked, and gave the boisterous parties described by
Spratling in the autobiography is partially revealed in the photograph of
the apartment's interior and suggested further by two items from the
scrapbook sent to David, each a signed colored print from a pen-and-ink
drawing: one, apparently from a rooftop perspective, of the St. Louis
Cathedral rising darkly against the night sky surrounded by the lower
brightly lit buildings of Cabildo and Orleans Alleys, lettered "621 Saint
Peter Street, New Orleans"; and the other, a single bed in the apartment's
interior, placed against the same kind of side window shown in the photograph, open and fastened against the low, slanted roof. It was during
their last months together in this attic place that Spratling and Faulkner
planned and completed what was to become a celebrated little book, but
which there is no reason to believe was originally anything other than
what Spratling said it was: "a sort of private joke."

In the fall, Spratling, in addition to his teaching and organizing a series of lectures on outdoor sketching during October at the Delgado Museum, was working over the large number of drawings from the 1926 summer in Mexico, preparing an interpretive text before sending them off to *Architectural Forum*. Faulkner by then had returned to New Orleans, having completed his second novel, *Mosquitoes*, in September. Although the biographical record shows that he was by then already conceiving the kind of characters that would populate his fictional world for the rest of his life, the array of Vieux Carré figures he had blended together in the plot of *Mosquitoes* may have lingered sufficiently in his mind for him to fall in with the idea of another kind of satiric treatment of them. The concept of *Sherwood Anderson and Other Famous Creoles* may well have been Spratling's, for he would probably have been more interested and familiar than Faulkner with the kind of pictorial art contained in what Spratling affirmed both in the autobiography and "Chronicle of a Friendship" as their model, a collection of satirical drawings by Miguel Covarrubias called *The Prince of Wales and Other Famous Americans*, published in the spring of 1925.

The young Covarrubias, who then unknowingly would become one of Spratling's closest friends in Mexico, had established himself within two years of his arrival from that country as the premier caricaturist of prominent figures in the glittering world of art and entertainment in New York City. Most of his renderings not only emphasized the prominent facial features vulnerable to exaggeration but also seemed to assess uncompromisingly, sometimes even wickedly, a personality of the subject.[5] The collection of sixty-six portraits opened with that of the Prince of Wales, who through extended U.S. visits had become by 1925 a familiar figure within the "famous" world occupied and in a sense created for Americans by the rest of the group. Though a "foreigner," he often seemed in his yearnings to be one of us, and his slight, top-hatted, gloved figure, placed by Covarrubias against a racetrack setting, seemed with its dark-circled eyes and suggestion of aristocratic dissipation to reveal qualities suddenly as apparent as those in many of the other drawings: the unconcealed brutishness of Jack Dempsey in the ring, the slight sneer in the laughing expression of Charlie Chaplin undisguised as the little

5. Carl Van Vechten, preface to *The Prince of Wales and Other Famous Americans*, by Miguel Covarrubias (New York: Alfred Knopf, 1925), 3.

hobo, the sense of clever superiority in the beady side-glance of the pre-
sumed yokel Will Rogers, or the absolute boredom in the drooping eyes
of Lillian Gish as with hands crossed piously on her breast she sustained
forever the image of the woman-child. The last drawing in the collection
was a self-portrait of Covarrubias himself, seeming with extended hands
to be presenting his cast of characters.

The first drawing in the Faulkner-Spratling book was also that of the
titular figure, the closing one that of the authors; the Spratling drawings
were a Vieux Carré microcosm of a society of artists and writers less
broadly pictured than that by Covarrubias. But the parallel with the earlier book was more than organizational. Anderson, too, somewhat like
the Prince of Wales, had during his few years in the Quarter also become
a member of the "Creole" group—its premier member in the sense that
he was the only truly famous one. But he also was a "foreigner," always
the midwesterner who seemed only a visitor and a commentator on how
different New Orleans was from the rest of the America he knew better
than anyone else. However, the self-consciousness in Anderson's work
and the gradual disappearance of the originality and stylistic power of
the earlier fiction which established his reputation were already becoming evident during the 1924–1926 period in which he, Faulkner, and
Spratling were friends in New Orleans. In the *Times-Picayune* review
(December 7, 1924) of the autobiographical *A Story Teller's Story,* for
which Spratling furnished a drawing of Anderson, a writer, states Anderson, "just can't take himself too seriously," yet he goes on to declare that
the new work "is probably one of the most American books that has ever
been written." An adverse review of the book, appearing a few months
later in the *Dial* ("Half-Truths," by Llewelyn Powys; April 1925, 330–
332), noted that a "curious self-consciousness has now crept in," and
although there are some fine passages reminiscent of the earlier Anderson, many others have "scarcely a page which does not contain a sen-
tence either slipshod or soft." Some of the stylistic tendencies parodied
by Faulkner in the passage below actually appear in this same issue of
the *Dial,* in "A Meeting South," Anderson's fictionalized account of his
introduction to Faulkner in which, embarrassingly as it turned out, he
was taken in by Faulkner's colorful stories about his past. Thus the
Faulkner-Spratling appraisal of parody and caricature seem to capture a
certain transitional interval in the career of the foremost "Creole" in the
book. To both Faulkner and Spratling there was something dispropor-

tionate about him: his commanding stature, both physical and reputa-
tional on the one hand; and yet on the other, what both his oral and
written style were becoming: often ponderous and groping for the subject. Spratling's drawing emphasized this image, showing the large figure
sitting in a chair much too small for it, dressed in Anderson's familiar
extravagant style, and on the floor a copy of *Tar*, an account of Anderson's midwestern childhood which had just been published earlier in
1926.[6]

But it was Faulkner's two-page foreword, signed "W.F." and immediately preceding the caricature, that went to the heart of the satiric portrait, burlesquing the heavy, repetitious, almost unctuous style which
Anderson's writing was recently displaying. A portion recounted an "interview" between Spratling and Anderson, the self-acknowledged "out-
lander":

> When this young man, Spratling, came to see me, I did not remember
> him. Perhaps I had passed him in the street. Perhaps he had been one of
> the painters at whose easel I had paused, to examine. Perhaps he knew me.
> Perhaps he had recognized me when I paused, perhaps he had been aware
> of the fellowship between us and had said to himself, "I will talk to him
> about what I wish to do; I will talk my thought out to him. He will under-
> stand, for there is a fellowship between us."
>
> But when he came to call on me, I did not remember him at all. He wore
> a neat business suit and carried merely a portfolio under his arm, and I did
> not recognize him. And after he had told me his name and laid the portfolio
> on the corner of my desk and sat opposite me and began to expound his
> plan to me, I had a kind of a vision. I saw myself being let in for something.
> I saw myself incurring an obligation which I should later regret, and as we
> sat facing one another across my desk, I framed in my mind the words with
> which I should tell him No. Then he leaned forward and untied the portfo-
> lio and spread it open before me, and I understood. And I said to him,
> "What you want me for is a wheelhorse, is it?" And when he smiled his
> quick shy smile, I knew that we should be friends.

The foreword closed with Anderson giving advice to American artists,
advice which he himself seemed consistently not to take: that they should
not regard themselves or their art too seriously and should cultivate an

---

6. Subsequently, Anderson may have been "running out of things to write about": See
Kim Townsend, *Sherwood Anderson* (Boston: Houghton Mifflin, 1987), 234–35.

ironic sense of self. The parody was, at the very least, amusing, although Spratling recalled in "Chronicle" that when they showed it to Anderson shortly after the book was printed, "he didn't think it was very funny." Anderson's reaction probably contributed somewhat to the growing coolness and ambivalence between himself and Faulkner, although that is another story. But even though the satire may not have been as mild, as "warm and delicate" as Spratling after forty years defended it as being, it nevertheless contained a kind of oblique tribute to Anderson's reputation and generosity: after all, he *had* been a "wheelhorse" to many young writers, including Faulkner, who, like Spratling in the little interview scene, had with high hopes laid their work before the great man.

The additional Spratling drawings, of thirty-eight French Quarter habitués, differed considerably from the Covarrubias ones, which in no way attempted a likeness necessarily congenial or complimentary to the subject. Spratling was not assuming the perspective of objective observer, seeking to capture the reality behind the famous persona; or, as Caroline Durieux would do later—with her "American" perspective reversing the Covarrubias stance—achieve in her Mexican series a kind of social commentary through her caricatures of group figures. Rather, Spratling was drawing his friends, and the portraits seemed consistently affectionate. A few had captions suggestive of in-jokes furnished by both Spratling and Faulkner, and a few—like some of Covarrubias's—were frontal likenesses with little exaggeration of facial features, such as those of Keith Temple, Moise Goldstein, and Ellsworth Woodward. But most placed the subjects within a humorous but recognizable context of their professional mediums. Many of those represented in the gallery had already been re-created in the characters participating in the endless, often vacuous discourses of Faulkner's *Mosquitoes,* although none of them would have known that in December of 1926, since the novel would not be published for another four months. And all of them, too, in their writing, preservation efforts, painting, photography, and music, had created a certain distinctive style and atmosphere of artistic and intellectual life within the few square blocks where they lived and worked. Thus in this sense they were counterparts of the humbler, even seamier "other" side of the Quarter that Faulkner had observed in his "New Orleans" sketches. Certainly the collection captured an important moment in that time and that place, a moment that would soon pass. Musician Harold Levy, whose portrait appeared in the gallery, had moved to the Vieux

Carré in the same year as Spratling and had become a particular friend of Faulkner's. After almost fifty years, he recalled *Sherwood Anderson and Other Famous Creoles* as only "a memento of a special time. . . . But for those of us who were a part of that time, it is a very special book indeed."[7] And for Spratling, in one of his best phrases, the book was "a sort of mirror of our scene in New Orleans."

Most of that scene would remain intact throughout the rest of the decade, but for Spratling it would be considerably changed during 1927. By then the Andersons had permanently left New Orleans for the mountains of southwestern Virginia, carrying along houseplans that Spratling had prepared for them during the previous spring. And within a few weeks after the publication in April of *Mosquitoes,* Faulkner would also leave the city, more or less permanently for Mississippi. His departure, of course, terminated the companionship commemorated by the drawing of the two at the end of the "famous Creoles" gallery, the high-spirited nature of which is suggested by the inevitable bottles beneath the wicker chair occupied by Faulkner, the Daisy air rifle on the wall, and the apostrophe to "Art."

That companionship was commemorated further in *Mosquitoes,* in which Spratling wrote that "I figured as one of the characters," and in which others from the "scene," such as Lillian Friend and Anderson himself, merged into the cast of personalities on board the *Nausikaa,* whose halting voyage into bad weather and clouds of mosquitoes recalled the well-known incident in the spring of 1925 when Anderson rented a yacht for a day's outing on Lake Pontchartrain with his New Orleans friends and visitors from New York. One particular episode in that novel, part of the generally sympathetic portrayal of the Anderson-like character Dawson Fairchild, seems curiously and intimately connected with Spratling, who was, of course, one of the original passengers. Fairchild, a novelist, "a man of undisputed ability and accomplishment" and who has "a kind of firm belief that life is all right," begins to reminisce in the temporary presence of Mark Frost—the character who Elizabeth Anderson felt was most like Spratling—about his boyhood, telling an odd but strangely realistic story of his juvenile fascination with sex: how, at a country family reunion in Indiana, he slipped into the men's side of the

7. Levy, quoted in Stella Pitts, "The Quarter in the Twenties," *New Orleans Times-Picayune, Dixie,* November 26, 1962, p. 44.

outdoor privy and put his head down through the hole, hoping to see what he could of the pretty, blond-haired girl who had just entered the women's side—what he saw were her blue eyes looking across to his, her long golden curls swinging below; and as the middle-aged man recalls the comic incident, its memory intensifies his sense of "youth and love, and time and death."[8] Faulkner here seems to have appropriated a Spratling story, for the same tale, with the young Spratling as the "hero," appears at the close of the "Alabama" section of the autobiography, where Spratling remembers it, also at a family reunion, the one held in his honor during his first visit to the home-place in forty years and where, he wrote, he saw again his cousin "Mary Lou," the now-matronly, grown-up little blond girl who laughed with him at their memory of the incident "until tears rolled down our cheeks."

The story, of course, may have originated with Faulkner, but as told by Spratling, called into memory in the very surroundings where it ostensibly occurred, it has the quirky ring of authenticity. And it is doubtful if he ever knew that the person to whom he told it in New Orleans some thirty-odd years earlier was soon characteristically re-shaping it into his own fiction. It is, at the least, interesting to contemplate the circuitous way in which an incident from an Alabama boyhood in 1912 found its way into the fictional portrait of one of the great figures in American letters, and how, under the transforming and intuitive hand of a yet greater figure, the incident as recalled from Fairchild's midwestern memory becomes one of the surest—indeed, touching—passages in the novel marking that character's sense of his declining power, an awareness that Anderson himself in 1925–1926 was beginning to perceive.

But for the life of William Spratling, the little story may have other uses. His journey back to Alabama in 1962 to receive an honorary doctorate from his alma mater was undoubtedly one of the happiest and most fulfilling experiences of his later years. And his choosing to close the autobiographical account of that euphoric family reunion with the artlessly bawdy story of what happened with the pretty blond cousin, an episode which by then had assumed cheerful childhood associations, may be seen as another example of the Spratling persona under construction. But, after all, his life after fifty years indeed had triumphed over the unhappy prospects he had so often placed in the epistolary record of those

8. William Faulkner, *Mosquitoes* (New York: Boni and Liveright, 1927), 232–34.

years and which he could not easily have forgotten. The story, however, was passed along—probably in the St. Peter Street attic, given Faulkner's tendency to make immediate use of his fictional sources—when that triumph was still unrealized. Certainly it would be a mistake to assume that a series of intimate revelations were shared by Spratling and Faulkner about their hopes at this critical stage in the career of each. Faulkner's privacy in such matters is well established, and there is no significant indication that Spratling was any different. Still, the possibility of Faulkner's re-locating his creative future to northern Mississippi took shape in that hot lofty space overlooking the Cabildo Alley into which he and Spratling had strolled countless times toward Jackson Square and the river. Although, as the biographical record shows, he had almost completed the first of the novels with that new setting before leaving the city, New Orleans to be sure had served him well in his apprenticeship: through the talented people he had met, observed, learned from, and been encouraged by—not the least of whom was Spratling—and through his absorption of "the rich, brooding air of the past that hangs over the city even now and that in the 1920s was much more intense and pervading."[9]

But what of Spratling? Financially, the famous Creoles book had been most successful, with the printing late in 1926 of 450 copies having a quick sale; and he might well have expected a good return from his share of the sales from the forthcoming *Old Plantation Houses,* now scheduled for publication late that year. Perhaps he too, however, though in a sense different from Faulkner's, had begun to feel he had about "used up" the possibilities of New Orleans for whatever creative future he might yet achieve. He was not a southerner, and had no deep sense of place to which he might return, drawing there on the sources of familiarity and ironic relationship that such a journey might produce. Like Faulkner, however, during the months on St. Peter Street he also, as we have seen, had begun to perceive an emerging potential for self-renewal. He had been to Mexico for a few weeks in the previous summer and was planning to return in the next. Even so, in the spring of 1927, an investment of his future in that direction still did not seem likely.

9. W. Kenneth Holditch, "The Brooding Air of the Past: William Faulkner," in *Literary New Orleans: Essays and Meditations,* ed. Richard S. Kennedy (Baton Rouge: Louisiana State University Press, 1992), 50.

That his career was taking on a certain repetitiveness, however, is indicated in an article he published in the May issue of *Architectural Forum,* "The Architectural Heritage of New Orleans." Gracefully written and full of passing observations of unique details in this or that building, the piece is yet on the order of the familiar excursion through the Quarter streets, and his drawings illustrating the text are old ones, dated 1924, with one having appeared in *Picturesque New Orleans,* and an allusion to a mahogany-bronze stairway detail in a house on Barracks Street having already been drawn for his and Curtis's 1925 work on ironwork. The subject of the architectural significance of the Vieux Carré and the need to preserve it was not a new one for Spratling or for those who had for years labored in this direction, the preservation movement having achieved by 1925 considerable success when a city ordinance set aside a preservation area within the Quarter boundaries. In fact, he concludes the piece with the observation that the many distinctions of the old town were by then beginning to be appreciated; and in a small supplementary article—on the varied use of fanlights in its residential architecture, which he wrote a few months later—he observed further that "sightseeing busses continue to bustle people through the quarter in ever-increasing numbers." And he probably knew also that his lament in the article—that its titular subject had not been properly addressed—was even then being answered in the work in progress by his early mentor N. C. Curtis, who would after some delay publish in 1933 his authoritative *New Orleans: Its Old Houses, Shops, and Public Buildings.*[10]

In October of 1927, as he began the fall exhibition season with shows of some of his recent drawings, Spratling would have read an extensive newspaper article that may have caused him to reflect on just what direction his career might then take. Written by one of the "famous Creoles," Frederick Oeschner, and entitled "New Orleans Man Wins Wide Notice," the piece was essentially a summary of the Spratling achievement and reputation. Not only had his writing and art over the years gained praise in New Orleans, they also were now held in high regard by architectural publications in the East, including those more sophisticated ones

10. The volume was published by the old-line Philadelphia firm of J. B. Lippincott. Curtis reached back into his own Auburn days in dedicating the book to Mrs. Charles C. Thach, wife of the college president; she and her husband, as we have seen (Chapter 2), had shown a special interest in the young Spratling.

especially devoted to criticism; and, moreover, in addition to contracts for further publications in the *New York Times* and *Scribner's*, Spratling was beginning to turn his attention to the arts in Mexico, where his work was winning even more acclaim than in this country. Still in his twenties, the article continued, he was nonetheless one of the "oldest inhabitants of the Vieux Carré" and for six years his quarters, first in Orleans Alley and then in St. Peter Street, "have been a rendezvous for a small group of friends who admire without flattery, who criticize without unkindness, and who are themselves occupied in artistic and scholarly pursuits."[11]

As he read the piece, flattering as it was, especially in its appraisal of a certain quality of life he had helped to create amidst his surroundings, Spratling might well have agreed that it was all demonstrably true. He had worked very hard. And the gradual elimination, begun in his college years at Auburn, of his self-consciousness and doubt, had now, it would seem, been completed through his ready engagement with the range of talented and distinctive personalities represented in the *Sherwood Anderson* gallery, which was probably more a mirror of *his* scene than it had been of Faulkner's. Certainly in the fall of 1927, he had plenty yet to do, but as the article suggested, much of that would have to be pursued elsewhere—and not just during the next summer's break from the academic enclosure. Thus, early in the new school year, he possibly began to consider some kind of transition toward a less encumbered kind of life.

Whether he decided just then to resign his Tulane appointment is not clear. His autobiographical account of the movement from New Orleans to Mexico, cast in the usual conflicting chronology, suggests a certain decisive bravado, stating that after three summers in Mexico he "had been caught up in the rhythm of life there," and the offer by Cape and Smith of a contract to write a book about Mexican life promised a certain financial independence and thus gave him a justifiable reason to leave Tulane. This is wholly misleading; the Cape and Smith firm was not even organized until the spring of 1929, almost a year after he had left Tulane. Actually his resignation from the School of Architecture was effective on June 6, 1928, before he departed for his third Mexican summer. And a July letter from an employment agency in Chicago to N. C.

11. Frederick Oeschner, "New Orleans Man Wins Wide Notice," *New Orleans Morning Tribune*, October 16, 1927, p. 2.

Curtis, whom Spratling had obviously listed as a reference, asking for a recommendation on Spratling for placement in a possible teaching position indicates that he was then very much uncertain of his immediate future.[12]

There may, of course, have been some behavioral incident that led to the break with Tulane, but the continuing esteem for him and his work reflected in local newspaper accounts during that academic year would seem to belie this. The critical period of resignation early in the summer of 1928, however, and of the final transition between New Orleans and his southward future may have been mediated by the prospect of another appointment for occasional lecturing on colonial architecture at the National University; his credentials for such were now stronger than ever. But the more likely financial encouragement came from the emergence of two commissions for writing and drawing to be performed that summer in Mexico, with both undoubtedly resulting from his impressive publications that spring in the *Forum* and *Scribner's.* One was to illustrate a series of articles on the politics of Mexico for the *World's Work,* a journal of contemporary politics and international relations published by Doubleday. Spratling could have done most of these human-figure and architectural scenes from his sketch pad without leaving New Orleans. The other contract, however, with the widely read popular magazine *Travel,* could not have been more fortunate in its timing or projected content: three essays on Mexican cities with text and drawings entirely by Spratling—obviously a justification for extensive travel and further development of what might become a major publication project. What he seems then to have had in mind was a collection of several of the illustrated essays whose form he had gradually made his own special province, like those on Savannah, Natchez, and Guanajuato, in which a brief but perceptive text on history and ambience would be mirrored in architectural renderings. These would perhaps be "personalized" in the manner of his Cane River portraits and interviews. The "bright fragment" of Taxco would be the place he would draw and describe most extensively.

To be sure, resigning the teaching appointment meant giving up the one steady source of income that he had. But given the almost astonish-

---

12. L. A. Thorensen of The Engineering Agency, Chicago, to N. C. Curtis, July 17, 1928, N. C. Curtis Papers, Manuscripts Department, Tulane University Library.

ing range of his supplemental employments, he may have felt that the time commitment for the, at best, modest academic salary was no longer worth it. His prospects, in fact, for a long-term academic career, if indeed he had even been temperamentally suited for one, did not seem particularly bright. He still did not hold a college degree, and after six years of teaching at Tulane (not nine, as he states in the autobiography), his academic rank was still that of instructor. His recognition by the AIA was for his achievements as an architectural artist, a medium in which he had no peer, but not as a designer of buildings. He could certainly do valuable things within the architectural firm, but the possibility of his moving to the professional level of an N. C. Curtis, a Moise Goldstein, or a Richard Koch was unlikely—once more, even had he possessed the temperament for that kind of future. But one phrase in the autobiographical rationale was clearly accurate. His beginning involvement in the "rhythm of life" in another country held the promise of responding anew to the restlessness and nervous energy that always marked Spratling's career. And it promised also to quicken further the antiquarian sensibility that the New Orleans years, including his drawing excursions to Normandy, France, and Italy, had both liberated and strengthened. At this time he may have perceived too that the rhythm of life in the Vieux Carré itself was changing: it had been "discovered," as indicated by his allusion to the busloads of tourists in the "fanlights" article published early in 1928. Certainly it no longer offered the elasticity of opportunity for his talents that had been the case in 1922.

In late October of 1928, Spratling's return to New Orleans from his extended summer in Mexico was extensively chronicled in the *Sunday Times-Picayune*. He "came back to his St. Peter Street attic" bringing with him new sketches which "many of his admirers believe to be the best of his career." His return also, the account continued, "brought confirmation of the report that he has severed his connection with the school of architecture at Tulane and intends to free lance." Thus five months after what was apparently a quiet resignation from the university, Spratling was fully committed to the risk of earning his living through his art and writing. He had as yet no contract for writing the kind of book that *Little Mexico* would become; rather, he seemed to be planning to utilize some of his recent drawings for what the newspaper article described as "his book on the cities of Mexico." But what is additionally interesting in the long article's content is the image of Spratling it records at this transitional moment, an image fully visible in the "mirror of our scene" and one that may serve to complete the New Orleans chapter in his life.[13]

The two drawings illustrating the feature story under the three-column caption "Spratling Pictures Mexico at History-Making Time" are themselves suggestive of this transition. One is a drawing, in the increasingly heightened Spratling style, of the cathedral at Cuernavaca, Mexico's oldest church; the other, a pencil portrait of Emilio Portes Gil, since late September president-designate of the country. The portrait, dated September 20 and signed by Portes Gil, had been executed in his office on the morning of his official appointment; and most of the succeeding article was devoted to Spratling's seemingly well-informed and moderately optimistic interpretation of the significance of the Portes Gil presidency and its prospects for Mexico. Almost exactly six years before, Spratling, just turned twenty-two, had hurriedly arrived in New Orleans to accept an unexpected appointment that had dramatically eliminated his sense of uncertainty and depression. Now, here he was, readily identified to readers of New Orleans's largest newspaper in his multiple persona of "Spratling, architect, artist, teacher, traveler, and student of affairs." To the young man from Alabama in the fall of 1922, such mercurial distinction would have been unthinkable. And perhaps it is appropriate to leave him here, poised, as it were, on the edge of a new beginning and a new kind of eminence. That further identity, however, had already begun to take shape during the three previous summers of sketching and writing in the country Spratling was soon to make his own. To review the nature of that portion of his apprenticeship, we should thus return to the summer of 1926, when he boarded ship in New Orleans and steamed out into the Gulf, for the first time not turning eastward to Savannah and Genoa, but heading further south, toward Tampico and Vera Cruz.

13. K. T. Knoblock, "Artist Finds Gil Trying to Awake Pride of Nation," *New Orleans Sunday Times-Picayune*, October 14, 1928, p. 30.

Dr. William P. Spratling
Courtesy Spratling family

Dr. and Mrs. Leckinski Ware Spratling (Uncle Leck and Aunt Miriam)
Courtesy Spratling family

David Spratling, 1912, the year the Spratling children were separated
Courtesy Spratling family

Roamer's Roost, the family home, Gold Hill, Alabama, as sketched by
Spratling, 1924
Courtesy Spratling family

ROTC cadet Spratling, 1918
Courtesy Auburn University Archives

Spratling sketch for a page in the 1922 Auburn University
yearbook, *The Glomerata*
Courtesy Auburn University Archives

Spratling's senior yearbook photograph
Courtesy Auburn University Archives

Spratling's college home, his cousin Leila Terrell's boardinghouse
Courtesy Auburn University Archives

Auburn architecture dean Frederic Biggin
Courtesy Auburn University Archives

Aboard the SS *Oskaloosa,* summer, 1921
Courtesy C. W. Warner

CHARLES
COLEMAN
THACH
LL.D.

PRESENTED·TO·THE·COLLEGE·BY·THE
CLASS·OF·NINETEEN·TWENTY-ONE

Spratling's bas-relief sculpture of Auburn President Charles
Coleman Thach
Courtesy Auburn University Photographic Services

Architect-preservationist N. C. Curtis, Spratling's first mentor
in New Orleans
Courtesy Nathaniel C. Curtis, Jr.

"End of balcony with wrought and cast rail guard and bracket from Brulatour Mansion (now the Arts and Crafts Club)"

"Wrought gate and post detail from old Exchange Bank, Royal Street," Spratling's caption read.

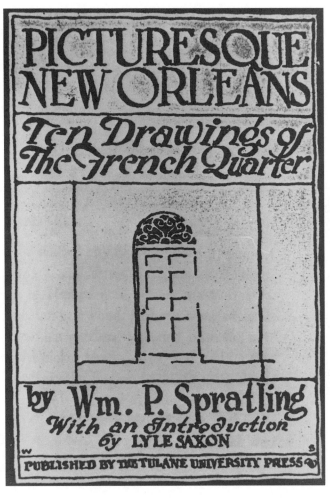

Cover of Spratling's *Picturesque New Orleans*

St. Louis Cathedral, sketched from the St. Ann Street side of
the Place D'Armes. From *Picturesque New Orleans*
*Courtesy The Historic New Orleans Collection, Museum/Research
Center, Acc. No. 1950.58.18.3*

Spratling's sketch of his friend William Faulkner, which
appeared in the *Sunday Times-Picayune*, April 26, 1925

Spratling's drawing of Sherwood Anderson, ca. 1925
*Courtesy William Faulkner Archives, Rowan Oak, Oxford,
Mississippi*

Elizabeth Anderson, reverse photocopy of a drawing by
Spratling, 1925
*Courtesy The Historic New Orleans Collection, Museum/
Research Center, Acc. No. 1970.22.3*

John Dos Passos, drawing by Spratling
Courtesy Manuscripts Department, Tulane University Library

Interior of the St. Peter Street apartment shared by Spratling and Faulkner. Seated in the wicker chair is Hamilton Basso.

Courtesy William Faulkner Archives, Rowan Oak, Oxford, Mississippi

SHERWOOD ANDERSON &
OTHER FAMOUS CREOLES
.A GALLERY OF CONTEMPORARY NEW ORLEANS &

DRAWN BY WM. SPRATLING &
ARRANGED BY WM. FAULKNER

WPS

PUBLISHED BY THE PELICAN BOOKSHOP
PRESS IN ROYAL STREET NEW ORLEANS
MCMXXVI

Cover of *Sherwood Anderson & Other Famous Creoles*

SPRATLING DRAWINGS FROM *Sherwood Anderson & Other Famous Creoles*

Lillian F. Marcus

Caroline Wogan Durieux

Spratling and Faulkner

Natalie Scott, ca. 1925
Courtesy Manuscripts Department, Tulane University Library

WAVERLY, ST. FRANCISVILLE

ANNOUNCING THE INTENDED PUBLICATION
FOR THE SPRING OF 1926

OLD

PLANTATION
HOUSES

IN

LOUISIANA

BY WILLIAM P. SPRATLING
TEXT BY NATALIE SCOTT

Announcement for *Old Plantation Houses in Louisiana*
Courtesy Spratling family

DRAWINGS BY SPRATLING FROM
Old Plantation Houses in Louisiana

Woodlawn
Courtesy The Historic New Orleans Collection, Museum/Research Center,
Acc. No. 1959.156.4

Bel Air
Courtesy The Historic New Orleans Collection, Museum/Research Center,
Acc. No. 1959.156.13

4

Un Viajero Alucinado: An Enchanted Traveler in Mexico

"At Tlaxamaloo there were Aztec palaces or the remains of them . . . and on the heights above that place . . . Aztec thrones with steps cut in the living rock. Here, in these things, one felt the dark mysterious fabric, that vague cultural background of old Mexico. But at Taxco there was the shadow of Spain of the Renaissance, with the cathedral to symbolize its civilization. Yet I often wondered to myself how much cities such as Taxco belong to the New World, whether they are indeed living cities or merely so many bright fragments of an imposed civilization." It was three years after his first trip to Mexico that Spratling published these initial impressions of Taxco, which were written for *Travel* magazine under the title "Silver City of the Clouds." And by the time they appeared, in July of 1929, he was on the verge of making arrangements to buy a house in the town he described in the subtitle of his article as "A Forgotten Gem of Colonial Spain." During the three Mexican summers between 1926 and 1928, the major transitional period in Spratling's life, he had traveled throughout the country, becoming what a Mexico City newspaper described as *"un viajero alucinado,"* an enchanted traveler. He recorded those journeys in hundreds of sketches and in a number of elegantly illustrated essays that expressed his growing awareness of "the dark mysterious fabric" of ancient Mexico which he would explore in the art form shortly to be created in his newly adopted Taxco. The little town was itself a "bright fragment" of those very impositions of the Conquest that his friend Diego Rivera was in that same year beginning to indict in the magnificent revolutionary frescoes on the walls of the Cortez Palace just to the north in Cuernavaca. And in its pastoral remoteness Taxco also to Spratling must have seemed centuries away from the urban energy beginning to penetrate the ambience of the Vieux Carré.

There is no reason to believe that Spratling had any particular knowledge of these historically interconnected layers of Mexican culture prior to his first visit in the summer of 1926, or indeed that he had any special qualifications for the initial temporary appointment as lecturer on colonial architecture which he stated in the autobiography he held in the summer sessions of the National University of Mexico. But Spratling was always a quick study. He may not then in the late twenties intuitively have understood his good fortune—any more than he had earlier in the decade when he first came to New Orleans—that for the second time his arrival in a new and strange environment coincided there with a series of intense cultural moments. But if Mexico was for him, experientially, a New Orleans writ large, he demonstrated no less in the one place than in the other an energetic determination to find for himself a setting in which his innate talent and personal social gifts could flourish. Not the least of these gifts was his seemingly uncanny ability to meet just the right people. And as his New Orleans movement into the artistic life of the Vieux Carré had been quickened through the connections of his friend and advocate N. C. Curtis, he was equally fortunate to bring with him into Mexico the friendship and introductions of the young archaeological scholar Frans Blom.

Spratling was in his second year of appointment at Tulane when Blom became associated with the institution, following some two or three years of intense experience in excavation and restoration at the great Mayan centers in southern Mexico and Guatemala. He became one of Spratling's two closest academic colleagues, the third being Oliver La Farge, who joined the faculty early in 1926. "We three young professors were inseparable," Spratling remembered, recording that all three commuted daily to and from their residences in the Quarter out to the University. Like many of his other friendships during the New Orleans period, these were also influential on Spratling's artistic and intellectual development. During the fall of 1924, when both were post-graduate students at Harvard, Blom had recruited La Farge, who had already been involved in the extensive anthropological fieldwork among the Indian communities of the American Southwest, to become his assistant leader of what became in 1925 the "First Tulane University Expedition to Middle America." The expedition was impressive in itself, covering during the spring and summer a 1,200-mile route through the most southern states of Mexico into Guatemala, passing beyond the limits of the ancient Aztec and Totonac cultures of the west into the Mayan of the east, and observing with careful notations sites that had not been comparably studied scientifically since the middle of the nineteenth century.

These notations were published in 1926 and 1927 under the title *Tribes and Temples,* a book Spratling would have heard discussed as it developed in manuscript once Blom returned to New Orleans in the fall of 1925 and La Farge moved down from Harvard a few months later. Apart from its scientific importance, the book would have been especially suggestive to Spratling, who was then with Blom's encouragement planning his first summer's trip to Mexico. Its wide array of photographs and drawings, some by La Farge, would probably have given him a first glimpse of Aztec clay seals and figures, of carved stone idols in the forms of animals, including a most strange one of a serpent crowned with a plume of feathers. More significant, however, was the form taken by the work, as the authors, wishing to maintain a style "satisfactory to the scientist" and yet to address the general reader "unacquainted with the history of the ancient inhabitants of Central America . . . decided to make this report in the form of a book of travel." It was, in fact, this very pattern of a narrative style—relating an ongoing story of discovery, a clarity of detail, and an evocative description of unknown places—that Spratling himself would largely adopt a few years later in the writing of *Little Mexico.* And perhaps above all else, it was from *Tribes and Temples* that Spratling first perceived that a subterranean layer of pre-European custom and feeling persisted in the daily life of isolated Indian communities in Mexico, an awareness to which he partly gave expression in the passage on Taxco quoted above.[1]

With their considerable linguistic abilities, practical archaeological experience, and combined scholarly knowledge of the Mayan world as well as those of the Navajo and Hopi, Blom and La Farge provided for Spratling another dimension of fraternity and cultural influence in addition to those already richly available in the Vieux Carré setting. He and Faulkner shared cooking expenses with La Farge, and it was inevitable that the two young faculty members would find their place as "famous Creoles" in the *Sherwood Anderson* collection published only a short time

---

1. Frans Blom and Oliver La Farge, *Tribes and Temples: A Record of the Expedition to Middle America Conducted by the Tulane University of Louisiana in 1925* (New Orleans: Tulane University of Louisiana, 1926) 1:1–4. See also D'Arcy McNickle, *Indian Man: A Life of Oliver La Farge* (Bloomington: Indiana University Press, 1971), esp. 37–49.

after the first volume of *Tribes and Temples* appeared. Blom is pictured as "the Tulane Champollion," drawn as he lifts the top of a miniature native hut from which runs one of the scantily clad Indian girls described with some enthusiasm in his book. La Farge appears with long legs and arms curved awkwardly, reading a copy of *Scribner's*, and is identified in one of Faulkner's more droll captions as being from "Harvard, a kind of school near Boston."

In the summer of 1926, Spratling replicated the voyage southward that Blom had taken a year earlier, with La Farge joining Blom in Mexico City: first to the export city of Tampico, with signs everywhere of the sordid but powerful mercantile presence of foreign oil companies, thence to Vera Cruz, and from there the long train ride north, always climbing, to the capital. Spratling's trip was principally financed by a contract with *Architectural Forum* for drawings of Mexican colonial architecture with, as usual, an interpretive commentary. It is likely that Spratling, with Blom's encouragement, proposed the arrangement and that the journal approved it within the wide context of the rising interest of American intellectuals in the art, archaeology, and indigenous culture of Mexico.[2] However, although the autobiography contains passing references to a number of well-known writers and artists from his own country whom Spratling came eventually to know, Americans as he understated it "who were doing things in Mexico at that time," there is no indication that he ever considered himself an integral part of any kind of "American community" there. The commercial side of his nature, always stimulated by the memory of frugal experiences growing up in Alabama and manifested in the seemingly endless elasticity of his multiple employments in New Orleans, was surely attracted by the possibility of what additional economic connections the *Architectural Forum* contract might foster. The romantic side of his character, on the other hand, continually expressed in his reflective writings on the architectural settings of older cultures in Europe, New Orleans, and, as we shall see, in Mexico, was perhaps initially attracted by qualities in the Mexican scene that also seemed to offer to figures like D. H. Lawrence, Hart Crane, Katherine Anne Porter, Edward Weston, Carleton Beals, and many others new in-

2. For a valuable and comprehensive discussion of this topic, see Helen Delpar, *The Enormous Vogue of Things Mexican: Cultural Relations Between the United States and Mexico, 1920–1935* (Tuscaloosa: University of Alabama Press, 1992).

terpretive possibilities: a country easily accessible, with a colorful and passionate history of conquest and revolution, and yet containing a certain primitive life, one relatively untouched by creative exploration.

There is little autobiographical information on Spratling's three summers in Mexico, but his initial accommodation in Mexico City and subsequent progress to the sites of his first sketches were facilitated by the letters of introduction given him by Blom. He met Rivera in this way as well as a number of young painters and architects, plus Gerardo Murillo—known widely as "Dr. Atl," the influential senior interpreter and recorder of the country's folklore and popular arts, and a seminal figure in the initiation of the Mexican mural renaissance. And whatever Spratling's initial feelings may have been about this new and unexplored frontier, the first fruits of his summer's work indicated his immediate and congenial response to a setting that evoked attitudes and feelings he had earlier expressed in his drawings and writings about New Orleans. His first "Mexican" publication exhibited, as always, his fusion of sensitive pencil drawings of characteristic architectural monuments with brief perceptive observations on the wide cultural context within which they were designed and built. These appeared in 1927 in the July and August issues of *Architectural Forum* under the title "Some Impressions of Mexico," and the drawings were probably the best work of his career up to that time. In fact, the layout of thirteen full-page renderings confirms Spratling's stature as an architectural artist, since such an extensive array was extremely unusual for the *Forum,* which, like other professional journals in the discipline, typically published articles illustrated by photographs and diagrammatic floor plans, not by sweeping freehand drawings such as these.

Indeed, in the midst of a gradual recognition by artistic audiences in the United States of the flowering of Mexican painting, especially that of the bold new muralists, little attention had thus far in the twenties been given—even in professional journals such as the *Forum*—to the country's magnificent heritage of Colonial architecture, especially to those qualities that had transformed its European origins into something truly Mexican. Important illustrated works in Spanish, such as Dr. Atl's *Iglesias y conventos de Mexico,* had not been translated, and thus Spratling's drawings and observations were among the very first communications northward of this dimension of what was already being called the "Mexican renaissance." The term had actually been used as early as 1922 by Walter H.

Kilham in his *Architectural Forum* articles, with photographs, on post-Colonial architecture in Mexico. Although he considered the native influence on imported forms from Spain, he used the term in its European descriptive sense of revival or re-appearance, not as a term identifying the flowering of a national artistic sensibility in Mexico, a part of which—to Spratling and Dr. Atl—was the new awareness of a "truly Mexican" architectural style that emerged from the Colonial blending.[3] Especially in Spratling's interpretations of the great Colonial churches of the seventeenth and eighteenth centuries, he captured with his delicate chiaroscuro, in a way that a photograph could not, their sense of mass and depth, distinctive patterns of ornamentation, and complex variation of terminal facades, and above all confirmed his fascination with the astonishing range and shape of their glistening domes and cupolas with "their primitive adornment with tiles, which convert their breast-like bubbles into a sort of jeweled ware of rare enamels."

He wrote in Part I of "Some Impressions" that Dr. Atl had estimated there were over four thousand domed structures of antique origin in the country. He had, of course, sketched centuries-old buildings in northern Italy. And on his European trip after his first year in New Orleans he would have seen in Spain the Baroque legacy of the master architect José Churriguera, whose large-scale, massive, elaborately ornamented designs had influenced the religious buildings of New Spain during the extraordinarily intense period of construction activity in the eighteenth century, when literally thousands of them were built. Certainly there were domes in Spain, he wrote, "but with the Mexican domes it is difficult to resist the thought that here there is something new, something closer to the earth, something created out of a passion that was more personal." Spratling's perceptions of Colonial architecture may have been influenced by his early association with Dr. Atl. But to him the defining quality of these buildings was something like that which he had already contemplated in the Creole architecture and ornamental ironwork of old New Orleans: the fusion or modification of European principles and motifs under the artistic hands of native craftsmen. Here, however, in New

---

3. Kilham's articles were entitled "Mexican Renaissance," Parts I and II, and appeared in the November 1922 and January 1923 numbers. He published a larger study under the title *Architecture of the Vice-Regal Period* (New York: Longman, Green, 1927). The book was probably known by Spratling.

Spain—now "old Mexico" to Spratling—this fusion had taken place on a much wider and more complex scale. Renaissance and Baroque structural ideas from Castile and Iberia, transported by Franciscan and Dominican friars adept at masonry construction, had yet received from thousands of Indian builders a "curiously naive and primitive quality that is unique," a certain vigor and colorful irregularity that was "rich in beauty, a little savage, and even in some instances bearing the unmistakable outward symbolism developed by this deeply mysterious race."[4]

What Spratling in his first summer saw, drew, and wrote about, existed, of course, in a country contiguous with his own. Here, however, the indigenous culture, unlike that in the United States, had not been essentially destroyed by the European conqueror but had persisted in what were indeed "mysterious" ways. It was an understanding that would inform his writing and both personal and entrepreneurial involvements in Mexican life for the next forty years. It was an understanding too that other interpreters of the Mexican renaissance in the second half of the decade were to assume also as their research and travels, as those of Blom and La Farge, carried them back to the junctures of pre-Columbian and Conquest history. And if the concept of "renaissance" involves not merely "re-discovery" but rather a new way of looking at the past that leads to a heightened consciousness of its relevance to the present state of a given culture, then perhaps Spratling could have seen no better example, at least in the plastic arts, than the murals being completed in that year of 1926 by his new friend Rivera at the University of Chapingo outside Mexico City. Here in a powerful new work of the contemporary world the tireless painter rendered the first of his interpretations of the human history of Mexico, drawing the form and content of many of his images from the ancient and Christian sources embedded in that history.[5]

Prior to his first visit to Mexico, Spratling would not likely have been introduced to this new vitality in Mexican art. Some attention had been given to it, mostly to Rivera's early work, but primarily in periodicals of limited U.S. circulation, and it would be toward the end of the decade before a learned and thoughtfully comprehensive assessment of the sub-

4. William Spratling, "Some Impressions of Mexico," part 1, *Architectural Forum* 47 (July 1927): 1.

5. See Desmond Rochfort, *The Murals of Diego Rivera* (London: Journeyman Press, 1987), 44–49.

ject would appear in Anita Brenner's *Idols Behind Altars*. Spratling in his writings or correspondence never seemed especially interested in the powerful social and revolutionary energy that permeated this art, but from his first appraisals of Colonial architecture, especially religious architecture, he caught something of the larger "idols behind altars" thesis in that these massive and yet graceful domed structures, with their fusion of native values and motifs with *conquistador* models, were an art form truly Mexican and part of the historical continuum leading to the "renaissance" inherent in the contemporary work of Rivera, Mérida, Orozco, Siqueiros, and many others. And it was especially interesting to him as, back in New Orleans for the fall term and preparing his Mexican notes and sketches for publication, he reflected on the contrast between the frustrating attempts at architectural preservation in the Vieux Carré and the stance of the Mexican government. There, under a recently implemented authority, a federal commission not only supervised the preservation and remodeling of old buildings but gave tax credits for ten years to property owners who in their new structures employed designs and traditional materials consistent with the commission's aim of sustaining the country's architectural heritage. "Where I live," Spratling wrote, "in the old quarter of New Orleans, there has always been the question of preserving the traditional French and Spanish work from demolition by commercial demands," but despite the periodic appointment of mayors' committees, he continued, "eventually the individual property owner comes out supreme in any controversy."[6]

This notation of the serious commitment of a politically disunified country to preserving the integrity of its historical monuments was obviously of more than passing interest to Spratling. And it was characteristic of his assimilative mind that he would link the architectural symbols of power in New Spain of the seventeenth and eighteenth centuries with the contemporary spirit in Mexican art, some of which in its revolutionary fervor would excoriate the history of conquest and suppression lying behind their construction. He may not, could not, have understood the wrenching political experiences shared by many of his newfound Mexican colleagues. But during that first summer under their influence, especially that of Rivera, who only recently had written eloquently of the innate sensitivity of Mexican children to form and color, Spratling

6. Spratling, "Some Impressions of Mexico," part 1, p. 8.

quickly came to see the quiet strength and beauty inherent in the "wonderful things" that people in remote sections of the country had always made with their hands: "gorgeous and intricately designed textiles made by the savage and absolutely untutored Indians. This in spite of four centuries of oppression and of many devastating revolutions!" In these aptly titled "impressions," Spratling had already begun to see what he could never have seen in New Orleans: an unconscious aesthetic pervasiveness in the daily life of a social order. A concept of art as a luxury was impossible for Mexico in the twenties, as the most authoritative chronicler of the early mural renaissance would write, "art was everywhere"—in the textiles, of course, that Spratling admired, but also in carved or painted votive offerings, miniature portraits exchanged by lovers, colorful murals adorning the walls of the most ordinary of shops, small sculptures for specialized religious or black magic rites, and "those marvelous toys worth a few cents, beautiful as Han tomb figures. The output was so varied as to be unclassifiable . . . so close to all, so thrust under everyone's eyes as to become invisible."[7]

Spratling would have written his essays describing his encounter with all this in the fall of 1926 as he was also pictorially recording the considerable range of his acquaintanceship among "famous Creoles"—from President Dinwiddie of Tulane to Lyle Saxon and "Pops" Whitesell, the Royal Street photographer, to all the writers, architects, and artists in between, each one of whom had affected the character and quality of his New Orleans life. It was, to be sure, a talented and sophisticated group, who had themselves created a minor "renaissance" in this oldest part of one of America's oldest cities. But its mood was temporary, and Spratling may especially have sensed this as he tried to delineate the elemental resurgence of artistic energy he had just witnessed in Mexico, a resurgence he found "reassuring," connected as it was to the "enduring qualities of the indigenous race."

Spratling's published essay-drawings from the second Mexican summer of 1927 began to appear early in 1928. The transition from the artistic scene of New Orleans to that of Mexico is indicated in a note to Uncle Leck and Aunt Miriam, dated March 15 from New Orleans, in which he

7. William Spratling, "Some Impressions of Mexico," part 2, *Architectural Forum* 47 (August 1927), 168; Jean Charlot, *The Mexican Mural Renaissance, 1920–1925* (New Haven: Yale University Press, 1963), 29.

asked "Have you seen the April *Scribner's?*" The note was accompanied by an offprint of yet another publication in *Architectural Forum,* this one from the February 1928 number, entitled "Guanajuato, the Most Mexican City." His focus for his second Mexican summer had turned to the northwest of Mexico City, and the four drawings in this piece continued to emphasize, as had those from the previous summer, architectural scenes whose scale and mountainous enclosures permitted a three-dimensional perspective unavailable in his earlier New Orleans sketches. Yet midway in this transitional period from one home to another, the casual intimate quality of Guanajuato and its intrinsic architectural interest reminded him of New Orleans. And although his penciled explorations by now were beginning to range over the whole country, this small locale characteristically attracted him because, unlike its better-known neighboring city of Guadalajara, it had retained—even with the practical introduction of reinforced concrete as a building material—an architectural integrity that for four centuries had been "in perfect accord with the traditions of her early Spanish Colonial period." Even more than the warm earth tones he had admired in the buildings of northern Italy, the dazzling colors of Guanajuato's stone, stuccoed adobe, and enameled tile stood in brilliant contrast to "our discreetly gray cities of the north," and to him the city seemed more replete with "paintable color" and unpretentious beauty than any city in Mexico.[8]

Spratling exhibited his Mexican work in a show at the Arts and Crafts Club in the fall of 1927 that also included pieces by N. C. Curtis. The Spratling section included thirty-three pictures, both pencil and watercolor, with some probably being the Cane River portraits, since one reviewer noted that the exhibition indicated Spratling's recent interest in figure drawing. Most of the review assessments concentrated on drawings of the Mexican churches and old houses that had begun to appear that summer in the *Architectural Forum* series:

> Here is an artist who never fails to get an interesting view, oft-times bird's-eye views, from unexpected heights . . . [a] fortunate ability to combine a spacious arrangement and at the same time to suggest far distances. These are soft and lovely in their lead-grey lines, some broad as the stroke of a

8. William Spratling, "Guanajuato, the Most Mexican City," *Architectural Forum* 48 (February 1928): 217.

brush, others as fine as an etcher's needle, an amazing mastery of the pro-
saic pencil.[9]

Spratling's growing Mexican affinity in what was to be his last academic year at Tulane was emphasized further when at his invitation the
influential editor of *Mexican Folkways,* Frances Toor, who had been visiting Spratling on her way to the University of Texas, delivered a lecture
at the club on the opening day of the exhibit. The range of his summer
travels there and the impression he and his work were making on those
most fully involved in the dramatic flowering of the arts in Mexico are
indicated by references in an essay by Dr. Atl published in *Architectural
Forum* as a companion piece to Spratling's on Guanajuato. Atl, an authoritative student of Mexican architectural history, entitled his essay
"Mexico and the Ultra-Baroco"; written for a North American readership, it was a compressed statement of his more elaborate thesis in *Las
iglesias y conventos de Mexico* that the astonishing proliferation (at its
maximum, ten churches monthly!) of religious architecture in New Spain
during the late seventeenth and eighteenth centuries assumed a style consonant with the enormous wealth of the Catholic Church and the colony's political and social unification. This architecture found its identity
in what he termed the "Ultra-Baroco," a language of European origin
but fully enriched aesthetically by anonymous masons, builders, and
even master designers into an expression characteristically tropical and
Mexican. And it was to the "admirable drawings" and "artistic sensibility" of William P. Spratling that Atl turned as illustrations of "the con-
structive tendencies and the plastic value of this truly Mexican style."
His "deeply sensitive" drawings, Atl wrote, especially in their fascination
with the dome and cupola, are the "wonderful fruits" of his several trips
throughout the republic and express more fully than any graphic reproduction could the spirit and character of this "first intellectual effort of
'New Spain,' " the first independent artistic expression that emerged
from the blending of the native and Spanish races.[10]

High praise, of course, for a young man who had experienced no more
than six Mexican months and whose economic status was sufficiently

9. Vera Morel, "Sketches by Local Artists Attract Many to Art Club," *New Orleans
Morning Tribune,* October 19, 1927.

10. Dr. Atl, "Mexico and the Ultra-Baroco," *Architectural Forum* 48 (February 1928):
223–24.

precarious to make his professional future uncertain. But as Spratling sent a copy of the Atl piece and an offprint of the Guanajuato drawings back to Alabama, he may well have perceived the intrinsic connection between his involvements with Colonial architecture and what in "Some Impressions of Mexico" he had called "a new feeling in the republic toward what is truly 'Mexicana.' " His drawings and interpretive essays had something of a kinship with the work of a Frances Toor and with that of those anthropologists and archaeologists from the United States who were working in the field—at the great pre-Aztec site of Teotihuacán, for example, which Spratling visited northeast of Mexico City. All of this activity, however unintentionally, was yet defining Mexico with its pervasive sense of myth and ancient sacramental traditions as a counterpoint to the great country to the north, whose twentieth-century sense of itself was increasingly historic and scientific.

After two summers, the possibility of an ironic Mexican exile—from a sense of home he had never possessed—may have been attractive to Spratling. But there is no indication at all that either his initial or permanent residency there contains any conscious attempt to record the impression of Mexico on the artistic self, as many talented painters and writers of fiction finding their way southward in the twenties were beginning to do. From the first, his acquaintanceships and orientation were toward the heart of the country and the native spirit. To be sure, he could never, even had he tried, have penetrated that spirit sufficiently to catch a glimpse of Mexico within a Continental vision, such as Dr. Atl's rather breathtaking conception of Ultra-Baroco religious architecture in eighteenth-century Mexico constituting "with its innumerable examples, an intermediate point between the Aztec Teocali and the New York skyscraper." Nor could he have fully understood Rivera's half-mystic, half-pragmatic sense in many of his murals that a subject of great painting and its execution in this hemisphere would be a uniting of the emotional power of the South with the technological possibilities of the North.

Still, as Spratling at the end of his second summer began the long voyage northward, leaving behind once more the geographical confines of the older, mothering culture of the continent, he must have felt confident that his extensive sketch-pad and notebooks were rich in professional promise, at least for the one contracted publication in *Architectural Forum* and almost certainly for a fall Arts and Crafts Club exhibition. His fascination with the curve and its displacement in his work of the linear and vertical planes in the structures of New Orleans and old plantation houses would eventually find its significant place in his silver designs. But for the moment, its presence in defining the essential plastic values of a major phase in New World architecture—praised by so eminent a critic as Dr. Atl—surely seemed predictive. Publication of the Guanajuato drawings was already set for February, and, in fact, Spratling seemed to have some assurance that other publications of the Mexican work would follow, since in the note to Roamer's Roost about the April *Scribner's* piece on Cane River, he wrote that additional *Forum* articles would appear in the May, July, and August numbers "and more later."

Despite Spratling's enthusiasm, the sequence did not continue. Just why it didn't is not clear. Most likely, the large number of drawings which had already appeared in the "Some Impressions" and Guanajuato articles over a seven-month period, between July and February, 1928, had seemed enough for the journal's purposes, concentrated as they were on traditional religious architecture. And Dr. Atl's accompanying piece on the definitive character of Spratling's work in this regard may have closed off the subject. However, the contract with *Travel* for the essays, with renderings, on selected Mexican cities offered Spratling an opportunity for his most extensive travel yet within the country.

Throughout the summer of 1928, he used Mexico City as a point of departure for daily excursions and week-long trips, those to the south carrying him beyond Taxco to Oaxaca and to the Isthmus of Tehuantepec. The extent of his travel and the nature of his visitations, as well as the visibility of his presence in the country, are recorded in a laudatory essay published in the Mexico City newspaper *Jueves de Excelsior*. Entitled "Un Viajero Alucinado en Mexico" and printed in late September, the full-page article reproduced three sketches, two of Cuernavaca, from the summer's work of the "enchanted traveler," and praised Spratling as "the new friend whom Mexico has indeed won": now for the third time he "finds himself in our country, immersing himself in the soul of our people, living among them, surprising them in their most intimate moments" and with his drawings and notes recording "the types and customs which distinguish us from other lands and other peoples." The piece is valuable for its description of Spratling's itinerary of some twenty locations, several visited in the company of the American painter and muralist George Biddle. He traveled especially, the essay continued, to "the cities that best represent the spirit old and new of this Mexico of paradoxes, and he has visited too the towns of less importance, which have not been mentioned by other travelers, and which, nevertheless, have their special charm, their importance as source of types." Also to the Mexican essayist, Spratling's sketchbook record of his trip to Tehuantepec—"the area most striking in life, in color, in sensitivity in our country, different from everything we know in geography and ethnology . . . where the women walk like birds and the houses are rich in legend"— was indicative of his leisurely, careful, and direct manner to "master the subtleties of form . . . to capture all those things which the man in a hurry will not have the chance to see again." But the essay is equally valuable in documenting Spratling's growing Mexican identity as writer and artist: through his publications in *Forum* and *Scribner's* and more recently in the *World's Work* "we have been getting to know the fine work of this young master who enjoys a cordial relationship with those in our country who can best show him the way." In fact, Spratling's affinity for that "way" seemed entirely natural because of his New Orleans background. His views on the merging of Spanish and native Indian tendencies in colonial architecture were extensively quoted and, to the Mexican journalist, carried a certain authority because of the "spiritual anthology" represented by his drawings of the Vieux Carré, a setting also marked in its history by the "unmistakeable influence and color" of Negro and French creole harmonies.[11]

At the end of what must have been a long yet productive summer, such public notice was reassuring to Spratling, and he characteristically sent a copy of the newspaper to Uncle Leck and Aunt Miriam, writing in pencil at the bottom of the page, "These are some of this summer's drawings—the best part is where I'm quoted in Spanish (perfect!)." The typically optimistic tone of his notes to Alabama, signed "Billy" as usual, was sustained in a scribbled "all's well"; but this was compromised slightly by an additional "I'm awfully broke." This would not seem to indicate that the gamble of cutting loose from academe was proving a disaster. He probably had just not been paid in full for the *Travel* pieces, the sketches for which had been done but the essays not yet written. The note confirmed his plan "to return next week by boat to New Orleans and then to New York." The lease on the St. Peter Street apartment was

11. "Un Viajero Alucinado en Mexico," *Jueves de Excelsior*, September 27, 1928.

still in force, and by early October he was settled in for a short stay, as indicated by the *Times-Picayune* interview on the 14th. From Mexico he had arranged for a show of his summer's work at the Arts and Crafts Club, which was reviewed with customary praise on the 29th in the *Morning Tribune,* describing his "integrity in even the slightest sketch and a more personal expression." The latter comment referred to his inclusion of a number of human-figure drawings, along with the architectural ones, some from the Cane River excursion and several that had already appeared in the first of the *World's Work* articles in September. It seems likely also that he had in advance gained approval for an exhibition at the club for a few works by Diego Rivera and had brought the pictures northward with him. That show opened on October 14, and minor though it was, it still was one of the first exhibitions of Rivera's work in the United States.[12]

There seems little doubt that by this time Spratling had committed himself to try a long-term residence in Mexico, and his visit to New York in November was in part a preparation for it. His arrival in New York, about November 10, was anticipated in a letter from Natalie Scott to Lyle Saxon in late October, congratulating him on the publication of *Fabulous New Orleans.* Saxon was temporarily living in New York, and Natalie knew also that Faulkner was there ("Tell Bill Faulkner I dreamed about him the other night! Nothing Freudian—if he is uneasy"). It was a reunion of sorts for Spratling, and he recalled it briefly in the autobiography, missing the time by a year but still remembering, accurately it would seem, that in "the fall of 1927, Bill and I were again together in New York, living down on Christopher Street."[13] That was the location of Saxon's apartment, where Faulkner stayed for the several weeks he was there, as Spratling probably did also. Faulkner's visit was to supervise the cutting on *Sartoris,* which Harcourt Brace had agreed to publish, and to see if anyone would be interested in his new manuscript. Spratling's mission was no doubt equally practical: either to confirm or to propose, probably the former, important publications that would draw further on his interpretations of Mexican culture during the three previous sum-

12. "Mexican Artist Features Exhibit," *New Orleans Times-Picayune,* October 14, 1928, p. 21.

13. Natalie Scott to Lyle Saxon, October 29, 1928, Scott Papers, Manuscripts Department, Tulane University Library. Faulkner's biographer establishes the fall 1928 New York chronology. Blotner, 422 ff.

mers. Given their imminent appearance within the next four months, it seems likely that he had already received conditional approval pending the submission of final copy. First, his series on Mexican architecture would be continued in the prestigious professional journal *Architecture*. Second, *Scribner's,* apparently on the good reception of his April essay, had agreed to publish in its January 1929 number "Figures in a Mexican Renaissance," which, illustrated with several pencil portraits in the Cane River style, would be one of the first important messages northward to a popular readership about the powerful surge in the arts then completing its first decade in Mexico. And, finally, it was probably during this visit that Spratling's reliability as an interpreter of the artistic and literary scene in Mexico received further credence through his commission to write a periodic "Mexican Letter" for Irita Van Doren's "Books Abroad" Sunday sequence in the New York *Herald-Tribune,* with his first column scheduled to appear in March.

If Spratling departed New York before Christmas with a couple of hundred dollars in payment for some of this, he knew that the money would go much, much further in Mexico than it would have in what was now his former home in New Orleans. In fact, as Natalie Scott observed in a letter to Lyle Saxon as she herself, a few months later, was thinking about joining Spratling in the Mexican move, it was becoming almost "too costive" to live there, and both she and Spratling confided to their good friend the prominent French Quarter preservationist Elizabeth Werlein that they felt each could live on $500 a year in a town like Taxco.[14] It is possible also that he left the city with some encouragement about the book he badly wanted to write, one not yet clear in his mind but one that would be something personal and original about Mexico and his new life there. Such an expression of potential interest would have come from Harrison Smith, who was shortly to leave his Harcourt Brace editorship to form a new house in partnership with the English publisher Jonathan Cape. They may have been introduced by Faulkner, whose friendship with Smith would have been initially helpful to Spratling. One of the new firm's first contracts was to publish the manuscript

14. Natalie Scott to Lyle Saxon, February 19, 1929, Scott Papers. The Elizabeth Werlein allusion was recalled by her daughter, Elizabeth Werlein Carter, in her oral history project at Columbia University; she also remembered that "Spratling was one of Mother's favorite young men." Recorded and communicated to the author by Ann Waldron (biographer of Hodding Carter), February 3, 1994.

Faulkner had brought along with him to New York: *The Sound and the Fury;* and during the company's brief life of three years or so it would publish also *As I Lay Dying* and *Sanctuary,* as well as, of course, Spratling's *Little Mexico.*

As Spratling began his fourth voyage south, this time with no plans to return, the year of 1929 seemed at least moderately promising. With his imaginative sensitivity to the resonances of time and place, he knew that he would be living in an environment where important artistic things were happening. But, beyond the immediate future, how he could further respond to this environment was not yet clear. What would bring this response into being, giving a focus to his entrepreneurial energy and considerable personal gifts—and would, in fact, make 1929 the pivotal year in his career and bring him into a permanent identity with Taxco—had actually already begun, in the summer of 1928. It was then that his friendship with Diego Rivera had become one of close mutual trust and respect; and it was then also that he developed an increasingly agreeable relationship with the most prominent American family in Mexico, that of Ambassador Dwight Morrow and his wife Elizabeth.

5

"Passionate Hieroglyphics" and the Move to Taxco

> Going to see the paintings of Diego Rivera in the courts of the Secretaria of public education straightens you out a little bit. They give a dramatic sequence to all this brightness and white glitter, to the terribly silent welling up of life everywhere. In tense earth colors that have a dull burnish to them he has drawn the bending of bodies at work, the hunch of the shoulders under picks and shovels of men going down into a mine, the strain and heave of a black body bent under a block of marble. . . . Some of it's pretty hasty, some of it's garlanded tropical bombast, but by God, it's painting. . . .
>
> Go around to the art galleries in New York. Look at all the little pictures, little landscapes after Cezanne, Renoir, Picasso, Corot . . . little fruity still lifes, little modern designs of a stovepipe and a bisected violin . . . stuff a man's afraid to be seen looking at . . . a lot of warmed-over truck, leavings of European fads.
>
> —John Dos Passos, "Paint the Revolution,"
> *New Masses* (March 1927)

On March 30, as the SS *Baja California* slowly made its way from New Orleans downriver toward the Gulf, Spratling wrote to Carl Zigrosser, director of the Weyhe Gallery in New York, assuring him that "after much delay, am at last underway for Mexico" and that he would write again when he reached Tampico.[1] Given its date and content, the letter is a specific indication of the defining transition in Spratling's career. While in New York he had arranged with Zigrosser to act as agent for the potential sale of a collection of American and French paintings to be exhibited in Mexico City for an extended period, and the letter in part was by way of explaining that there had been some slight difficulties in

---

1. All references to the correspondence of Carl Zigrosser are from the Carl Zigrosser Papers, Annenberg Rare Book and Manuscript Library, University of Pennsylvania.

meeting insurance and customs specifications but that all was now re-
solved. This was the first of several commercial engagements within the
expanding relationship between the art worlds of the United States and
Mexico he would make over the next three years as he sought a living
in his new country, prior to the unexpected emergence of his designer-
silversmith identity in the tranquil little town of Taxco, which he had
described in a strangely anticipatory essay published in the month just
previous to this one. That living and that new identity would be earned,
perhaps even in part created, under the hardest of circumstances, as the
Great Depression, already in this spring of 1929 implicit in a nervousness
on Wall Street, would inexorably find its way southward.

The letter to Zigrosser was written after Spratling had essentially completed his occasional though consistent journalistic career, first begun in
1925, in which he had recorded his artistic and verbal impressions, assuming the stance of the resident observer or brief visitor in a few historical settings of the southern United States, or else the persona of the
American traveler in the older cultures of Europe and, of course, Mexico.
Three of the six essays completing this phase, all published in 1929, had
already appeared by March, and the other three, describing his travels in
the summer of 1928, would be printed in a few months and had probably
been delivered before he left New York. Henceforth, his voice and pencil
would be those of the fully acclimated expatriate interpreter, and, in fact,
the first example of these, his initial "Mexican Letter," had appeared in
the *Herald-Tribune* on February 29, the day before he boarded ship in
New Orleans.

All six of the essays provide a synthesis, first, of Spratling's immersion
in the idea of a "renaissance" in the artistic life of Mexico, of which his
own interpretive drawing and writing we should now see were indeed a
small part; and, second, of his awareness that this cultural response to
the country's complex history seemed to oppose the continuing dislocation of its politics. But the essays, all illustrated and written during the
months when Spratling was on the verge of making the decision to move
his future to Mexico, are further integrated in that they confirm—beyond
whatever practical reasons would lead to that decision—his discovery of
a greater example than he had yet appraised of the drama inherent in the
juxtaposition between past and present that had informed almost every
subject he had chosen to draw or write about since first arriving in New
Orleans in 1922. The romantic side of his nature responded enormously

to the "return" of Mexico's pre-Columbian and Colonial past in the art of muralist, painter, architect, and native craftsman, and also such activity as he observed in La Merced, one of the poorest markets in Mexico City, where children in their early teens under the tutelage of a prominent sculptor were cutting in stone images of native animals "directly in line with the Aztec tradition."[2]

While this was, he wrote, "evidence of something new and vital taking place in the shell of things that are past," he never construed this vitality, which was surely a sign of spiritual and historic unity, as powerful enough to bring together in any widespread political unity the disparate communities throughout the country that existed as small nations complete in themselves. By his third Mexican summer Spratling had already begun to penetrate and accept the strange sense of isolation pervasive in these populations, which he illustrated by a brief encounter with an elderly Indian, laden with multicolored baskets on his way to La Merced:

> "Did you make these in your home?" I asked.
> "Si, señor!"
> "But where is that?"
> "En mi tierra," (in my country) he says.
> "But where is your country?"
> "Por allá Tepepam, señor."
> Tepepam is a village less than ten miles from the capital!

And rather than sell a basket to Spratling at a price higher than he could get in the market stall, he would instead walk the additional twenty blocks where he could bargain, gossip, and eventually sell out for less than his production costs.

This curious impracticality, vagueness, and feeling of misdirection, utterly incomprehensible, Spratling wrote, to "the foreigner," were not at all unlike the sense of indigenous "native" elusiveness and non-rationality which George Orwell during these same years in the late twenties was experiencing as a police officer in Burma and would interpret as part of the ironic colonial imprisonment of the "sahib" figure. To Spratling, with no official frustrations at stake, however, all of this was appealing in its steady unawareness of the twentieth century, and, within a few years, he would explore it further in *Little Mexico*. He was, in fact, before even

2. William Spratling, "Mansions of the Conquistadors," *Travel*, August 1929, p. 29.

settling down in Mexico, already defensive about its exploitation by absentee landlords, and was bitterly resentful of condescending American journalists who pessimistically and superficially surveyed the country and its alleged backwardness and futility through the lens of the relative efficiency of the U.S. government.[3]

Though drawn by the many contrasts and connections between the life of modern Mexico and its colonial past, Spratling nevertheless felt that the country was making social and governmental progress even though he took the long view—accurately, it would seem, from our almost seventy-year perspective—that it would take many years "for Mexico to be herself in the sense of being a country of, and for, Mexicans, not the Spanish; of being more of the American continent than of Europe." He admired the country's popular strongman, President Plutarco Elías Calles—with whom he made a sketching appointment. But under his transitional stance of the foreign, though sympathetic, interpreter, he could, like Orwell, also perceive the political irony in the scene before him. In some of his finest descriptive writing he described an image of that scene—the spectacle he witnessed on the night of September 16, 1928, the celebration by all Mexico of *la Independencia,* the grandest day of the year, whose wild and clamorous enthusiasm Spratling compared to that in France on July 14.

> This vast space in front of the *Palacio* is so jammed with people one can scarcely move in any direction. Fireworks of the most extravagant description explode overhead and burst into thousands of stars. Bells of the cathedral, vaguely seen in the dim light from the flames in the square below, are, strangely enough, not being rung. Nevertheless, the towers are crowded with the gravely watching figures of literally hundreds of *campesinos* and *obreros.* The long facade of the palace, brilliant with the light of a thousand searchlights and with balconies hung with brocaded red velvet, is almost Roman in its splendor—a curious display in a popular government. The diplomatic corps and other elegantly gowned people can be seen thronging the balconies and the brilliantly illumined salons of the second floor.

Then, at eleven o'clock, President Calles appears on the balcony, rings the historic bell and, with hands upraised, greets the great throng: *"Viva Mexico! Viva la Independencia!"*

3. See, for example, the series of three articles, the first one illustrated by Spratling,

The crowd bursts into wild cheers, goes mad for the space of some minutes. Hats fly into the air amid cries of *"Viva Calles; Viva Mexico! Viva! Viva!"* It is as though there were only one party—with no political factions, insurgents, or other problems existing in the country; as though all the aims of the Revolution had been accomplished facts and there remained the single impulse of an intense nationalism.[4]

Spratling may have considered this essay on Mexico City, "Mansions of the Conquistadors," to have been the centerpiece of the volume on the cities of Mexico he was still planning. Certainly, even with his extensive travels in both Europe and the United States, there seems no reason to doubt his assertion that he found in its blend of cosmopolitanism and feudal splendor, in the sense of savagery and barbarism latent in the red volcanic stone of the massive buildings laced, he felt, with the blood of "thousands bent to the will of the conqueror," a city such as he had never encountered before. Of the six essays he published in this year of 1929, which together seem to mark a transition between the northern part of his life and the southern, this one contains, in addition to its rare—for Spratling—statement of social criticism, the widest range of allusion to the many faces of Mexico, the ironies and contradictions of its fantastic history, which had already appeared separately in some of his earlier writing. And in his now typical style, carefully keeping in mind his unprofessional but yet knowledgeable *Travel* readership, he arranged this complexity into an impression of place and cultural ambience through a blending of historical reference: the conqueror Cortez and the little Catholic priest Hidalgo, father of the 1810 revolution; and through revealing contrast: the curious intransigence of the *campesino* basket-seller's "trade psychology," as opposed to what Spratling perceived as the efficiency and heel-clicking energy of the Calles administration.

As a montage of Spratling's past and present Mexico, the essay is comparable to "Figures in a Mexican Renaissance," which, though less analytical in content than many of his others, was yet the one through which he probably contributed most for North American readers an identification of the artistic and educational awakening of their southern neighbor. The descriptive "renaissance" term was not at all original with Spratling,

that appeared in the *World's Work* in 1928 by Henry Kittredge Norton, entitled "What's the Matter with Mexico?"

4. Spratling, "Mansions of the Conquistadors," 31.

having appeared since the early twenties in several journal accounts directed mainly toward assessments of the emerging power of such painters as Rivera, Orozco, Mérida, and Montenegro, whose work was seen as initiating for Mexican art a brilliant revival in its rejection of the old European masters and creative absorption of indigenous pre-Columbian and Hispanic sources. And, once the mighty subjects of Mexico's history of conquest and revolution began to appear in monumental proportions, especially in the public frescoes of Rivera, it became gradually clear to many artists and writers about art in the United States that the most important painting being done anywhere on the continent—perhaps the most significant ever and certainly the most comprehensive—was being done in Mexico. To John Dos Passos the "passionate hieroglyphics" he saw on the three-storied walls of the Secretaría in Mexico City, "probably a good half-mile of them," contained to be sure the obvious symbolism of hammer and sickle. But there was an organic impetus behind all of it that had nothing to do with Russian importation; it simply explained to a population that largely could not read (but could walk) the origins and nature of their spiritual and economic condition. It was this latter quality, the actuality of a popular graphic art, subsidized by the government, whose humane content spoke directly to the life of the people that was obviously of some significance to the proletarian sensibility of the *New Masses* audience for whom Dos Passos wrote. But what made painting such as this transcend the familiar pedestrian modes of Marxist art and put to shame the imitative character and exclusivity of much of that in the United States was the expression of the message in a plastic form and pictorial technique of surpassing originality. "If it isn't a revolution in Mexico," Dos Passos concluded, "I'd like to know what it is."

To the stream of travelers who came southward to view this revolution in painting, actually to see its principal symbolic figure at work on the Secretaría murals, the socialist message was insignificant in itself, as it was to Spratling—and indeed would be to subsequent history. What was breathtaking in this new kind of art was the majestic scope of its mythos, seeming in its incredibly elastic array of panels to capture, as the young California painter Ray Boynton described it, "the struggles and hopes and labors and festivals of that vast folk who have lived on the land and tilled the soil and carried on the labors and the wars and have an immemorial identity with the land of Mexico."[5] The American artist-

5. Ray Boynton, "Rivera," *Mexican Folkways* 2 (August-September 1926), p. 28.

visitor to such a mural scene in 1926 or 1927 may well have felt there was something disturbing and yet vaguely desirable in the creative un- folding in awesome forms of this wide and fully integrated human story, an expression unachievable in the artistic consciousness of his own plu- ralistic nation. Of course in those years neither such a visitor nor Sprat- ling—who in his own appraisal of Rivera for the *Scribner's* essay adopted the stance of paying a personal call to the worksite—could have known the end of the Mexican mural story, having seen only a portion of the uncompleted Secretaría panels and not, of course, those greater ones yet to come in the next few years at Chapingo and Cuernavaca and in the Palacio Nacional. In later years Rivera would reflect on the total accom- plishment of the Mexican muralists, feeling that what gave their work originality and universal value was that they

> for the first time in the history of monumental painting—ceased to use gods, kings, chiefs of state, heroic generals, as central heroes . . . [but] the man of the fields, of the factories, of the cities, and towns. . . . Also for the first time in history, from the semi-mythic past to the real, scientific, foreseeable future, an attempt was made to portray the trajectory of the people through time in one homogenous and dialectic composition.[6]

If "dialectic," with its implied interpretations of history as tension be- tween contradictory forces, was a word Spratling would not have thought about in 1927–1928 when he wrote his "renaissance" assess- ment, "homogenous" was one he might well have chosen. And "trajec- tory," with its suggestion of an ascendant curve, was a design concept that had fully penetrated his architectural consciousness in the last three years and that, in its association to him with the pattern of Mexican history, finds a strange correlation with Rivera's usage. The curve was an architectural form unknown to pre-Conquest Mexico, and in Spratling's fascination with the thousands of domed religious structures that had relentlessly made their way across New Spain, he came to see these sym- bols of political and ecclesiastical power as enshrining the very historical tensions that made the social trajectory of the Mexican people seem an exciting possibility: enclosing beneath the sweeping curves of their cupo-

6. Rivera, quoted by Luis Cardoza y Aragón, "Diego Rivera's Murals in Mexico and the United States," in *Diego Rivera, A Retrospective*, ed. Cynthia Newman Helms (New York: Norton, 1986), 187.

las, for example, images of biblical saints or even a Jesus with Indian faces, or on the multicolored tiled surface of the great dome of Taxco's Santa Prisca itself a row of gleaming Aztec suns surmounting the inscription "Gloria a Dios en las Alturas."

Spratling's essay on the principal as well as representative movers in the Mexican renaissance does not attempt to develop the "idols behind altars" thesis, which was already, even as he wrote, under definitive analysis in the work of Anita Brenner and would be published also in 1929. What he had to contribute to that subject was largely confined to his essays on Colonial architecture, although in *Little Mexico* he would address further the persistent presence along the ascending trajectory of the nation's violent history and its spiritual and artistic awakening of a suppressed but undestroyed primitive culture. In 1927–1928 the early important books by American scholars and observers incorporating the social and artistic consequences of the revolution of 1921 within the long continuum of Mexican history were just beginning to appear, and journal news of the "renaissance" had primarily been confined to those circulated to limited artistic and political subscription. The piece by Spratling certainly sustains the image of contemporary Mexican painting, in his phrasing, as an "all-inclusive" representation of "the toil and strivings of the nation," with the new masters finding and assigning values to their art that suddenly were indigenous, not merely accessory, to the social fabric. But the value of the essay is its early delineation for the wide and literate U.S. readership reached by *Scribner's Magazine* of the homogeneous interconnections between the muralists and the rest of that fabric.

The essay begins with Spratling calling up personal and familiar greetings to a responsive Rivera seated high on a scaffold at the Secretaría, and then proceeds through a series of vignettes of six principal "figures" who have erected "constructional vistas" for the nation. Very much in the manner of "Cane River Portraits," there are pencil sketches of each figure, but here each has personally inscribed the drawing. As usual in his perfected short-essay manner, Spratling's style is concentrated, suggestively observant, and augmented with details that yield a quick authentic impression. The balance is especially admirable, with no more space given to the imaginative social consciousness of Rivera and Orozco than to the extraordinary stature and efforts of Moisés Sáenz in pursuing his governmental charge of developing rural schools for educating the nation's large native Indian population, bringing them into effective suffrage and political consciousness; or to the fresh and vital architecture ("a primitiveness of line that is almost Aztec") of young Carlos Obregón in his designs for public buildings in Mexico City; or to Dr. Atl's catalytic impulse among the arts; or to the coordinating folkloric research and editorial contributions of *Mexican Folkways*' Frances Toor, "the one American there who has consistently devoted herself toward preserving what is traditionally and indigenously Mexican in art."[7]

The essay, published in January 1929, seems to unite Spratling's first two summers in Mexico, perhaps all three, but references to the "Calles administration" indicate it was written before July 1928, when President-elect Alvaro Obregón was assassinated and Emilio Portes Gil was installed as interim president. All six of the sketches are dated "1927" and an allusion to the celebrated *Wall Street Banquet* panel in the Secretaría mural, which Rivera completed in mid-summer 1927, suggests that Spratling probably composed the essay during his last academic year in New Orleans. Not only the signed sketches but also the many personalized and familiar details seem to corroborate that by the end of his second Mexican summer Spratling had established a sympathetic kinship with all that the six "figures" represented. Illustrated too, as in almost all of his writing, is the integrative character of his perceptions. He seemed to feel obliged to give some legitimacy to the "renaissance" term beyond its casual association with a concentration of genius and creative energy, and he wrote that the classical Renaissance of fifteenth-century Italy had emerged from "no stranger background" of change and social evolution than that of twentieth-century Mexico. And, had he known of them, he might have seen even closer comparisons with other times and places in our own century to which we have applied the term *renaissance*: Ireland, the South, Harlem, where to a united population the quietly persistent presence of a high order of creativity was called up and given direction, as Spratling saw happening in Mexico, by the dramatic remembrance and discovery of values native to their traditions and history,

7. William Spratling, "Figures in a Mexican Renaissance," *Scribner's Magazine* 85 (January 1929): 14–21. For a further commentary by Spratling on the work of Obregón, the "figure" closest to his own discipline, see "The Public Health Center, Mexico City," *Architectural Forum* 55 (November 1931): 589–94. The new center, which contains murals by Rivera, was called by Spratling "the most Mexican building . . . done in Mexico since the Conquest."

a discovery made against a shared experience of internecine strife and social dislocation.

Once more, Spratling could not participate emotionally in that shared sense of native communion which, for many young Mexican artists, fused the agony of their experiences in revolutionary campaigns with a new awareness of what Dos Passos described as "an enormously rich and uncorrupted popular art" in textiles, pottery, toys, and even in the mural decoration of tavern walls in villages throughout the country. Ultimately, however, in his own creative confrontation with the white metal lying beneath the hills of Guerrero, Spratling would resurrect and assimilate into a new art form this very tradition, becoming, indeed, a "figure" himself. If we see much of his writing and drawing as a kind of intellectual and psychological preparation for this achievement, then the dual essays on "Indo-Hispanic Mexico" published in the months immediately following the *Scribner's* piece are particularly suggestive. Their subtitle, "Some Notes on the Manner in Which Indian Form and Impulse Has Persisted and Continued Through an Imposed Culture," projects the same thesis that his American colleague Frances Toor developed in an essay, written in the same year, about the remarkable artwork of Mexican children, especially poor Indian children, in the government-supported "Open-Air Painting Schools": that though the Conquistadors and all the subsequent exploiters had been able to subjugate and disinherit Mexico's native population, they had not killed off the Indian's artistic impulse and plastic creativity, whose continuing expression—as if "guided by ghosts of the past"—had made the Mexican Renaissance possible. Spratling's elaborately illustrated set of essays (sixteen sketches, some full-page) brings to completion the brief allusions made in his earlier writing to architecture *poblana*, the native expression: how the presence of Indian psychology and sense of tropic form working through the thousands of laborers, masons, sculptors, and decorators who built the massive Colonial churches brought a forceful simplicity and joyous personal touch, especially in surface and decorative patterns, to the otherwise severe and traditional Spanish style.[8]

8. Frances Toor, "The Children Artists in the Mexican Revolution," *Mexican Folk-ways* 4 (January-March 1928): 6–23; William Spratling, "Indo-Hispanic Mexico: Some Notes on the Manner in Which Indian Form and Impulse Has Persisted and Continued Through an Imposed Culture," parts 1 and 2, *Architecture* 59 (February 1929): 75–80; (March 1929): 139–44.

Spratling's verbal and visual evocations of the ghostly hands that centuries before had creatively subverted the very symbols of their conquest
are a genuine if minor contribution to the Mexican renaissance of the
twenties. The hands that had carved or painted on hundreds of facades,
portals, or interior frescoes monkeys, fruit, interwoven palm branches,
cornstalks symbolically draped with flowers, personal sun and moon
portraits, or even inscriptions in the Aztec language had bequeathed to
all Mexicans an art impulse that, in Spratling's phrase, had "persisted
and continued through an imposed culture." After a century of revolutionary travail, this impulse, especially in the work of Rivera and the
early muralists, had now surged triumphantly into full view of the art
world of both America and Europe, but as Dr. Atl and others of Spratling's predecessors had described, it had always lived a quiet life in the
beauty and primitive elegance of the materials of daily existence—
clothing, eating utensils, playthings—made in isolated Indian communities throughout the country. Spratling, of course, had been a slightly late
arrival on this scene of recognition and resurgence. But his quick and
responsive adaptation to it has helped our own understanding of the phenomenon. It is one thing to read the astounding statistics, for example,
of the number of domed Spanish colonial churches built in or around the
ancient sacred Aztec city of Cholula (365!), but Spratling's tower-level
sketch in "Indo-Hispanic Mexico" (part two) of the great basilican Capi-
lla Real (itself having 39 domes) with other church structures in the distance catches in a kind of spatial-historical perspective the religio-
conquistador mentality, whose policy was that each pagan pyramid or
temple should be either replaced or be superimposed with church or
monastery.

The place-names and drawings which appeared in the two parts of
"Indo-Hispanic Mexico" establish the range of Spratling's travels in the
summer of 1928. As mentioned above, he traveled at times in the company of George Biddle, who in a few years would use his own observations of the Mexican model of government support for artists as
instrumental in helping to establish in the United States during the
Depression years the Federal Art Projects program. In this last of his
summers-as-writer, Spratling seemed consistently to be drawn to scenes
that, however unknowingly, stored up for release in his future residency
a full perception and appreciation of the interwoven primitive-colonial
presence firmly embedded in the character of modern Mexico. At Xochi-

milco, for example, for Spratling in 1928 "a morning's walk" from Mexico City but now one of its continuous suburbs, he saw a preserved, unified way of life existing among its interconnected system of canals and islands that, in microcosm, must have recalled the actual site of today's Mexico City, Tenochtitlán, Montezuma's capital, whose complex network of causeways, water thoroughfares, and floating islands enclosed the civic, agricultural, and religious life of its 300,000 inhabitants and had dazzled the eyes of Cortez and his followers four centuries earlier. Spratling recorded also what was of particular interest to him architecturally, that the Indian impulse of decorative, personalized construction was still unconsciously alive. He witnessed, for example, in the village of Tonantzintla, not far from Cholula, the repair of a church (where a carved group of "most delightfully naive saints held up their skirts just over the doorway") by several Indian villagers who had been engaged, without pay and entirely on their own, for over two years in skillfully painting and regilding the elaborate vaulting of the interior wrought by their seventeenth-century forebears.

Spratling's summer of 1928 served to deepen his sense of "renaissance" and increased his integrative perception that many contemporary young Mexican architects, such as the "figure" of Carlos Obregón, were comparable to the great modern painters of the decade in that their designs were utilizing forms and solutions directly connected to the lives of ordinary people. In his exposition, however, of how the simple, direct, and humane artistic expression of the Indian hand had continuously touched and given an indigenous spirit to the architecture of conquest, he needed, as contrast, a relatively "pure" expression of the Spanish Baroque and of Colonial residential building. This he found in the quiet and unpretentious city of Taxco, which is the principal focus of the first part of "Indo-Hispanic Mexico." Spratling had been urged to visit Taxco, he wrote in the *Travel* article, by the enthusiasm for its provincial simplicity of Miguel Covarrubias, Roberto Montenegro, and other artists whom he had met in Mexico City; they "seemed to have just discovered it for themselves." When he first saw the town, essentially abandoned since the late nineteenth century, the huddle of a few stores, a cantina, and an inn or two could not obscure for his architectural eye the dingy splendor of the great Church of Santa Prisca, already two centuries old, which dominated the central plaza and looked toward clusters of symmetrical red-roofed houses, integrated by slender twisting pathways that climbed a hillside so steep that fifty feet away from the plaza one would be a hundred feet above it. And it is typical of Spratling's cultural explorations during this "*viajero alucinado*" period that he would also have caught within the town's ancient history the connection between these images of New Spain and the mines of Montezuma.

Those mines now, Spratling observed, being worked in only "a desultory way," had originally, of course, with the quantity and purity of their silver ore, formed a basis for Aztec wealth and for that of the sixteenth-century European conquerors. But a decline into spasmodic production had rendered Taxco an obscure mining village, though still a stop on the twisting mountainous road to the Pacific, where for centuries, as a Spratling contemporary would put it later, "the Manila galleons unloaded treasures from the Orient and the southern seas, returning with thousands of gold and silver coins which circulated as common currency throughout the Asiatic world."[9] It was not until the mid–eighteenth century, however, when the town, under the impetus of the entrepreneurial schemes of the mysterious José de la Borda, assumed its most characteristic Colonial form. It had risen anew as a kind of monument of thanksgiving, especially the re-building of the magnificent Santa Prisca Cathedral, to God and the Blessed Virgin for having looked with favor on de la Borda's activity, which had managed to extract millions in silver from the local mines. Whatever providential connection may have there been at work, it would have depended on the crushing and deadly toil of thousands of Indians. And Spratling, always with an eye for the suggestive detail, may well have perceived on that first visit in the spatial juxtaposition of the great church itself with the "Little Black Footsteps," the name of the small cantina hard by its side, something of the town's human history, the connection between wealth and the endless parade over the centuries of grimy workers returning from the deep hillside shafts. Still, the architecture of the town, accommodating the steep mountainside location, had remained essentially unaltered in what Spratling called its "Spanish ingenuity," where construction details of even the smallest pink stone houses had fitted themselves into a consistent pattern, lying undisturbed long after silver production had declined to a trickle. "It is a little world," he wrote, "in which to take walks."

9. Daniel F. Rubin de la Borbolla, "William Spratling, pionero," in *William Spratling* (Mexico City: Centro Cultural Arte Contemporaneo, 1987), 14.

Shortly before Spratling's first Taxco visit, the city had been "rediscovered" by the newly self-conscious Mexican government, and identified as a national monument with a congressional decree that its physical appearance could not be altered or extended without the approval of museum authorities. To Spratling, who remembered the problem of Vieux Carré preservation, such an assurance must have increased the attractiveness of Taxco, perhaps as a quiet retreat for visiting and writing, perhaps even as an inexpensive place to live despite its remoteness from the capital art scene—if, of course, one had the money to make such an arrangement. It seemed most unlikely, however, that there was any money to be made in Taxco, since Mexico had neither the capitalistic sensibility nor the investment capacity to revive the region's dormant mineral wealth.

"Taxco's period of real prosperity existed so many years ago that no one there now remembers it . . . and there is to-day real poverty in the little town . . . places like Taxco are having to wait a long time for their revival of prosperity, and then what it will do to them when it arrives is another thing." There is an oddly predictive quality about this almost idle speculation, as quoted from the "Indo-Hispanic" essay, for even as that essay was being written, the new National Highway that would connect Mexico City, Cuernavaca, and the Pacific Ocean at Acapulco was already under construction. Within three years or so Taxco, though no longer as in centuries past centrally located on what was once the main road of the Western world, would nevertheless now be readily accessible from the new highway, ready indeed to be described in a caption by the *New York Times* as "Taxco of the Aztecs Now Greets the World."[10] And for our story, of course, the town was also becoming "ready" for what William Spratling would bring to it. Within that story there is indeed an ironic correlation in the two details that seemed on Spratling's early visit to define the city's colonial presence, its suspension in time. First, the streets. Unintentionally hostile then to automobile traffic, they zigzagged upward toward the small plaza in front of the *parroquia*, their smooth surfaces laid in intricate patterns of black and white marble which had been traversed for endless decades only by pedestrians and patient burro trains. Today, the marble bits lie beneath rough cobblestones over which

10. Brick Berry, "Taxco of the Aztecs Now Greets the World," *New York Times Magazine,* April 24, 1932, 18.

hordes of small foreign-car taxis bounce and rattle, carrying tourists from all over the world who have come to see the picturesque city and to buy the silver displayed in the scores of shops that evolved from Spratling's own. And, second, of course, the *parroquia* itself, the Church of Santa Prisca, which in 1928 Spratling sketched with a perspective from the south, calling it "the baroque in its most glorious development." Some forty years later, his funeral service would be conducted there.

If that summer of 1928 was singularly momentous in anticipating the emerging shape of the Spratling identity as he and the community of Taxco came closer together, it was a summer that also brought him to another place where this identity would be given further direction. He had visited Cuernavaca then, eventually using the visit as basis for one of the three *Travel* articles he would publish in 1929, "The Friendly Capital of Rebel Mexico." Though that piece was the least effective of the three, the sketches of the sixteenth-century Franciscan cathedral were well executed and Spratling characteristically used them elsewhere, in the "Indo-Hispanic Mexico" series and in the flattering *Excelsior* newspaper account of his travels and interpretations of Mexican life. On the copy of the latter article which he sent to Uncle Leck and Aunt Miriam, one of his handwritten notes stated that he had recently completed, and successfully sold for publication, sketches of Interim President Emilio Portes Gil and of Ambassador Dwight Morrow. The Morrows had arrived in Mexico City in the previous October, and Spratling may have met them first early in the summer when he came down from New Orleans, or possibly in Cuernavaca itself a few weeks later. Already by then the couple had become irretrievably fascinated by the garden-like city, whose mild temperatures, beautiful flora, and proximity to the capital made it for them a convenient retreat even as it had served the emperor Maximilian and Carlota and generations of well-to-do Mexicans. The Morrows' decision during their second year to purchase a small weekend house there proved enormously fortunate for Spratling, leading him into a relationship with the family that would significantly mark his life for years to come and would also unexpectedly yield him the financial means to settle permanently in Taxco.

As Spratling today may seem to us one of the most interesting and original Americans who traveled through the expatriate experience of the twenties, so he must have appeared to the Morrows, who despite their apprehension at the difficulties of the ambassadorship, had almost since their arrival found unanticipated pleasure in the Mexican scene. Spratling's knowledge of that scene and his growing commitment to it, together with his demonstrable personal gifts and his affinity—not necessarily intentional—for people of intelligence, authority, and influence all must have helped the relationship along. In addition, the house that the Morrows purchased belonged to Frederick Davis, a friend of Spratling's whom he had met on his first visit to Mexico. Manager of the Sonora News Company, Davis had been one of the earliest designers of jewelry emphasizing folk motifs; too, he was a wealthy collector of Mexican art and antiquities, a practice Spratling was beginning to pursue during his summer travels, and Spratling lived initially at Davis's address in Mexico City, at 17 Avenida Madero, when he first settled permanently in the country. By the time Spratling departed for his last year in New Orleans, in the fall of 1928, the Morrows had already begun to acquire adjoining property in Cuernavaca and to expand the house with a series of courts, fountains, gardens, terraces, a small pool, and a tower that commanded a fine view of the city and distant mountains. It is not clear whether by then they had decided to record in narrative and, with Spratling, in plans and sketches what they would call their "Casa Mañana," but at least Spratling must have felt that their friendship was another resource he could count on when he returned, possibly even some employment.

And, indeed, within a few weeks of his arrival for permanent Mexican residency in 1929, he was engaged in making drawings of the expanding number of additions to Casa Mañana. He wrote to Dwight Morrow on May 10 from Cuernavaca:

> Many thanks for your kind hospitality—which I've enjoyed.
>
> I've made notes for about 5 drawings and expect at least 2 or 3 to be really decent. Will finish them in Taxco and bring them up to show you about the end of next week.[11]

The one hundred dollars payment for this initial work was, to say the least, critical to Spratling's usual marginal finances. Except for the payments for journal articles he had brought with him from New York, he

11. The letters from Spratling to Dwight Morrow are in the Dwight Morrow Papers, Series X, Box 4, Folder 129; the letter, below, from Morrow to Diego Rivera, Series X, Box 4, Folder 60; Archives and Special Collections, Amherst College Library, Amherst, Mass.

probably had no other expected income until the beginning of the summer session at the University in Mexico City, where he had been awarded
another appointment. The letter also indicated his further gravitation
toward Taxco, whose seedy charm and architectural integrity—not unlike those of the Vieux Carré, but without its intellectual atmosphere—
had obviously already become attractive to him. For the Cuernavaca
work, the town was also convenient, only forty miles southward, and
certainly a place where, at a comfortable boardinghouse, he could live
cheaply.

The patience, discretion, meticulous research and planning which had
been characteristic of Morrow's pre-Mexico successes in the realm of
law and international finance were also qualities that contributed to his
notable diplomatic achievements in Mexico, such as resolving the long-
standing U.S.-Mexican contention over oil leases and concessions and
the even more highly charged tension between the Mexican government
and the Catholic Church. Contemporary American historians of Mexico
such as Frank Tannenbaum, Stuart Chase, and Lesley Byrd Simpson uniformly praised his tactful sensibility in his ambassadorial conduct. And
to Morrow's first biographer, the Englishman Harold Nicolson, who had
completed his own distinguished diplomatic career in 1929, Morrow was
attractive as a biographical subject not only for his astuteness in international diplomacy but also for his image as the "perfected type" of civi-
lized American. And, too, there may well have been a further affinity, as
Nicolson, during the years following Morrow's death when the biography was being written, would doubtless have discussed with Elizabeth
the delight and affection the Morrows had taken in planning the gardens
and additions to Casa Mañana. These were the years, the early thirties,
when Nicolson and his wife, Vita Sackville-West, were beginning to plan
and develop what were to become the famous gardens at their home,
Sissinghurst Castle, in Kent. These gardens were "a portrait of their marriage," their son wrote later, just as those of the Cuernavaca house,
which Spratling of course pictorially recorded, were the most personal
and binding image of the Morrows' Mexican life. But at least equal to
all of this was Morrow's refusal in negotiations to assume any kind of
ethical superiority. There was something, too, about his disarming small
stature and slightly awry appearance. As Nicolson observed,

> his insatiable friendliness, his utter simplicity, the very exuberance of his
> good will, held them enthralled. He applauded their food, their climate,

their agriculture, their hats, their ancient monuments, the bamboo cages in which they kept their tame parrots, their peasant industries, their patriotism, their volcanoes, even their finances. Here at last was a North American who neither patronized nor sneered.[12]

Like Spratling, he was "a new friend whom Mexico had indeed won"; and his successful arrangement shortly after his arrival with the most romantically heroic figure of the decade, Charles Lindbergh—the Lone Eagle himself—to make a dramatic non-stop flight to Mexico City was made to widely popular acclaim.

Consistent with this genuineness and sincerity was Morrow's passion for decorating the Cuernavaca house with Mexican handicrafts and historic objects of art; and here again Spratling, the young American—both the Morrows were over twenty years older—who seemed to have endless talents, was again most helpful. Soon, and for at least a year, he became a kind of friendly business-agent for investigating and authenticating pottery, for example, that might be suitable for the Casa Mañana setting. He would send up from Taxco consignments for inspection, sometimes bringing them himself following his extended trips to Indian villages, mostly within the state of Guerrero.

Dear Mr. Morrow:—

I am enclosing the bill for the jars which you asked for this afternoon. The cost of getting them out is so out of all proportion with what they actually cost that I rather hesitate to put it down.

There were five expeditions, one to Chilacachapa (only one piece resulting), two to Tuliman (nothing the first time) and two to Guapa. Also, incidentally I was able to get a couple of pieces while in Acapulco. The trips were of from three to seven days and the expenses totaled 270 pesos; with the cars to Iguala and back and to Cuernavaca the total for expenses comes to 350 pesos.

To these costs I am adding an equal amount to cover my time and incidentals. (Over a five-weeks period these trips must have occupied more than two-thirds the time). So that the bill comes to $350 (dollars). If it seems too much please simply reduce it to whatever you think it should be,— seriously.

12. Frank Tannenbaum, *Peace by Revolution: An Interpretation of Mexico* (New York: Columbia University Press, 1933), 174; Stuart Chase, *Mexico: A Study of Two Americas* (New York: Macmillan, 1934), 278–79; Lesley Byrd Simpson, *Many Mexicos* (New York: G. P. Putnam's Sons, 1941), 306; Harold Nicolson, *Dwight Morrow* (New York: Harcourt, Brace, 1935), 310.

The next time I am in Cuernavaca (possibly tomorrow) I shall be glad to make a little catalogue identifying and locating the various examples. And if you and Mrs. Morrow should decide you need more I think it will be much easier to get them now. I've had an assistant, an Indian boy in Iguala, who is very intelligent about these things and who I can send to buy any time.

By the date of this letter (August 16, 1930) and subsequent payment of charges to Spratling a few days later, Morrow had returned from playing a leading role in the London Conference on Naval Disarmament, had been elected to the U.S. Senate from New Jersey, and was clearing up his Mexican tasks prior to leaving the embassy in September. But for the Spratling story, the letter is of interest in part because of its return address: number 23, Calle de las Delicias, Taxco. In the previous year he had published writings and drawings of this town which would, he stated, have to be patient as to the revival of its prosperity. Now, for the first time, and in that place, he was an owner of real estate, of a house that would be not only a home but also a place of business that would hasten that very revival.

In addition to his involvements with the Morrows and the Cuernavaca house, Spratling was energetically pursuing other possibilities of income during the spring and summer of 1929. He was, of course, teaching at the National University's Summer School and lived for most of 1928 at 17 Avenida Madero, often visiting Taxco for short periods. But the summer session seemed no longer to have the appeal of earlier summers, when it had given him the chance to meet many of Mexico's leading artists and intellectuals. "I'm giving a lousy class," he wrote to Zigrosser, "pain in the neck," and added that what he really wanted to do was "get back to Taxco and finish my book," which seems a likely reference to the Casa Mañana drawings but may also suggest he was already working on the manuscript that would become *Little Mexico,* although as yet he apparently had no contract for publication. Also, ever since his return he had, following several bureaucratic delays, finally managed to mount at the National University in Mexico City the exhibition of American and French Modernists he had brought down from the Weyhe Gallery in New York and was encouraging Manuel Toussaint and other Treasury officials to acquire the pictures for a permanent collection. He wrote to Zigrosser on July 23 that although Toussaint especially was being rather casual about it, the exhibit had been received very favorably and there was some talk of an official purchase, "but don't bank on it." Both he and Rivera had given university talks—he on the American pieces, Rivera on the French (Rivera's "was a pip")—and he had arranged for Morrow and the French minister to visit as well as for Paramount News to do some filming. Two weeks later, prospects for a sale of at least some of the exhibit looked better, he wrote on August 7, and "you may count on me, as well as Diego and a few others to do all that is possible to effect the acquisition." Any sale, of course, would have helped Spratling's finances, as would the small commission he might earn from the placement and sale at the Weyhe of the work of Carlos Mérida and of Rivera's assistant for some years, Paul Higgins. Despite the steady urgency of his financial condition, Spratling was a sincere champion of artists such as these, whose merits, he felt, should be recognized in the United States. Mérida, relatively unknown there, is a good example. "He has something special," Spratling wrote in the same letter, and, in his brief and deft assessment, perceived that the abstract restraint, Parisian influence, and absence of social ideas in Mérida's work made him a unique figure among the painters of this renaissance movement. Naturally interested in capitalizing on the growing reputation of Mexican and Latin American art, Zigrosser regarded Spratling's judgments and recommendations with both aesthetic and commercial respect. He was extremely grateful to Spratling, he wrote on March 20, for "using your good offices with Rivera in our behalf," referring to the gallery's negotiations over a period of several months in 1929–1930 to secure further paintings and drawings of Rivera, who had exhibited at the Weyhe in January of 1928.

In his telegram to Zigrosser on March 20, 1930, confirming that Rivera would provide the requested paintings and drawings, Spratling noted also that he had come up to Mexico City for the day and that Rivera was in Cuernavaca. By then, probably since January, Spratling was living permanently in Taxco, commuting frequently to Cuernavaca as was Rivera who, with his new wife, Frida Kahlo, was living temporarily in the Morrow's house while they were in London for the Naval Conference. Still painting the frescoes at the National Palace, Rivera was also working for the greater part of each week on a new commission, this one authorized by Morrow in the previous September for a series of murals in the Cortez Palace at Cuernavaca. These paintings, whether considered as complete in themselves or as an extension of Rivera's idealized conception of Mexico's history already begun on the walls of the National

Palace in Mexico City, are unquestionably one of the great works of art in the Western Hemisphere—perhaps the greatest public work. Spratling's significant role in their initiation was certainly one of the most fortunate turns of events in his career, leading to at least a partial stabilization of his personal finances in yielding him the means for purchase of the house in Taxco. But it was not unlike other situations throughout his life that often found him not just at the right time and place, knowing the right people—this time the Morrows and Diego Rivera—but in a condition of possibility that his own quick assimilative personality and intelligent opportunism helped to create.

It was characteristic of Morrow's generous and optimistic responses to the circumstances of life that he would wish to leave some kind of substantive permanent commitment to the genuine affection for Mexico and its people that he and Elizabeth had developed. He had the personal wealth to do so, and there is every indication that they planned to retain Casa Mañana and to return there from time to time once the ambassadorship was over. It was natural that the location of this commitment should be in their beloved Cuernavaca, but as to the form it should take, quite likely, Spratling may have had something to do with that. He tells in the autobiography what seems to be, at least in part, a fanciful story in which, first, he convinces Morrow that Rivera is Mexico's greatest painter and that he might be persuaded to accept a commission for murals at the Cortez Palace; and, second, suggests to a rather naive Rivera how the amount to be charged for the commission might be derived—by assigning a dollar value to every square meter of wall space to be painted. This technique, so the story goes, yielded a figure of $12,000, which Rivera doubted that Morrow would pay, but when the ambassador agreed, the grateful Rivera gave Spratling a $2,000 commission, which allowed him to buy the house in Taxco.

The Morrows, of course, active in the arts and intellectual scene, would not have to be convinced of Rivera's stature; they already knew it, and would certainly have been familiar with the magnificent frescoes recently completed at the Secretaría and the Agricultural College at Chapingo. But the idea of a major mural painting outside of the capital, on the walls of the last residence of the Conqueror, and in Morelos—the land of Zapata—with its violent history and revolutionary associations, was indeed ingenious. And though the prospect would have appealed immediately to Rivera's mythic imagination, the idea of the commission itself may well have been Spratling's and it was probably he who first discussed it with Rivera.

Spratling's version of the meeting between Rivera and the Morrows poses Rivera, as head of the Communist Party in Mexico, reluctant to make a visit to the U.S. embassy, especially to discuss a commission to be paid by the capitalist enemy. The problem was solved by Mrs. Morrow's issuing a social invitation whereby the group convened, then strolled over to the residence to discuss the matter, with Spratling and Allen Dawson, Morrow's secretary, interpreting. Other versions of the whole arrangement suggest corrections to Spratling's, but it must have been quite a meeting. Actually, Rivera had recently been expelled from the Party for certain policy differences with other leaders. But his socialist sympathies and commitment ran deep. And there he stood, described by Spratling as clad in a new suit, a Texas hat, with a .45 pistol strapped about his ample waist, towering over the diminutive Morrow, who was, after all, the friend of Calvin Coolidge and for thirteen years had been a partner in the financial house of J. P. Morgan, whom Rivera in the previous year had caricatured, along with John D. Rockefeller and Henry Ford, in the Wall Street Banquet panel of the Secretaría mural. The unlikely meeting was tempered, no doubt, toward a successful conclusion not only by Spratling's friendship with both parties, but also by the beauty and verve of Frida Kahlo, who must have been in attendance, by the graceful presence of Elizabeth Morrow, to say nothing of the skill and openness of Morrow himself who, despite his "capitalist" background, had already forged a trusting and friendly relationship even with President Calles.

What probably won over Rivera as much as anything else was Morrow's assurance that he would have complete freedom as to the mural's subject and treatment. While Spratling's statement that he accepted Rivera's offer of a sub-commission, much to the approval of the Morrow family, would seem to ring true, Rivera's own autobiographical recollections are quite different:

> My commission from Morrow had been arranged by my friend, the American architect, William Spratling. Spratling had come to live in Mexico and was seeking some way of earning his livelihood in my country. I expected him to accept the customary agent's commission but he would not. Aware of his needs, I used an indirect means to make the payment. I asked him to buy me a house in Taxco, and then I signed the property over to him as a gift.

That Spratling would refuse an amount of money probably larger than any that had come his way for years seems rather unlikely, but Rivera's friend and first major biographer also asserts the same: that Spratling refused the commission, and adds only that Rivera gave him a painting instead.[13]

Despite these contradictory versions, it is clear that the $12,000 payment to Rivera was to be made with the understanding that Spratling would be directly involved in the complex arrangements necessary before the actual painting could begin. He was to be the link between Rivera and the Morrows, who knew by late November that they would be leaving Mexico at the end of the year for the London Naval Conference and that, if Morrow accepted the offered appointment to an unexpired term as senator for New Jersey, their ambassadorship to Mexico would soon be over. Official permission for the project had to be secured, and the physical condition of the sixteenth-century palace assessed. It was apparently left unclear as to just how improvements to the building were to be paid for, and though Rivera and Spratling hoped that governmental support would emerge, Rivera stated that eventually he had to bear the costs himself. But in the several weeks between the time of the initial agreement and Spratling's bringing to completion the preliminary details, Rivera's conception of the scope and symbolic content of the mural had assumed its essential imaginative form.

Elizabeth Morrow noted in her diary for December 3, an entry devoted mostly to her husband's frustration and uncertainty over accepting the appointment as senator, that Rivera called at the official residence "to arrange about the Cortes-frescoes at Cuernavaca."[14] Quite likely he brought with him a letter written on the same day to her from Spratling describing the state of the project, in which she was perhaps more interested even than Morrow. The letter contains what seems to be the first specific statement of Rivera's plan for the paintings—a plan he had shared with Spratling. The letter's tone of haste and urgency, while due

13. Diego Rivera, with Gladys March, *My Art, My Life: An Autobiography* (New York: Citadel Press, 1960), 168–69; Bertram D. Wolfe, *The Fabulous Life of Diego Rivera* (New York: Stein and Day, 1963), 272.

14. Elizabeth Morrow, quoted in Nicolson, *Dwight Morrow*, 352. Several years later, Elizabeth Morrow published this and other diary entries under the title *The Mexican Years* (New York: Spiral Press, 1953).

in part to their desire to communicate to the Morrows before they left the country that the project was in motion, may also have suggested that the process of payment needed to begin also.

Dear Mrs. Morrow—

I am addressing this to you instead of Mr. Morrow hoping it gets to you sooner. No use going into the details of many delays etc. and it is so late now that I must write hurriedly.

The governor has supplied all official consent and promised help necessary. I have had Pancho go over the roof of the palace with me to estimate costs and Diego plans to get him started almost immediately with repairs to the building.

Diego has expanded in his enthusiasm the original idea and plans to (sometime in the future) complete the scheme on his own if contributions from the government do not materialize. He wants me to tell you that he has dedicated the entire back gallery to Cortes because 1st Cortes is reputed to have been most fond of that view and 2nd because it overlooks the principal locale of the convent. The vaulted corridor (connecting front with back) will eventually be the linkage of the Independencia and Morelos (who it happens was imprisoned just off that very corridor) and the front gallery with Zapata—who made his proclamation of repatriation of the land to the Indians from that balcony.

The study itself seems to me well organized (if not detailed). Due to the short visual distance afforded by that gallery the majority of figures will be very slightly larger than lifesize. I hope you like it. . . .

We miss you all awfully,

> as ever - yours,
> Bill Spratling

Rivera authenticated the contents, adding in his own hand *"Feliz año nuevo, Diego Rivera."* Spratling included a photostat, apparently a sketch by Rivera of what the letter described, and added in a postscript that Diego wished to add that he must "guard" the original because large detailed studies were yet to be made of each figure in it.[15]

On December 5, the day he left for the north, Morrow made the anticipated response:

15. All references to the correspondence between Spratling and Elizabeth Morrow are from the Morrow Family Papers, Sophia Smith Collection, Smith College, Northampton, Mass.

My dear Diego Rivera:

I am sending you by Mr. Spratling my check for $2,000 as an initial payment in connection with the mural paintings that you plan to do on the rear gallery of the second floor of the Cortez Palace at Cuernavaca. I understand that the total cost of the work will be $12,000. The subsequent payments can be arranged to be made from time to time as the work progresses. Mr. Allen Dawson will be back in Mexico in a short time, and Mr. Spratling can take up with him the manner and times of payment.

He added that, before leaving, he would confirm the arrangement with Mr. Estrada, minister of foreign affairs, who would, he was sure, be entirely agreeable. Morrow, with his typical modesty, wanted—in vain, as it turned out—the Cuernavaca frescoes to be regarded as a symbolic gift of friendship from the United States, and he concluded that "I shall ask Mr. Estrada to treat as confidential the fact that I am making the contribution to enable this work to be done, and I make the same request of you."

Clearly, Spratling was in the middle of all this, and the second payment of $2,000, authorized by Dawson on January 29, 1930, may have been the amount either that went to Spratling or that purchased for him the Taxco property. Whatever form his reward took, he felt that he had earned it, placing in the *File* a recollection that for months he would often have to monitor Rivera's progress, sometimes fetching him by car to "drag him down to Cuernavaca." What is important here for us is that Spratling, as much as if not more than anyone else, saw from the very beginning this great work of cultural synthesis and artistic power take shape, moving from Rivera's mind into sketch and cartoon, then into its magnificent architectonic distribution on the loggia walls of the palace as *The History of Cuernavaca and Morelos*. Rivera saw in the conquest of Cuernavaca and the subsequent experience of the region a metaphorical commitment to his mythic vision of Mexican history. Ranging in sequential panels from the subjugation of the Aztec pre-Columbian world by the European Christian invader, including a panel showing the actual construction of the palace itself, to the ultimate defiance of that subjugation by the modern revolutionary hero Zapata of Morelos, the mural pictorially unites, against a vast historical theme of the loss and reclamation of a truly Mexican identity, the Indian and Hispanic dual heritage of contemporary Mexico.

What impression it all made, if any, on Spratling's own imagination is difficult to say. However, as we have seen, from the beginning of his

Mexican experience his selection of subjects and his treatment of them—as indeed would be true of those he would draw, design, and write about for the rest of his lifetime there—were charged with a strong sense of this duality and its continuing presence in the life of the nation. No such equivalent existed, of course, in the homogeneous history of his own native country, although possibly his affinity for the Mexican condition may have been quickened by his formative years in the South, and especially New Orleans, with their pervasive feeling for a past always seen as tragic and critical to identity. Spratling was perhaps the first to publish a description and organizational interpretation of the Cuernavaca frescoes, which he wrote for Frances Toor in an issue of *Mexican Folkways* especially emphasizing Rivera's achievement. The issue, which must have been costly to produce, contained over thirty fine, clear photographs of the paintings, plus a full-page reproduction of a Rivera self-portrait, and was the first time, Toor wrote, that a complete group of Mexican frescoes had been published; and now that they were finished, she continued, given their location in the tourist center of Cuernavaca and the strong contradictory reactions their version of Mexico's past elicited, they were already becoming something of a shrine.

In one of his finest critical perceptions, Spratling too saw their significance, but in a kind of cultural perspective that, rendered at the very moment, as it were, of their completion, is itself impressive. He saw the remarkable Mexican decade of the twenties with its integration of an indigenous heritage finding its meaning and definition in the figure of Rivera and the Cuernavaca murals, which were completed by the artist, following his return to Mexico in 1921 from his European apprenticeship, in his own tenth year of participation in that reaffirmation of native values. Rivera had emerged from the Revolution of 1910, Spratling felt, as one of its few "actualities," a solid cultural entity who had transcended the disintegration of the various revolutionary groups, consistently retaining his socialist ideology which, in the mature style of the new frescoes, had received its most superb plastic realization. Art and the national identity had crystallized. "Being done at this particular time they become especially significant," he concluded, "somehow marking in Mexico an epoch. They complete something."[16]

16. "Diego Rivera," *Mexican Folkways* 6 (July-August 1930): 162–96. This issue, like others, was delayed for several months owing to the journal's financial problems, and Spratling probably wrote the article in the fall. This issue was mailed to subscribers after

It might be observed that Spratling too had completed something. Some twenty months before, in his voyage of commitment aboard the *Baja California,* he had initiated a kind of minor anti-odyssey, leaving his homeland for permanent residence in another country. He had been lucky, of course, in his encounter with cultural situations that readily accommodated the particular talents he brought to them. Thus far, it had all been worth the risk, especially since now toward the end of 1930, as he was entering his own thirtieth year, he could look down across the *barranca* high above the square and survey from his own house the quiet meandering life of the town. The ambience of Taxco was about as far from that of New Orleans as he could get. As we have seen, he had written and published in the previous two years an account with sketches of the town's architecture and of its re-discovery. During his first year of residence there he made arrangements to contribute some of those drawings to an official history of Taxco being conducted by Manuel Toussaint, who had handled for the Treasury the exhibit and sale of French-American paintings Spratling had brought down with him in the spring of 1929. The conclusion of that history summarizes the attractions of the town, its picturesque character, its monuments and buildings, its climate, its tranquillity, and *"las horas doradas"*—the golden hours—which silently pass there: "Tasco, within the limits of its possibilities and of the site on which it is located, is admirable."[17] Spratling, of course, would participate in the enormous expansion of those possibilities. However, before he could do so, the good fortune that had followed his journey southward seemed for a time to disappear.

July 1931, since in another article there are references to events occurring in the first half of that year. Rivera completed the Cortez Palace murals in November 1930.

17. Manuel Toussaint, *Tasco, su historia, sus monumentos, características actuales y posibilidades turísticas* (Mexico City: Publicaciones de la Secretaria de Hacienda, 1931), 217.

6

Hard Times in the Silver City of the Clouds

"Most awfully in need of money   Would you possibly consider five hundred on my work on Cuernavaca monograph or accepting security my house I beg you not think it an abuse of your kindness and please do not hesitate say no."

"If possible lend advance hundred by wire Mexico today urgent."

"Need money desperately beg you wire here today hundred or all you can on account Rivera drawings or watercolors from Harrison Smith . . . please write about sale or your purchasing."

"Beg wire hundred today."

This series of telegrams, the first to Elizabeth Morrow on January 8, 1931, the others to Carl Zigrosser in mid-November and early December of that year, frame a period of considerable financial stress for Spratling. It was a year also that illustrates the impressive range of his capability. He must have hoped that his hard work during that period would lead to increased recognition, to some measure of financial stability, and perhaps to further commissions within the rich and internationally visible context of Mexican art and history. All of these hopes, of course, would eventually be realized, but in the short term they would not; in fact, during the first half of 1932 he would experience the first major failure of his creative and energetic style of engagement, a failure that involved a betrayal of trust by one of the very patrons attracted by his ascending reputation. It was a disappointment he would remember for the rest of his life.

Just prior to this period of personal and professional stress, however, Spratling's immediate prospects must have seemed reassuring to his commitment to a permanent Taxco residency. A few months earlier he had written in his essay on Rivera and the Cuernavaca murals that they completed an epoch, going on to project that this was but a beginning for what he called the "new currents" initiated by the prominent pioneering figures of the renaissance. And, as his friend René d'Harnoncourt would predict within a month or so, this relatively new self-awareness of Mexican art and its recognition of the strength of its survival after four centuries of foreign intimidation would continue to flower, but probably no longer revolve around the influence of a single master. The occasion for this observation was the first major exhibition in the United States of the arts of Mexico, which opened at the Metropolitan Museum of Art in October 1930. The financing organization was the Carnegie Corporation, but once more it was the support and initiative of Dwight Morrow's enlightened ambassadorship that lay behind this public revelation of Mexican culture. And once more it was Spratling to whom he turned for assistance.

Spratling's statement of his significant involvement in this important exhibition seems at first glance to be one of several insertions in the autobiographical file that create for the early and middle years a persona of exaggerated proportions and achievement consistent with his self-image toward the close of his life, when he had, in fact, achieved wide-spread recognition. The published file of remembrance is notable for its absence of modesty. And yet one is often reassured to find in the account of events having a larger recorded history that Spratling's versions of his role in them is moderately accurate. He wrote in the autobiography that he was able "to anchor" himself in Mexico when Morrow "asked me to organize an all-encompassing Mexican art exhibit for the Carnegie Institute. Once I had this laid out," he continued, they arranged through further discussions that René d'Harnoncourt be put in charge, with his success there being helpful in his eventual ascendancy to the directorship of the Museum of Modern Art. As usual, Spratling's chronology seems confused here. He had already been in Mexico for at least six months before the exhibition possibility became firm, and what "anchored" him was apparently the result of his agency for the Cuernavaca murals, although he may well have been paid for the service he did render to the exhibition. However, the nature and extent of that service are uncertain.

He clearly did not "organize" the exhibit in the sense of assessing its character and scope; that was entrusted to Homer Saint-Gaudens, director of fine arts for the Carnegie Institute in Pittsburgh, who traveled throughout Mexico for this purpose during the month of November 1929. And it was through Morrow's "kind offices," as stated in the exhibition catalog, that d'Harnoncourt was recommended to Saint-Gaudens as the person "best fitted to develop the details of this exposition," choosing and assembling the works and arranging for the initial showing in Mexico City before the exhibit moved north for its U.S. tour.[1] There is no mention of Spratling here or in the Metropolitan Museum *Bulletin* description of the exhibit's inception and development. Nevertheless, he did have a part in it, although, as in the story of the Cuernavaca frescoes, he was a background figure, someone who knew how to get things done in bringing the cultural desires of the two countries into a public fruition. Besides being an American, he was not important enough to be listed either on the honorary or advisory committees for the Carnegie exhibit of Mexican arts. Yet he had the trust of the Morrows, whom he had been helping for months in securing native art objects for Casa Mañana, several of which would find their way into the show.

On November 8 Allen Dawson wrote from the embassy to Spratling in care of a "Señora Victoria," at whose boardinghouse in Taxco he was staying, that "four of us will drive down Sunday in Elisabeth's car with lunch-basket to bring you back to Cuernavaca to meet the St. Gaudens." The Morrows habitually spent weekends in Cuernavaca, and Saint-Gaudens presumably was to be their guest there, discussing the nature of the exhibit before beginning his travels throughout the country. For Elisabeth, Spratling's favorite of the Morrow children—the second daughter, Anne, having been married the previous May to Colonel Lindbergh—an outing to Taxco would have been pleasant, since she was especially interested in Spratling's plans for possible residence there and of course also in his drawings for Casa Mañana. However, it seems obvious that Spratling was someone Morrow wished the Carnegie director to meet, someone important enough to fetch from Taxco for a Sunday discussion, possibly about Saint-Gaudens's itinerary, possibly about what contributions might be made by Spratling's friends, such as Rivera, Covarrubias, and the painters whose work he had championed commercially, but surely also about native arts in isolated sites in the state of Guerrero. Thus not only did Spratling have at least some involvement at the front end of the project, he still was rendering it some service—organizational apparently—the following June, when he wrote to Zigros-

1. American Federation of Arts, *Mexican Arts Catalogue of an Exhibition Organized and Circulated by the American Federation of Arts*, with a preface by F. A. Whiting and an introduction by René d'Harnoncourt (New York: Southworth Press, 1930), ix.

ser from Taxco that he had to be in Mexico City from June 15 to the 25th to "work on Carnegie Exposition." The 25th is the date that the exposition officially opened, showing there until July 5 before it traveled to New York for the fall season.

While it is of minor importance to set the biographical record straight and to clarify the slightly erroneous impression that Spratling's word choices in the autobiographical file sometimes create, the significant observation to be made about his association with this important Mexican-U.S. partnership is that by 1929, after only a relatively short "permanent" residence in Mexico, he was already recognized as a knowledgeable and serious collector of native art. The major contributors of items for the large exhibit were Morrow himself, d'Harnoncourt, and Fred Davis, but Spratling made loans of over twenty pieces, ranging from nineteenth-century silver saddle decorations, painted gourds and tiger masks, and eighteenth-century and contemporary *retablo* paintings (small individualized votive offerings), to contemporary pottery from Guapa in Guerrero. He discussed these latter pieces in a learned and carefully detailed essay which he wrote in the late fall of 1930 and published the following February under the title "Some New Discoveries in Mexican Clay." The article was illustrated, of course, the eight drawings of the elegant pottery with their design motifs of winding ferns, maize grass, sun, and stylized bird figures being different from anything he had published before. Potters in Guapa spoke little Spanish, most speaking Aztec, Spratling wrote, and while the pattern of rudimentary design gave their creative work an intimate connection with their daily existence, it "did not in the least explain what is certainly one of the most sophisticated of the indigenous arts of the continent, found among circumstances furthest removed from civilizing influences and in one of the most primitive regions in Mexico." The essay records his arduous journeys into the almost unbearable heat of this and other villages in the *tierra caliente* of lower Guerrero, journeys from which he brought back to Cuernavaca not only decorative pottery such as that for which he billed Morrow in the August letter cited above but also objects which were themselves new forms of native art not seen before in the "outside worlds" of Mexico City and New York until they were included in the Carnegie Exhibition.[2] The in-

2. William Spratling, "Some New Discoveries in Mexican Clay," *International Studio* 98 (February 1931), 22–23, 78, 80.

formed authenticity of this fieldwork is enhanced by Spratling's customary tone of respectful fascination of the mysterious pervasiveness of ancient Mexican things. He was indeed a man Saint-Gaudens should get to know.

Dawson added a note to the Spratling invitation that his drawing paper had been left in Cuernavaca. He was, of course, in frequent visits there at work on the multiple drawings and architectural layout for the Morrow house and in correspondence with Zigrosser about plans to publish the book. But, in addition, his range of projects and involvements—trying to earn a living—was as varied in number as that in his New Orleans days. He was trying to put some form into the still disconnected parts of the manuscript he would be able to confirm by the following July that Harrison Smith would definitely publish. Also, in response to Zigrosser's desire to capitalize on Rivera's rising stature in the United States, Spratling was encouraging Rivera to do some lithographs for the New York market and was working up some of his own, which he was requesting Zigrosser to have printed by George Miller, the master lithographer who was engaged by the Weyhe. In anticipation of Zigrosser's visit to Mexico in late July of 1930 on a buying trip, he wrote: "I'm delighted you're coming—so is Diego. . . . He seemed very pleased with the idea of making lithographs—we talked about it at length. Also he has some canvases—done during the winter—which are pretty swell—probably the best small things he's ever done." And, following the visit, "you can depend on me to get after Diego for the lithographs. Write if there is anything else you want and when you find out from Stuart Chase what he wants for his book I'll be glad to communicate details to Diego."[3]

Several months before this, however, Natalie Scott had arrived on the scene, completing the plans she and Spratling had made in New Orleans for her re-settlement once he had secured some permanence in Mexico. True to her flamboyant style and well-known equestrian penchant—she is shown in her "Famous Creoles" caricature mounted, charging a tall building—she made most of the trip from New Orleans to Mexico on

3. W.S. to Carl Zigrosser, June 8, August 8, 1930. Spratling seemed often to act as an informal agent for Rivera, who, in this case, had agreed to illustrate Stuart Chase's forthcoming *Mexico: A Study of Two Americas* (1931).

horseback![4] She lived at first in Spratling's house, and their companionship gave a new dimension to his Taxco experience, as reflected in her colorful, long and gracefully written letters:

> Bill continues to let himself be diverted, in spite of my motherly counsels. We went to Iguala yesterday and had a most Mexican trip. Mariano started out with no spare, and the most antiquated group of tires ever called upon to support a car. We shortly had a blow-out, and . . . I was grateful for my vaccination for the tube looked as though it were suffering from an acute attack of small-pox. . . . When we reached the next shadeless spot, in sight of Iguala but not walking distance, we had the next blow-out. It got fixed just before Bill followed suit.
>
> I wish you had been along last week. We had a grand hike along the Huisteco, on horseback and then on foot—also hands, knees and anatomy in general. We even had to swing down one big rock on a limb of a tree.
>
> It was superb, though. We went out on the "turtle's" nose and there was the world and all before us. The whole state of Morelos. You know how these Mexican mountains have a trick of starting up with a leap right from the midst of level stretches. It was a colored relief map. Far white dots of towns, shining slivers of lake, the mountains, and the sky above intensely blue.
>
> And what in the distance but Popo himself, looking very splendid. His big truncated dunce-cap covered with snow, of course I should not speak of him so disrespectfully, and I couldn't have, to his face, for he looked kingly. Really, there were clouds all below him, and he looked as though he were moored in a sea of them, and likely to break loose from the moorings any minute and float off with them.
>
> Izta was at her best, too. I never saw so clearly before how she rated the title of The Sleeping Woman. She was covered with snow, too, and a perfect long white lady,—not a curve missing—with one arm hanging down. I wonder how *her* back would photograph?
>
> Bill and I are going to one of the year's big fairs on Sept. 8, at Tixchtla (that's as good a spelling as any). It is 3 miles on horseback away from Chilpancingo. Why aren't you here?

---

4. The story is authenticated in an interview with one of Natalie Scott's closest New Orleans friends, with whom she maintained a forty-year correspondence: Mrs. Samuel G. (Martha) Robinson. See Martha Robinson, transcription of tape-recorded interview in "Friends of the Cabildo Oral History Project," p. 16, Cabildo Oral History Project, Vivian Scott Papers. Tulane University Archives. The horseback trip probably began in Brownsville, Texas.

I worked this week, a little. I did a rough draft of a short story and had the most amusing time with it because I put Bill in, in all his grumpiness. I thought to put him to shame, but when I read it to him, he said he thought he was rather a "charming character". What's the use?[5]

The correspondence was with Zigrosser, he, Natalie, and Spratling having gone during his visit on an extended holiday to Acapulco. The letters between the three are full of the trip and of the photos Zigrosser took there and in Taxco. Spratling wrote to Zigrosser, "You're a peach & I'm awfully obliged to you. The pictures came yesterday and are charming. Natalie curled up with pleasure at the bathing scenes. I wonder if you could lend me the films for larger prints of my house—& the one of me dining. . . . Acapulco was marvelous—wasn't it?" And, a few days later, again to Zigrosser: "Tomorrow Natalie and I are off on a 10 day horseback trip to . . . points on the river Balsas (see map). It should be an interesting trip & Natalie's crazy to do it. I, naturally, have misgivings. Natalie speaks of you often and sends her very best."[6]

The physical grandeur of the Mexican scene, however, and Spratling's intimate connections to a cultural dimension of that scene experienced by few Americans could not fully remedy what seemed to be the continuing crisis of his personal finances. Unlike Natalie, who received at least a small but regular rental income from her ownership of New Orleans real estate, he could count only on his luck and entrepreneurial genius—which, as we have seen, often formed a happy combination. But when he boarded the SS *Baja California* for his anticipatory southern journey in March of 1929, Black Tuesday on the New York Stock Exchange was only seven months away, and its gradual economic erosions into the world of art were no less depressing than those in every other aspect of American and international life. By the summer of 1930 he had indeed secured the Taxco property, but he wrote to Zigrosser in June that he had been "ghastly broke." The collection of contemporary French and American paintings that he had brought down with such high hopes of a substantial commission from their governmentally sponsored exhibition and sale in Mexico City were by then packed and stored. "Perhaps some miracle," he wrote, "can still be worked to make them buy the lot—or 3/4 of it or something." A portion of the collection eventually was pur-

5. Natalie Scott to Carl Zigrosser, August 22, 1930.
6. W.S. to Carl Zigrosser, August 8 and 27, 1930.

chased by the Bellas Artes during the following spring when the Depression had worsened. But Spratling's commission was minimized (less than $15) because by then, of course, it was a time for bargains—incredible ones from our perspective; among the thirteen paintings purchased: two Picasso paintings at $35 each, a Dufy for $20, a Utrillo and Matisse for $25 each, a Rouault for $20, a Vlaminck for $17.50![7]

Yet Spratling received from the total arrangement with the Weyhe Gallery in this instance over $200 in commission for the New York sale of the Rivera lithographs he had encouraged and of the paintings he had gotten together and shipped north. And though he had to borrow a $30 check from Natalie ("being the only one with a bank account") as payment on his bill with George Miller for printing his lithographs, which he hoped to show himself at the gallery that fall, his spirits were good, and in his usual enterprising manner he was finding ways here and there to get by. By late August he was planning the New York trip, and though he wrote that "I shall certainly arrive broke!" he added that he had sent "the two best stone masks I had" to Zigrosser for gallery sale and that he could send four other of his best, each of which should be worth "400 or 500 apiece." This traffic in artifacts, selling and what he referred to as "idol swappin'," he would carry on for the rest of his life. Even this early, he already had a "collection": "I sold a small bunch of idols, unnecessary to my collection, the other day for 450 pesos"; "so," he added, "for the moment I am in funds." And, in reference to his labors for Morrow: "I ought not feel so puffed up over it, but Mr. Morrow owes me considerable on a collection of primitive pots he plans to make a gift of to the Metropolitan. At any rate—I shall arrive in N.Y. It will be Oct 15 or Nov 1."

He didn't make the trip. The lithographic prints of the thirty or so drawings he had sent up for a show, which Zigrosser apparently meant to sponsor, were not ready, but, as he wrote to Elizabeth Morrow in November, it was "also a lack of means. You and Elisabeth have probably decided that I'm a terrible sort of person. . . . And I had really counted on going the 10th of this month. But things just didn't work out." It was a long letter, one of several between the two over the next year about

7. Zigrosser dated his final settling of the account with Spratling as "July, 1931." I am indebted to John W. Scott for details of Natalie Scott's finances at this time.

detailed plans for the little book she was now planning to publish on Casa Mañana. The Morrows had departed Mexico and their ambassadorial life in mid-September and were now moving between their home in Englewood, New Jersey, and Washington, D.C., he having been overwhelmingly elected as Republican senator for New Jersey in June. In the present letter Spratling confirms that his architectural drawings of the various sections of the house and his pencil renderings of certain interior views are almost complete; he now wishes to have her thoughts on size, method of printing, "and any more ideas you may have." He added that he was shortly "sending you something you've (probably) been expecting—& which I hope you'll like. Diego spoke of sending it but he'll probably delay indefinitely—so I'm doing it. Something important." He told her too about the special issue of *Mexican Folkways* devoted to the Rivera murals and its inclusion of his essay.

> It should be a bang-up number. How many shall I have her send you? Aside from the text it should be worth having as a very complete record of that *obra*—for your friends. . . . Am writing Elisabeth today—but, as usual, I send her my love by you too.
>
> > Yours sincerely — affectionately
> > — Wm Spratling
> > Bill[8]

The book was more her project than her husband's, although as Mexico receded into the distance and their public life moved from diplomatic to legislative, it became important to both as a kind of personal memento—it was to be privately published—of their happy times in what she called "beloved Cuernavaca." How she felt about the house and its associations may be seen in two excerpts from her diary, one on the eve of their departure for the long period taken up by the London Naval Conference, and the other some ten months later in the last week of Mexico residence.

> Elisabeth and I are down here alone tonight. I wonder if it is our last night in Cuernavaca! I went up to the Mirador before breakfast; Popo and Ixta were clear and beautiful, sheer white against the sky. I looked hard for memory's sake! . . .
> Elisabeth and I had a lovely morning in Cuernavaca. We arranged the

8. W.S. to Elizabeth Morrow, November 28, 1930.

little Mexican kitchen with all our pots and pitchers and then we said goodbye to everything. We took a swim just before we left; the sun was so hot and the pool so blue! As I swam across in the sun, I looked slowly at all the loveliness. I said, "I will remember it all—the blue sky, and the gardener trimming the yellow mimosa tree above our wall in his big sombrero and white clothes, the blue plumbago, and the sprays of heliotrope, the gay awning, the big pots with geraniums, the pink arch, the Cathedral spire—everything!"

[entries for Friday–Saturday, November 29–30, 1929]

I'm all alone here tonight, except Emma and Jean, and the yellow cat! It is heavenly, peaceful and quiet after so many people all day. I'm writing out of doors, the air delicious and soft, the smell of limes floating everywhere. We went to see Diego's frescoes this morning—very wonderful— and *finished.* . . . Dwight makes his radio speech at 6:30. I was glad to be alone. I walked slowly all over the place, enjoying everything, and then went to the Mirador . . . in the glow of the sunset. Popo was not out but the sky was glorious and our little street ran from the pink church to the pink sunset. I looked hard at all that lovely sweep of hill and mountain. Will we ever come back again? I wished on the first star!

[entry for Sunday, September 14, 1930]

And in the ensuing months such memories were repeatedly called up as she gave talks about Mexico in Washington as she and d'Harnoncourt were involved in the ceremonial openings of the exhibition of Mexican art as it moved from the Metropolitan to other sites around the country. From her hometown of Cleveland, she wrote to Spratling in February, in a long letter mostly about the book:

René felt it was the "swellest" opening of the four that have been held so far, and I was very happy to have a share in it. We both told as amusing stories of Mexico as we could, and the exhibit was launched on the wave of our enthusiasm. My talk at the Colony Club went off splendidly. . . . I have to be careful here in Washington how I talk about Mexico. I am apt to show homesickness for that beloved place too plainly, and people here think that Washington is the only place to live.[9]

Spratling was soon to develop a somewhat comparable sense of place in regard to his tiny house in Taxco, and he must have had some sense of

9. Elizabeth Morrow to W.S., February 26, 1931.

the Morrows' affection for Casa Mañana. He was not himself involved in the actual expansion of the house as the Morrows in 1928 acquired the several adjacent plots of land that allowed its extension through a series of connected patios. Their Cuernavaca neighbor, Fred Davis, supervised the plans during the week, and Pancho, the town's master mason, performed the construction work. Spratling, however, watched it develop in his visits, especially during the late summer and fall of 1929, as he was assisting in securing decorative pottery and crafts and also in assessing the Cortez Palace site for the fresco work then assuming final conceptual form in Rivera's mind. It cannot be said that he was an intimate in the wide and distinctive diplomatic-social circle of the Morrows. Yet as a reflection no doubt of the personal and conversational charm that gave him ready acceptance in the artistic and literary order of the Vieux Carré, he frequently appears in diary entries for this period as a welcomed weekend guest: coming up for a swim and asked to stay for lunch, taking Elisabeth to the movies, "Mr. Davis and Bill Spratling here for supper Saturday night"; taking Elizabeth and Elisabeth to a public building in Mexico City to see Rivera at work; or arranging on a tour to Taxco and Acapulco their accommodations in his own rental lodgings: "We are here in Bill Spratling's boarding house, a very clean plain place, with lovely views in every direction and sweet-faced Mexican women to wait upon us. Elisabeth, Dwight and I are all sleeping in the same big room. . . . Elisabeth wild with delight over the place" (entry for Thursday, October 31, 1929). And almost a year later, Spratling was one of their few guests—two of them personal staff—on the last day of their last visit to Casa Mañana, two days before they left Mexico and their diplomatic service: "Cuernavaca too beautiful this morning! I went to see the frescoes again. Dwight and George, Arthur Springer, Bill Spratling and Mr. Nutter for lunch and swim. Perfect—the pool—in the sunshine. Gave toys to the children before leaving." (entry for Wednesday, September 15, 1930).

The detail of the toys and the children is incorporated into the scene—which Spratling perhaps witnessed—she affectingly describes in the conclusion to "Our Street in Cuernavaca," her essay that precedes the Spratling drawings and photographs of decorative furnishings in the publication *Casa Mañana*:

> The last day that we were in Cuernavaca we made a little fiesta and gave out toys to the children in the street. . . . We had the presents laid on

the dining-room table and my husband and I gave them out as fast as we could. The children were quivering with eagerness but no one pushed or shoved, even when it was seen that there would not be enough toys to go around. For the late comers we had only cookies and centavos, and . . . children from far beyond our quarter were running to the garden gate. We could not face any more wistful eyes, so we said goodbye quickly and got into the motor to return to Mexico City. As we turned the corner I looked back for a last sight of our street in Cuernavaca. The beautiful church was in the background, hanging over the little houses like a blessing, and in the foreground stood that group of happy children, crowding the cobbles from curb to curb, each with a toy in his hand waving and shouting "*Adiosito, Embajador!*" (Good-bye for a short time, Ambassador!) "*Adiosito, Embajadora! Adiosito! Adiosito!*"[10]

The highly personalized essay about the house, its development, its associations, assumes part of its significance, one feels, just because it was she who wrote it. But it was composed, for its first publication in the *American Mercury,* only a few months before Dwight Morrow's untimely death in October of 1931—cutting short what promised to be the most visible dimension of his brilliant career. Thus its contents, receiving as they did a visual corroboration from Spratling's pencil, obviously assumed an enhanced symbolic meaning as she persevered toward the book's eventual publication in 1932.

Spratling, along with Zigrosser, was intimately involved with the final form the book assumed. But however perceptive and sympathetic he was about its meaning to the Morrows, his commission for the drawings was critical to his finances. The amount was $900, which he proposed in a letter to her on January 31, 1931. The letter contained a suggested and elaborately detailed layout for the publication, and contained also a muted sense of urgency about the money.

> Please treat the whole layout as only my personal suggestion. I hope you will be very drastic about anything and everything you'd like changed in it. Including estimated costs for work by William Spratling. I would even suggest you consult publishers or architects to verify (or damnify) my awful rates. But the point is that, even though I have received an advance from you, you must feel free to even reject the whole idea. . . .

10. Elizabeth Morrow, *Casa Mañana,* drawings by William Spratling (Croton Falls, N.Y.: Spiral Press, 1932), n.p.

I wish it were possible for me to be in New York . . . in case you might find such advisable, I would be very glad to come and attend to the details of the production of the book, adding travelling expenses there and back (and perhaps the cost of a suit of clothes, which would be right sorely needed), to the estimate included.

The "advance" had been $500, which in some desperation he had requested by telegraph on January 8 in the passage quoted at the beginning of this chapter. Dwight Morrow telegraphed the money four days later, which Spratling gratefully acknowledged to her in the letter later that month: "Please forgive me for what must seem lack of gratitude or delay or both. I can't begin to thank you for the advance (which came at a time when I simply couldn't see daylight financially in any direction)."

This was not the only time that the Morrows would render financial aid to Spratling, and his correspondence with Elizabeth would continue for many years after the publication of *Casa Mañana*. Concurrent with that project was another publishing venture which also held special meaning for him and which promised to be not only financially profitable but also his most prestigious involvement in the world of Mexican art. As it turned out, however, it was probably the most frustrating and disappointing experience of his career. His idea of publishing a pictorial record with interpretive commentary of Rivera's fresco achievements seemed to have originated at least as early as the period in late November 1930, when the murals at Cuernavaca were being completed. The "something important" he had written then that he was sending to Elizabeth was a portfolio of annotated photographs of the Cortez Palace work. He wrote to her two weeks later, on December 12, that he had been delayed in sending it because he was unable to find in Taxco paper suitable for binding, and that perhaps she could take care of that herself: "It really deserves a decent, dignified binding. And as a work of Diego's the thing is so fine and so complete that (in my humble opinion), it should almost be worth publishing as a book. . . . But it's still in time for Christmas."

It is an interesting and even, in a sense for the Spratling story, a significant coincidence that this letter with its suggestion of a book on the Rivera frescoes should have been written in the same week as in New York City, at the home of John D. Rockefeller, Jr., a group was organized which would shortly be known as the Mexican Arts Association. Dedicated to the development of U.S.-Mexican friendship through artistic interchange and "through encouraging cultural relations," the group was composed of interlocking memberships drawn from America's wealthiest families active in the world of museums and philanthropy in the arts. Elizabeth Morrow, naturally, as the wife of the ambassador, was a charter member. Within six months the group had identified its first important project: a retrospective exhibition of Rivera's work at the Museum of Modern Art.[11] Many Mexican artists were then doing superb work, but it was Rivera who, even in the early stages of the Depression, possessed the highest visibility and was, as Spratling observed, a "perfectly marketable quantity." Spratling was to have no connection with the organization and subsequent catalog of the exhibition, which was to open at MOMA just before Christmas of 1931 and during its four weeks engagement would set an attendance record of some fifty-seven thousand viewers. All arrangements were under the supervision of Frances Flynn Paine, herself a wealthy art dealer and collector-advisor to the Rockefellers. Spratling, who had met her during her trip to Mexico a year earlier, didn't particularly like her officious and aggressive efficiency, but admitted in letters to Zigrosser that she had completely charmed Rivera: "Nothing can convince Diego that Mrs. Paine isn't the greatest woman in America. She came down commissioned by Mrs. Rockefeller and the Modern Art Museum to get all his stuff together for the show in December and to get verbal material from him for the very elegant publication the gallery is to put out. It looks like a Rivera winter."[12]

Given such a statement as to Spratling's own knowledge of who was in charge, it is difficult at first glance to reconcile the completely erroneous notation in the chronology appended to *File on Spratling* under the year 1930, "arranged one-man show for Rivera at that museum [MOMA]." This apparently posthumous allusion, by the person constructing the chronology and made in clear violation of the facts, can possibly be construed as a careless misunderstanding of something Spratling had said, perhaps in an interview. More difficult to reconcile, however, is the first part of the 1930 notation, "Edited *The Frescoes of Diego*

11. The meeting took place on December 9, 1930. An account of the membership and their relationships is given by Bertram D. Wolfe, *The Fabulous Life of Diego Rivera* (New York: Stein and Day, 1963), 297–98.

12. W.S. to Carl Zigrosser, September 24, 1931.

Rivera for the Museum of Modern Art, N.Y." This, together with the allusion in the autobiography (p. 35) that Spratling in 1928 had already received "proofs for my monograph (Museum of Modern Art)" on "Diego Rivera's frescoes in Mexico," appears to be the strangest of all the several false impressions yielded by this occasionally misleading autobiography. There is no record of such a publication under Spratling's name at MOMA or anywhere else. Neither is there any allusion to Spratling in the official catalog of the 1931 Rivera exhibition, which was prepared by Paine with notes by one of the senior museum staff. The exhibition actually included, in addition to the 143 paintings and works on paper, only 8 fresco panels: 5 "portable" ones recreated from themes of originals at the Mexican sites, plus 3 new ones based on New York topics.

Spratling may well have been considering a work on Rivera's frescoes as early as 1928, although this would have been before those depicting the epic history of Mexico—at the National Palace and at Cuernavaca—had even been initiated. The first book in English on Rivera was entitled *The Frescoes of Diego Rivera,* published by Ernestine Evans in 1929 (New York: Harcourt Brace), and that Spratling already a year earlier had "proofs" of a work with the same title seems unlikely. In fact, in his *Herald-Tribune* "Mexican Letter" of July 28, 1929, Spratling shows himself very much aware of Evans's forthcoming book ("which Harcourt Brace plans to issue this fall or winter") and expresses the hope that the volume will include some of the preliminary designs for the National Palace stairway murals in Mexico City, recently authorized by President Portes Gil and even then being drawn by the "maestro Rivera . . . daily working twenty feet aloft on a scaffolding." But exposing such errors to set the record straight is in itself a kind of mean and sterile occupation. Besides, one wishes somehow to vindicate the man in the file. And, once more, it seems that this may be possible, for beneath the confused chronology and apparent corruption of fact lies the memory, suppressed and re-fashioned, of Spratling's involvement in the book about Rivera that first appears to be referenced in the letter to Elizabeth Morrow quoted above. Such involvement actually pre-dates the Mexican Arts Association plan for the MOMA exhibition, for by the time Paine proposed that idea to a willing Rivera in July of 1931, Spratling was well advanced in arrangements with the German house of Ganymed, specialists in graphic design and large-scale color photography, for preparing plates of Rivera frescoes at their several sites.

The ambitious undertaking, apparently originating with Spratling, was the proposed publication, first, of a volume on the frescoes, with the high-quality color photography and additional black and white plates, plus the inclusion of the Cuernavaca works, being more definitive than anything appearing before. A second volume was tentatively planned, emphasizing Rivera's paintings and drawings. The plan had Rivera's support, and the unexpected emergence of the MOMA exhibition, which the two volumes would complement, could only enhance their visibility and potential sales. Spratling, with the advice of Zigrosser, was in charge of the design elements, including selection of the panels to be photographed, the ensuing plates, paper, and even typeface. There were to be at least twenty color plates: six from the Secretaría frescoes, three from the National Palace, six from Chapingo, and five from Cuernavaca. With his usual dexterity and work capacity, Spratling was busy throughout the summer and early fall making all arrangements for the photography while at the same time finally completing his writing of *Little Mexico* and finishing the layouts for *Casa Mañana*. Elizabeth Morrow, of course, knew about the Rivera book, and it was in a letter to her on July 23, 1931, primarily about her book, that he alluded not only to his involvement with "the photographers from Munich about the Rivera things for color reproductions" but also to the ambiguous term that thirty-five years later found its way into the autobiography: "the Rivera monograph." His allusion here and subsequently was not to an extended essay of critical analysis on a well-defined subject, not in fact to the kind of interpretive writing he was then completing for *Little Mexico*. Rather, he seemed to mean that he was preparing for the first volume a descriptive commentary, identifying the frescoes and perhaps placing them in some kind of Riveran artistic chronology. He made the distinction in his letter to Elizabeth: "I'm working awfully hard to finish [*Little Mexico*] for September 1st. There is also the Rivera monograph—which is much easier, being a purely editorial job."

The Weyhe Gallery was to be involved, perhaps as publisher but more likely as contractual agent for distribution rights. Zigrosser wrote to Spratling on June 17 suggesting that "it would be wiser to put forth our relations regarding publication of the Rivera book on a more explicit and business like basis," and outlining the gallery's potential connections to the project whether the book appeared under its imprint or not. The missing element in all this, of course, was the matter of financial support. Neither Spratling nor Weyhe had the funds to pay the considerable costs of photographing and printing the color plates. But by the time of the June 17 letter a third party to the enterprise had emerged, one that eventually was to be a disaster for Spratling. The letter was addressed to Spratling at the Park Avenue residence of Dr. and Mrs. James B. Murphy, wealthy art collectors whom Spratling had come to know at least by the time that the Carnegie Exhibition was being organized, since they contributed some of the pieces to it. He was on familiar terms with the Murphys, especially Mrs. Murphy—Ray Slater Murphy—whom he addressed in correspondence as "Ray," in contrast to his always formal "Mrs. Morrow," whom he probably knew better. The address on the letter suggests that Spratling was in New York by early summer completing arrangements with the Murphys to finance the project, though it was not clear then under whose publication imprint the book would appear.

Within a month, however, Ray Murphy was taking an increasingly authoritative hand in the matter, directing Zigrosser on the contractual negotiations with Ganymed and authorizing her bank to make the initial payment of $2,800 for the color photography Spratling was supervising in Mexico. It was in this correspondence that Spratling's elimination from the project was prefigured. "It should be made definite," she wrote, "that while Spratling is responsible for the choice of the plates, the ownership is mine. It should be made clear to the Ganymed that the plates are only to be delivered at my direction. Spratling's authority stops after correcting the proof of the plates, till a new contract is made covering the actual formation of the book."[13]

Whether that contract was ever made is not clear, but by the fall the project seemed completely dependent on her decisions. Spratling had been patiently monitoring the slow progress of the photographers, who by the fall had completed and submitted to him both color and black and white proofs of all the selected fresco panels except those at the National Palace. There had been several delays in the photographers' initially reaching Mexico City, and when Ganymed proposed an increase in price, Spratling responded to Zigrosser on August 7 that he was writing Mrs. Murphy, "who is the only one who can decide."

13. Ray Slater Murphy to Carl Zigrosser, July 17, 1931.

The delays widened the growing rift between him and the Murphys. "What about the Rivera book?" Zigrosser wrote on November 3. "When will you send us the photographs of the black and whites? Mrs. Murphy is getting restless." And by the 18th: "Confidentially, Mrs. Murphy is very annoyed at you. You had better watch your step. She has gotten the idea, God knows where, that you have given Von Stetten [the Ganymed photographer] numerous commissions to do reproductions on your own for another monograph of yours on Diego. She wants to get the book out in time for the Rivera exhibition. I doubt, however, whether that would be possible." By December 26, Spratling wrote that he had mailed on the 20th everything for the book, "complete dummy, text, photographs for black and white, and list of illustrations." He had himself paid for the black and white photos, but felt that Mrs. Murphy "has shown me so much suspicion and lack of sympathy—as though I were out to do her in some way—that I am afraid to even mention accounts to her. At the same time she cannot be unaware that I am desperately hard up."

By mid-January of the new year Spratling had received no word or, more important, payment from the Murphys for the book material he had sent forward. Zigrosser was now acting as a reluctant intermediary, writing on the 29th that Mrs. Murphy had reaffirmed that she had made no agreement about a second book, presumably part of Spratling's original plan, and that, moreover, "she has apparently changed her mind about including the black and white photographs in the original book. What was your agreement with her in the first place? Have you a copy of your contract? I judge, from what she said, that she is planning to bring out a loose leaf portfolio of the color plates alone. I wish you were here to straighten out the whole tangle." The next day, in a handwritten note, Zigrosser admitted that the letter was one "she practically asked me to write. I always told you that she was difficult, neurotic, and suspicious. . . . I don't know what she is up to in asking me to write this letter."

As early as March Spratling was gradually being isolated from the project: "Mrs. Murphy promised to write, but never a word. I suppose one of those nasty little things happened there that in Mexico is called "chisme". Certainly I can never speak to her again. I'm such a damn fool and so soft-hearted that it took me months and considerable pain to realize that something had finished."[14]

In May, he received from her a letter, ignoring all of his, asking that he send up artifacts (dance masks) for her collection and holding out the possibility he would still be responsible for correcting the color proofs from Ganymed. But by June, he had been cut off completely:

> We had better simply not mention the Murphys again. They, it seems, are through with me, and certainly I am with them. They allowed themselves the sensation of "paying me off," the amount about covering my expenses on the black and white material. They had wired for that on December 14th, though the Doctor in his letter said they never wanted it. O well, it has all been very painful, and, as I say, better not mention them or the subject again. You must know that I once had a great deal of affection for Ray, and it is only on account of that that I attempt this faint explanation. You, I am sure, will understand that it has rather smarted.[15]

The Murphys' plan proceeded—as Zigrosser had predicted—toward publication of the color plates in an unbound loose-leaf set, including some of the black and white photographs, which Spratling had supervised with such care. By September, Mrs. Murphy had identified Jere Abbott, associate director of MOMA, as editor, telegraphing on September 8 from her home in Seal Harbor, Maine, to Ernest Weyhe that he should "have Rivera portfolio for Mr. Abbott at your shop September thirteenth without fail." And in November, the Weyhe Gallery confirmed its role as future sales representative and distributor, with the publication to bear the imprint of the museum. Nineteen color plates and fifteen photographs were eventually, in 1933, published in portfolio for the museum by the Plandome Press in New York. Rivera made a presentation copy to "la Señora Dwight W. Morrow," signed and dated February 20, 1933, inscribing it, as translated, "as a token of grateful remembrance to your husband and of our friendship."[16]

14. W.S. to Carl Zigrosser, March 14, 1932.

15. W.S. to Carl Zigrosser, June 4, 1932.

16. Courtesy D. H. Hill Library North Carolina State University. The Plandome Press often printed museum exhibition catalogs; for example, printing in February 1931 "for the Trustees of the Museum of Modern Art" a thousand copies, again with Abbott as editor, of the Toulouse-Lautrec–Odilon Redon exhibition held in that month. Mrs. Murphy lent works to this exhibit as well as to the Rivera exhibit later that year, and it was probably her influence that led to her "fresco" set being published in this way.

Neither the front matter of the portfolio nor that of the bound volume contains any reference to Spratling. Yet the idea seems originally to have been his of a book focusing solely on the Rivera frescoes with the finest color photography revealing for the first time in published form the full power of their plastic conception. It had been his chance to have his name associated in an important way with a truly distinctive publication project with international distribution possibilities. He had undoubtedly worked harder at it, and longer, than anyone else. And now it had all slipped away. Mrs. Murphy's notion of accelerating the project to publication within nine months or so in time for the December opening of the Rivera exhibition was unrealistic, involving as it did much detailed correspondence between Mexico and Berlin. But the slow Mexican pace of everything had undoubtedly been too much for her New York impatience and thin line of tolerance. The delays had not been Spratling's fault, and although he did not manage his conceptual negotiations of the project as clearly as he might have, there seems to be no basis for the charge that he was secretly working with Ganymed toward a second volume. However, he had been a convenient person to blame and he was, moreover, financially at the mercy of the wealth and influential power of the New York art scene. It had indeed been "painful"—over a year's work and nothing to show for it, financially or professionally; and it had "rather smarted" not only because it had been a betrayal of trust and friendship but also because he had been used and then discarded.

This drama of high hopes and disappointment during Spratling's early Taxco years, unknowingly played out for us in his correspondence, is important in our attempt to come to terms with the character of this man who, at the end of his life, constructed in the eclectic file of the autobiography a public persona that moved blithely and almost without impediment toward increasing eminence. However, it would seem that the final, and authentic, form of the Spratling identity was fashioned as much by what was suppressed or omitted in the file as by what was placed in it. Spratling surely knew that his reference to "my monograph (Museum of Modern Art) on those frescoes" was misleading, implying the falsification which the posthumously arranged chronology of his life in fact sustained: that he had published for the museum an edition of the Rivera frescoes. But he knew, too, that there was a certain dogged accuracy in the reference. The portfolio edition contained the notations "Color Plates by Ganymed, Berlin" and "Copyright, 1933, by Ray Slater

Murphy, New York." Yet Spratling's hand had been continuously present in the organization and management of the whole project, including the very selection of which fresco panels and the details thereof were to be color photographs and thus appear in the final publication. In putting together the autobiography, he could not bring himself to mar the tone of the highly selective file of recollection by mentioning the trauma and betrayal of the experience. Mrs. Murphy is mentioned only once, but without rancor. Still, he had never forgotten "my monograph." Now he could at least give himself the credit that thirty-five years earlier he had been denied. And that is what he did.

It would indeed be a mistake to assume that the autobiographical file, given its occasional revelatory integrity, was to Spratling only a casual and egocentric re-invention of himself. And it would be also a mistake to assume that its ironic and relatively unruffled tone is dramatically at odds with that of the private self-expressions contained in his correspondence. There is, to be sure, plenty of anxiety in the letters written during the early Taxco years as he was trying to eke out a living without any kind of the steady, if modest, financial support such as that afforded by his teaching at Tulane. The year between his full involvement in the Rivera project and the time in June of 1932 when he was cut out of it completely is partially defined by the continuing urgency with which he attempted to sell off paintings or drawings he had either bought or "idol-swapped" from Rivera. In late September of 1931, for example, when he was simultaneously completing his drawings for *Casa Mañana,* working toward a self-imposed deadline for finishing the text of *Little Mexico,* and dealing with Ganymed on printing estimates for the Rivera book, he wrote to Zigrosser that he saw no way he could come to New York for the *Little Mexico* publication: "I am down to rock bottom again." As always, he was looking ahead to another venture, this time a book on the *tierra caliente* country south of Taxco, in which he had invested time and money on expeditions but had produced no material to show for it. Less than a month later, anxious about the sale of some Siqueiros lithographs he had sent to the Weyhe on commission, he wrote: "Haven't you any news for me? I am on the very edge." He had, he said, sent a Rivera drawing and very good watercolor ("Really a pip") to Ray Murphy first in the hope she would buy them: "I have to have the money. It is the only means I have to raise cash." He also remembered that his publisher-to-be, Harrison Smith, had in his possession three or four Rivera pieces, and he urged Zigrosser to secure them for sale and perhaps even place them with Jere Abbott for inclusion in the MOMA exhibit ("I've simply got to have some money").[17] But, although Mrs. Murphy five months later did buy the watercolor, Spratling's financial plight became so bleak that he was reduced to sending to Zigrosser in late November and early December the series of telegrams already quoted in which his pleas indeed seemed desperate.

Spratling's financial woes were, of course, but a microcosm of those permeating the New York art world then feeling the full brunt of the Great Depression. "Business conditions are unspeakably awful," Zigrosser wrote early in the new year, on January 30. "Nothing sells. Mr. Weyhe loses money every day. Salaries have been cut, etc. We all hope that we can hold out until the tide turns." Still, they had been able to respond to Spratling's plea. "It was awful nice of you and Mr. Weyhe to help out. The cash lasted about three days. So I am back where I was already. Won't you write and make me an offer for the drawings? And did you finally get those from Hal Smith?" How much he was depending on these sales is indicated by yet another telegram on January 14: "If you are interested in buying the two Rivera drawings and those from Harrison Smith beg you lend me two hundred wiring today." And two months later, when he was "bitched, financially speaking," he still hoped for the sale: "I feel a little shamefaced to be writing you urgently all over again about the Rivera drawings from office of Cape and Smith. . . . All you have to do is say whether you want them or not, and if so how much. But the point is, please write quick. Air mail, today for example."[18] There is here a kind of embarrassed ambivalence on Spratling's part because the stressful request appears in the same letter as his first recognition—the "considerable pain"—that the arrangement with the Murphys and his attendant financial possibilities were coming to an end. In the June letter referenced above, however, where he ruefully acknowledges the irrevocable conclusion to his association with the Rivera project, there is little, if any, sense of depression. He still had his horses, "and I make money renting them at two pesos a day to the tourist rabble," he wrote, perhaps

17. The letters were written on September 27, October 19, and November 10 and 22, 1931.

18. W.S. to Carl Zigrosser, March 14, 1932. The Weyhe Gallery did not buy the drawings.

remembering his enterprising skill only a dozen years earlier when he had rented out his overcoat at twenty-five cents an evening to his undergraduate friends at Auburn.

This summer of 1932, with all of its stress and disappointment, seems to have been the time when he accommodated himself fully to a permanent life in Taxco. In fact, his last letter to Zigrosser in that season is full of the young Spratling's customary sensitivity to the promise of the future. On August 18, he wrote that about all he had to live on were the occasional sale of a lithograph and the rent of his horses. Still,

> aside from finances, things here are fine. The weather is incredibly good and the hills are all green and sparkling. I'm breaking in a new horse—the prettiest I have. We get him out every morning from 6 to 8, and he's just getting to like it. I wonder if you like horses. Natalie has just returned from a couple of months in Mexico. Looking well, but somehow older. There are also lots of artists here now. You bump into them whenever you turn a corner. Where so much art will go to god knows.

A notation at the end of the letter—that René d'Harnoncourt, just then winding up the tour of the Carnegie Exhibition, had spent the weekend with him—might serve to mark the conclusion of the four principal involvements that during Spratling's first five years in Mexico had carried him into an intimate association with its awakened self-image. The highly successful Carnegie exhibit had been completed; *Casa Mañana* would shortly be in press; the trauma of the Rivera project, if not out of mind, could at least be reconciled with his knowledge of what he had accomplished and with the assurance of the great man's continuing friendship; and *Little Mexico,* after many delays, had finally been published earlier that year both in New York and in a special Mexican edition under the imprint of Cape and Smith. The latter would not bring him the financial rewards he had characteristically hoped for, but it would essentially bring to a notable completion his career of interpreting as writer and architectural artist cultural scenes congenial to his antiquarian sensibility. The depth and character of Spratling's apprenticeship to the future are implicit in *Little Mexico,* and thus it is proper that we examine it now, together with the several essays he was writing concurrently for the New York *Herald-Tribune.* The "Mexican Letters" series might be regarded as companion pieces to the book itself, showing on the one hand how ably Spratling had accommodated himself to the broad artistic vista of contemporary Mexico. *Little Mexico,* on the other hand, illustrated his extraordinary perception, as the reviews would affirm, of the nation's vast cultural sub-stratum lying beneath that immediately observable, one "drenched in mystery" and more in touch with the traditions of its pre-Conquest ancestors than with the politics and intellectual issues of the twentieth century.

Guanajuato, described by Spratling as "Mexico's most beautiful city"
From Architectural Forum, *February 1928. Courtesy Spratling family.*

The Shrine, Guadalupe
From Architectural Forum, August 1927. Courtesy Spratling family.

Cathedral, Vera Cruz
From Architectural Forum, August 1927. Courtesy Spratling family.

Dwight and Elizabeth Morrow, Cuernavaca, 1929
Photograph from Dwight Morrow, *copyright 1935 and renewed
1962 by Harold Nicolson, reprinted by permission of Harcourt Brace
& Company and the Estate of Harold Nicolson*

Diego Rivera, sketched by Spratling for "Books Abroad,"
New York Times, July 28, 1929

PANELS FROM RIVERA'S *The History of Mexico*
(*Cuernavaca and Morelos*), the Cortez Palace, 1930

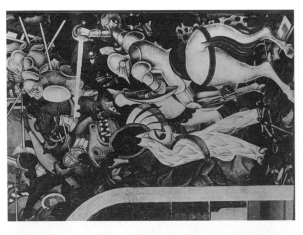

Battle of the Aztecs and Spaniards

Sugar Plantation

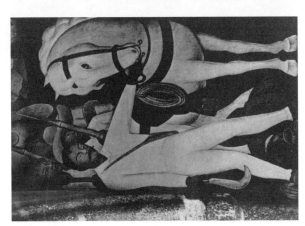

Emiliano Zapata

Spratling, painted by David Siqueiros, 1931
From File on Spratling *(Boston: Little, Brown, 1967)*

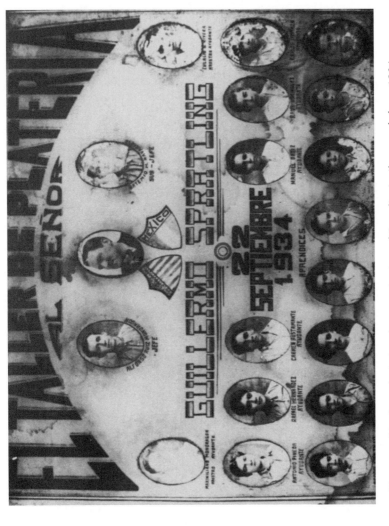

Photographic chart depicting the organization of Spratling's silver workshop, 1934
Courtesy Spratling family

Spratling, ca. 1932
Courtesy Manuscripts Department, Tulane University Library

Christmas card for 1937–38 holiday season from the Taller de las Delicias,
featuring a nineteenth-century lithograph of the Church of Santa Prisca
Courtesy Library of Congress

Spratling with Miguel Covarrubias and Spratling's
high school and college friend Gladys Steadham
(Stewart), Taxco, 1938
Courtesy Ralph Hammond

Mary Anita Loos and Rosa Covarrubias, ca. 1944
From Covarrubias *by Adriana Williams, Copyright ©*
1994. Reproduced by permission of Adriana Williams and
the University of Texas Press

Pre-Columbian clay figurines, Vera Cruz, from *More Human than Divine,*
photographed by Manuel Alvarez Bravo
Photograph © National Autonomous University of Mexico

Spratling at the ranch, ca. 1948
*Courtesy Spratling family. Copyright Juan Guzman, Reporter-Grafico, Mexico,
D.F. Av. Morelos 89 DEP. 8.*

Spratling with Lyndon and Lady Bird Johnson, Taxco, ca. 1962
Courtesy Spratling family

Spratling at Auburn to receive an honorary doctorate, 1962
Courtesy Auburn University Archives

Sketch of Spratling in about 1930 by Rene d'Harnoncourt
Collection of the Birmingham Museum of Art, Birmingham, Alabama;
Gift of Sarah d'Harnoncourt

Spratling in his last year, as sketched by Gillett Griffin
Courtesy Gillett Griffin

Spratling designs produced both in his lifetime and since
his death have borne several different hallmarks.
(For a pictorial sequence of hallmarks, see Sandraline Cederwall
and Hal Riney's *Spratling Silver*, p. 33.)

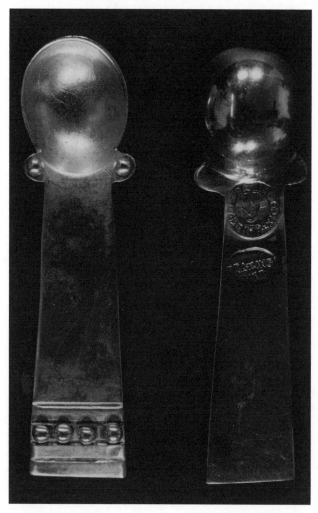

These salt spoons, probably produced in the 1930s, may
be "old" silver from coins or smelted silver ore (.980,
"purer than sterling"). The hallmark is one of Spratling's
earliest.

Courtesy Leigh Askins Smith

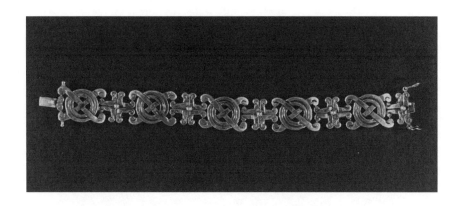

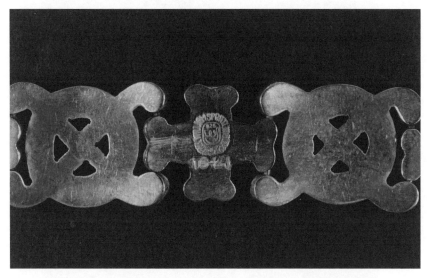

This Maya motif bracelet, purchased at the Spratling shop in the 1990s, shows beneath the hallmark the government mark (TS-24) assigned to the shop and guarantees sterling quality (.925 silver ore with .075 copper alloy).

DESIGNS BY SPRATLING
The photographs on the following pages are from the
Collection of Sucesores de William Spratling

Brooch, silver and tortoiseshell
Photograph by Gerardo Suter

Cigarette box, silver, with stylized jaguar motifs
Photograph by Gerardo Suter

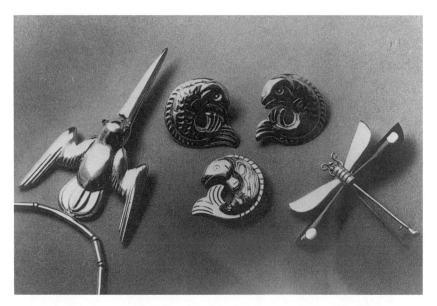

Hummingbird and fish motifs in brooch and earrings, silver; fish brooch,
silver and mother-of-pearl; dragonfly pin, silver and rosewood
Photograph by Gerardo Suter

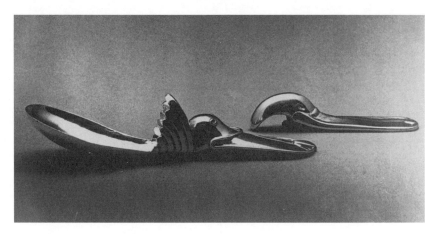

Duck sugar spoon, silver
Photograph by Gerardo Suter

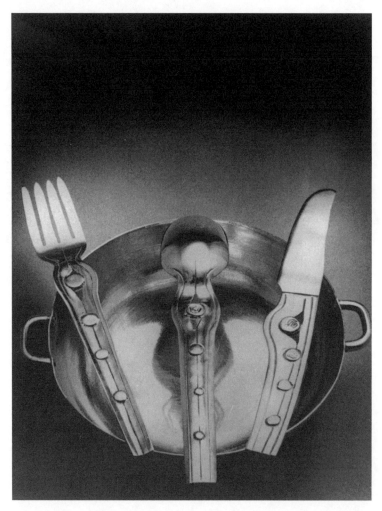

Child's place setting, silver
Photograph by Gerardo Suter

Stylized sun-motif brooch, silver with amethyst incrustations
Photograph by Gerardo Suter

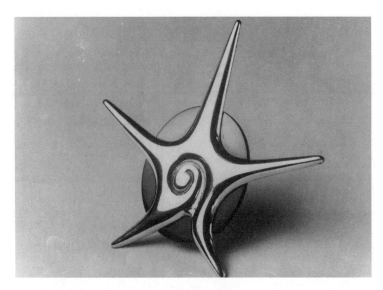

Starfish brooch, silver and tortoiseshell
Photograph by Jason Creagh

Coffee pot from the jaguar service, silver with rosewood handle
Photograph by Jason Creagh

Necklace, pre-Hispanic rock crystal beads, gold and green
serpentine
Photograph by Jason Creagh

Silver brooch from the early 1960s
Photograph by Jason Creagh

From the Alaskan period: bracelet, necklace with mask pendant, ivory, tortoiseshell, silver
Photograph by Jason Creagh

Alberto Ulrich, owner of Sucesores de William Spratling
today, with Don Tomás Vega, the last maestro to be trained
personally by Spratling
  Photograph by Jason Creagh

Don Tomás with one of his workers
Photograph by Jason Creagh

Entrance gate to Rancho Spratling, Taxco-el-Viejo
Photograph by Jason Creagh

7

New Designs from an Old Tradition: Verbal Preludes

"At the time of writing, Mexico is enjoying cool, bright mornings and slightly warmer afternoons refreshed with showers. It is probably the pleasantest time of the year here, and it is hard to realize that instead of escaping the summer season, as in New York, people—those who know and are able to—are rushing back to it. There is much going on here. People are doing interesting things." Thus begins Spratling's "Mexican Letter" in the "Books Abroad" page of the Sunday, July 5, 1931 *Herald-Tribune*. And what follows is a wide-ranging two-thousand-word profile of literary and artistic happenings in Mexico: the Guggenheim project of Carleton Beals, the renewed painting activity of Rivera and Jean Charlot, the folklore research of Anita Brenner and Frances Toor, a forthcoming novel with Mexican setting by Susan Smith, a brief review of new art work at the Galería Iturbide in Mexico City—especially that of Tamayo and Siqueiros—notations of publications on Mexican communism and the Revolution, the Taxco writing and painting of his New Orleans friends Natalie Scott and Caroline Durieux, and on and on. The page is centered with a large reproduction of a Siqueiros lithograph, which Spratling notes (not without a vested interest, of course, as the painter's informal agent) will be among several others to be shown in the fall at the Weyhe Gallery in New York.

It is indeed an impressive display and suggests that this kind of occasional writing and reporting was a significant part of Spratling's apprenticeship prior to his first effort to create a new industry from an old tradition. The essays he wrote for the New York *Herald-Tribune* Sunday "Books Abroad" page illustrate just how well he had educated himself on the arts scene in Mexico. And, of course, the pieces gave to his name a certain authority at the time when U.S. interest in that scene was at its highest point. Though the "Books Abroad" feature was discontinued during the Depression, for several years it ran every Sunday under the editorship of Spratling's friend from New Orleans days, Irita Van Doren. Columns by journalists Hugh Walpole (London) and Jenny Bradley (Paris) ran almost every month, and other Sundays were filled by pieces on literary events from Germany, Italy, Russia, and other European countries. The content of Spratling's occasional "Mexican Letter" was good enough to stand against stiff international competition.

The series, often illustrated by Spratling drawings which would re-appear in *Little Mexico,* sometimes took notice of the activities of American visitors, such as Susan Smith, Katherine Anne Porter, Carleton Beals, Malcolm Cowley, Caroline Durieux, and Waldo Frank; and he was not beyond complimenting books published in the United States by his friends Elizabeth Morrow (*The Painted Pig,* with illustrations by d'Harnoncourt) and one of the several cookbooks authored by Natalie Scott. But when a portion of one of the four-column essays was devoted to Mexican or Spanish publications, Spratling showed a studied intimacy with his subject: in giving lukewarm praise to a new biography of Blasco Ibáñez, for example, he seems to know well the principal earlier study of the writer, to which he compared the present one; and in noting the imminent appearance in Spain of hitherto unpublished Ibáñez fiction, his reference to Ibáñez's style (who "wrote with all the furious energy of the Valencian temperament") seems one of easy familiarity. Several of the essays in their eclectic content illustrate the range of Spratling's always careful reading, from a study of El Cid's eleventh-century Spain, to the first volume of an elaborate edition of the Catalan poet Joan Maragall, to a new biography of Ignatius Loyola, to French critical works on the Brontës. Perhaps most impressive is a long review ("Literary Notes from Mexico," March 8, 1931) of the translation into Spanish from the ancient Maya of the *Libro de chilam balam de Chumayel.* His review of the poetic, narrative, and prophetic content of the translation, which he seems to have read completely, includes an informed commentary on recent scholarship on Maya manuscripts and the difficulty of their translation, and provides a judicious estimate of the volume's importance, not only in what it reveals about "the most ancient civilization on the continent" but also its observations on the Conquest in Yucatan, seen through the eyes of the conquered rather than those of the victors.

But more often than not there was also room for extended reviews of books and issues relevant to those interpretations of Mexican art and history which he had already in his journal articles placed before a more limited readership. He seemed to see, for example, in a long and sensitive review of contemporary Mexican fiction that in its "new and amazing fertility" it had become a kind of late harvest of the renaissance epoch of the twenties, with the work of Martín Luis Guzmán (*El águila y la serpiente*) and Mariano Azuela (*Los de abajo*) utilizing for the first time as fictional material the social and human background of the 1910 revolution. And the *Herald-Tribune* reader of Sunday morning, November 10, 1929, must have been startled indeed to see almost leaping from the page the skeletal horseback rider of José Guadalupe Posada, the graphic illustrator of revolutionary Mexico whose re-discovery Spratling's "Mexican Letter" of that day would describe. Nowhere is Spratling's central linkage with the artistic world of contemporary Mexico better illustrated than in this review of a forthcoming edition of Posada's work. It was to be published under the editorial offices of the *Mexican Folkways* of his friend Frances Toor, but Spratling had already seen the selection of engravings to be reproduced, most of them the originals only recently found stored in a Mexico City print shop, and he had read the introduction by Rivera, who as a boy had known Posada, "as great as Goya," he wrote, "interpreter of sorrow and happiness, and of the anguished aspirations of the people of Mexico." Spratling understood that Posada's tiny etchings of the past had already, in their influence on the muralists, found their way into the national epics high on the frescoed walls of many public buildings, just as they would within a year appear on those at Cuernavaca. Aside from the artistic importance of the Posada publication to Mexicans, "for America," he wrote, "it will be an opportunity to see something Mexican done from the inside out."[1]

The latter phrase was one of Spratling's favorites, suggesting that by 1929 he had adopted a sense of himself as an "inside" writer interpreting things Mexican to an "outside" audience. It was a self-image that would continue to inform all of his work, including his graphic designs, and to sustain as well his disappointment in the superficiality with which many

1. William Spratling, "Mexican Letter," *New York Herald Tribune Books,* November 10, 1929. Spratling also, in a quotation on Posada by Anita Brenner, shows his continuing high regard for her *Idols Behind Altars* (1929), which he ranks in another essay with the sixteenth-century colonial treatise of Díaz del Castillo and Madame Calderón de la Barca's nineteenth-century *Letters* as the three "most generally interesting books that exist today in the English language about Mexico." Brenner had listed Spratling's January 1929 *Scribner's* essay in her bibliography.

American visitors of genuine talent depicted the life of the country. Two years later, for example, when his own designs were first beginning to take shape, he wrote to Zigrosser concerning one of the Guggenheim proposals—this one for the young artist Howard Cook—which he was now regularly being asked to evaluate, another indication of his "inside" status. Although he accepted Zigrosser's recommendation of Cook's great promise, "I didn't like his program, it being very broad and vague, taking much for granted about the country and representing the outside-in point of view."[2] While Spratling felt no messianic impulse to correct this perspective, there is a certain animated focus in his communications during these years to the outside audience of the *Herald-Tribune* that he was an informed and residential witness to the phenomenon of a country with an ancient heritage which, after surmounting the shock of revolutionary experience, was now consciously attempting to enter the modern world through the construction of a public culture. The newness of it all was rather lively, he felt, writing in the same "Letter" containing the Posada review that "while New York talks and carefully propagandizes the idea of a popular museum of modern art this government . . . calmly announces, and in the same moment opens a museum of modern Mexican art in a fine, big gallery on the ground floor of the National Theater." He was only slightly less enthusiastic in his essay of June 2, 1929, which was devoted entirely to an interview with Antonio Castro Leal (portrayed in a Spratling sketch), the new rector of the continent's oldest university. Then undergoing a complete reorganization of its curriculum and emphases in engineering, law, medicine, and even the fine arts— Spratling had attended concerts of the new symphony under the baton of Carlos Chavez—the University of Mexico, with extraordinary governmental financial support, was attempting to produce graduates who could "meet in a modern way the very special necessities" of the nation. His finest essay of the series, on the work of Orozco (April 14, 1929), skillfully explicates the radical concept, so foreign to his *Herald-Tribune* readers, that contemporary art in Mexico had itself come to function as a social necessity. His choice of illustrations for the essay, two drawings from a group called *Mexico in Revolution,* capture the compelling bitterness of an artist with less philosophic power than Rivera but with a greater emotional conviction—whether "the painting be of smug religious

2. W.S. to Carl Zigrosser, September 24, 1931.

pedants patronized by a cross-eyed God who plays favorites against the poor or whether the scene, as on the walls of the great stairway of the Preparatoria, depicts the pity of the early Christian fathers bent in compassion over a bruised and suffering people."

Spratling's last writing for the series in which he had served as a generous propagandist for the epoch he himself was helping to define was published on July 5, 1931. Later that month those arrangements were proposed to Rivera for what would be the wildly successful exhibition of his work in December at the Museum of Modern Art. That event, along with the widespread sale of Rivera's paintings to North American collectors and his acquisition of mural commissions in San Francisco and Detroit, confirmed his tremendous commercial and artistic popularity in the United States. The Rivera phenomenon suggested also the transition to what Spratling felt would be a new epoch in Mexican art following that indigenously integrative one of the twenties, which in his *Mexican Folkways* article on Rivera he had seen as ending with the completion of the Cuernavaca murals. He noted more than once in the *Herald-Tribune* series that though Rivera continued to be a "presence" even in his absence, still the work of younger artists could now be viewed in a certain relief against that of the past. The arrival in Mexico of the full effects of the Great Depression, however, thwarted such optimism and adversely affected too the genuine social and cultural achievements of the country which Spratling and a few others had praised to an outside audience. It was, ironically, within this new condition that the two most original of Spratling's contributions to the Mexican Renaissance appeared.

Little Mexico, after several delays, was finally published by the struggling house of Cape and Smith in March of 1932. Spratling wrote to Zigrosser in the previous September that he had just finished the manuscript. He had, however, given a copy earlier to Rivera, whose foreword, in the form of a letter to Spratling, was dated August 29, 1931. He expected a quick printing but wrote in early November that "Little Mexico, goddamit, has been postponed, for the reason that the same nasty customs has held up all my illustrations and Cape and Smith are just now getting them out." Years in both conception and composition, the book was obviously important to Spratling, and he was anxious about its reception. Zigrosser had sent a card of brief praise, but that wasn't enough. "It was damn nice of you to say bravo about the book. I'm delighted that you like it. However, you must write me sometime critically. I want to know what you really think of it, and what people up there in general say. . . . Why don't you tell me what Diego thinks of it. He'll never write."[3] And though in the same letter he stated that the Mexican edition had drawn editorial praise from *El Universal* as well as from both Anita Brenner and Carleton Beals, by the end of March his anxiety showed in a friendly rebuke to Zigrosser that

> there is simply never any answer from you, except, perhaps, a line, like when you wrote a card and said bravo about Little Mexico. I want to know more about that. . . . please let down a little bit and tell me what people are saying about the book. They seem to like it here. There's only been one serious review, which as an editorial in *El Universal* called it "El Primer Libro Sobre el Mexico de Verdad"—and "the white blackbird of all that mass of gray literature by visitors to Mexico."[4]

He need not have worried; the reviews were uniformly positive, all of them echoing Rivera's phrase of the "acuteness and grace" with which Spratling developed his portraits of the little Mexicans. The combination of "authentic scenes" and "beguiling sketches"—the integration of text and drawings—made the book admirably attractive and, as the reviewer observed in the *New York Times,* which reproduced four of the drawings, "of William Spratling it may be said with the most sincere banality that he writes about the things that he sees with a hand guided by the eye of the graphic artist." Other reviews, which must have pleased Spratling the most, praised his critical stance in presenting and selecting his content: his "deep sympathetic attitude toward the country in which he now lives," the fact that he was "honored" by the native confidence and was thus able to collect and tell "tales that no one had told before," and his ability to penetrate those "still secret regions of Guerrero, where a man from Mexico City is as much a foreigner as one from London." He had indeed "achieved something not altogether explicable" through his fusion of what Rivera called "irony and love," by which he pictured Mexico as though he had actually been a part of its "intense history and yet, detached, views it from the best of perspectives." Finally, all of these strains are implicit in the two most enthusiastic reviews, that of Stuart Chase—whose friendship with Spratling should not lessen his extraordi-

3. W.S. to Carl Zigrosser, November 10 and 22, 1931.
4. W.S. to Carl Zigrosser, March 30, 1932.

nary estimate—and that in the *Christian Century,* both of which perceived that the book had revealed the heart of the country:

> Mexico has claimed Mr. Spratling . . . in an embrace which he will never
> shake off. Because it has him in so warm a grip, he can communicate its
> way of life with an understanding and a sympathy which no other North
> American to my knowledge possesses. If he strikes the Northerner as a
> little mystical, it is only because little Mexico is drenched in mystery. I have
> been there and I can testify. . . .
>
> I wish everyone who loves Mexico, or who has any curiosity about it,
> or whoever read any book about the problems and the politics of Mexico,
> would read this book of Bill Spratling's. . . . It is essentially about that
> stratum of Mexican life, chiefly Indian, which lies beneath the surface of
> ordinary observation, and, like the submerged five-sixths of an iceberg,
> sustains the visible part. . . . For the student of Mexico to interview political
> leaders and get acquainted with the intelligentsia in the capital is well
> enough, of course, but not to know typical samples of the great unchanged
> and unchanging masses who live in the villages and constitute the bulk of
> the population and keep alive the traditions of their pre-conquest ances-
> tors, is not to know Mexico.[5]

Despite the book's fine critical reception, its sales and first life both
fell far short of Spratling's expectations. In his introduction to the 1964
reprint, Lesley Byrd Simpson, Spratling's good friend from those years,
recalled that in the spring of 1932 "came the heart-breaking word: Cape
and Smith, the publishers, had dissolved their partnership, and *Little
Mexico* was left an orphan."[6] As always, Spratling took the disappointment pretty well, well indeed coming as it did in the middle of his rejection by the Murphys. Characteristically he tried to get out of it what he
could, writing to Zigrosser in May an inquiry about selling in New York
for fifteen dollars a few copies of the special Mexican edition, signed
with an original lithograph and snakeskin binding, but by June he had

5. The reviews, in order of referral: C. G. Poore, "A Corner of the Mexican Maze,"
New York Times Book Review, July 31, 1932, pp. 2–3; review of *Little Mexico,* in *New
Orleans Times-Picayune,* February 21, 1932, p. 21; "Little Mexico," *Saturday Review of
Literature,* May 28, 1932, pp. 760–61; Stuart Chase, "On the Street of Delights," *New
York Herald-Tribune Books,* February 14, 1932, p. 5; W. E. Garrison, "Little Mexico,"
Christian Century, July 6, 1932, p. 864.

6. Lesley Byrd Simpson, introduction to *A Small Mexican World* (Boston: Little,
Brown, 1964), 4. All page citations are from this edition.

lowered the price to ten. But if the book did not remediate his worsening financial condition, it justified for him, perhaps more than anything else he had done, the "Mexican" identity he had at first casually but later through deliberate and permanent exile sought and assimilated.

That justification is also a revelation of why exile was attractive to Spratling. The book appeared in the same year as *Light in August*, the fourth Faulkner novel published since 1929, the year Spratling had settled in Taxco. These were novels, of course, in which his old St. Peter Street comrade had created from the story of the South, to which he had returned, the imaginative history of its decline as seen in its representative families. Faulkner's fictional landscape, in which the complex relationships between such families as the Sartorises, Compsons, and Snopeses are played out and in which memory is increasingly held hostage, has recently been viewed as part of the autobiographical impulse in southern fiction that attempts to discover the connection between the self and a world permanently displaced of its sense of myth and tradition by that of science and history.[7] However slenderly Spratling's own creative career may be related to this search, it is not difficult to see all of his writing as essentially autobiographical. The world that he found in Mexico and attempted over and over to interpret, with a sympathetic affinity anticipated by his essays on New Orleans, Savannah, Natchez, and the Isle Brevelle, had not suffered this kind of displacement. To be sure, the country's defining moments had been those of revolution and violence, which had, like the Civil War of the United States, brought the nation, or at least the consciousness of its governmental center, into the modern world. But to the vast majority of the Mexican population that were most intriguing to Spratling, the past had not lost its mystery and sacred power. *Little Mexico* is both a climax and a completion of this suggested autobiographical quest that gives a sense of unity and direction to a Spratling career so easily viewed as only eclectic and brilliantly opportunistic. The book records his affection and at times respectful commitment to his discovered affinity with a culture whose oldness and intransigent memory seemed odd and remote to that of his own native land.

Certainly there had been nothing quite like it written about Mexico before, and its originality—itself a new design capturing an old tradi-

7. See Lewis P. Simpson, *The Fable of the Southern Writer* (Baton Rouge: Louisiana State University Press, 1993).

tion—is something of a verbal parallel to the art forms in silver Spratling would soon be creating. His reference to the book's purpose in *File on Spratling* stated his desire "to picture normal life in a small Mexican village." It would not be, he added, a "Winesburg, Mexico," but "a brief sketch, words plus many drawings of places and people." The brevity of his sketches, however, is not the revealing difference between what he produced and his curiously recollected contrast with Sherwood Anderson. *Little Mexico* certainly is not about a series of bewildering and frustrating encounters with modern life but, rather, about a world oblivious to it. If Spratling had a model at all, it was not *Winesburg, Ohio,* but perhaps D. H. Lawrence's *Mornings in Mexico,* which he had probably read along with *The Plumed Serpent,* to which he had referred in one of the articles written during his first long visit to Mexico.[8]

In both Lawrence and Spratling there is the technique of the observant journey, the sense of wonder at a strange world, which the writer cannot make clear to his "outside" audience because it is contradictory to every mode of social and psychological testing that the audience knows. That world can only be described, non-judgmentally, of course, and perhaps even interpreted if one has made the effort to perceive the mythic measurement appropriate to it. Alien to that measurement is the sense of urgency and schedule which the *turistas* bring with them and around which the white *patrón* organizes his materialistic schemes. In Lawrence's absorption of the "native" perception, such obsessions were a "truly horrible monkey-like passion for invisible exactitudes."

> Now to a Mexican, and an Indian, time is a vague foggy reality. There are only three times: en la mañana, en la tarde, en la noche. . . . There is even no midday and no evening. . . . Manaña, to the native, may mean tomorrow, three days hence, six months hence, and never. There are no fixed points in life, save birth and death, and the fiestas. And the priests fix the fiestas. . . . But to the white monkey, horrible to relate, there are exact spots of time, such as five o'clock, half past nine. The day is a horrible puzzle of exact spots of time.[9]

To Spratling, a permanent rather than a temporary resident like Lawrence, a passion for the exactitudes of time was but one of the *ameri-*

8. William Spratling, "Some Impressions of Mexico," part I, *Architectural Forum* 47 (July 1927), 8.

9. D. H. Lawrence, *Mornings in Mexico,* with an introduction by Richard Aldington (London: William Heinemann, 1927), 48–49.

cano's embarrassing albeit unintentional forms of patronizing. Using, as did Lawrence, the perspective of one of his Indian or Mexican companions, he could understand why

> Angel slyly calls [foreign tourists] the *synchronizados* [*sic*]. He sees them as they arrive in the plaza and get out of their cars. . . . They stop to consult their watches before looking at the church. This obedience to Time seems to him incredibly funny, particularly when instead of sitting down on those nice benches in the plaza or looking about, they continue standing there for twenty minutes heatedly discussing whether they shall leave at two or two thirty. He does not realize that these people never enter into a country, that they merely travel.

Indeed, with their bland and casual air toward anything indigenous, they looked to Spratling as if, in a Marsden Hartley phrase, "they had just come in from grazing"; and he agreed with Angel that the tourists (who, ironically, would become his best customers within two or three years) were like "synchronized sound movies, which have captions in Spanish and motivations and reactions which reject reality."[10]

Both Lawrence and Spratling, observing from their remote southern sites of Oaxaca and Taxco, respectively, felt that, as Lawrence put it, in no country "more than in Mexico does human life become isolated, external to its surroundings, and cut off tinily from the environment." And in one of his several brilliant descriptions, this one oddly modern in its scientific phrasing, Lawrence saw the search for human contact as a kind of centripetal force that would bring hundreds of Indians through the vast curving spaces between their remote villages and the central axis of a market-day location. To Spratling, the curved domes atop Taxco's Santa Prisca, which were the legacy of Cortez and the first European tourists and of King Philip's religion, served as a kind of physical axis for the *mexicanitos,* the "Little Mexicans," drawing them from the hills to market day in Taxco, a happening similar to scores of others throughout the immense distances of this great mid-continent country. Perhaps the force that brought them was indeed a search for further human contact or, incidentally, to pay tribute to the Virgen de la Luz, but the whole affair was a solemn ritualistic fusion of cultures. On such days the town be-

---

10. Marsden Hartley, quoted in W.S. to Carl Zigrosser, June 4, 1932; Spratling, *A Small Mexican World,* 171–73.

came something more, he wrote, than merely conventionally picturesque, for then "a subtle and unsuspected relationship between bourgeois and primitive Mexico becomes an actuality. If it is not purely Mexican, it is everything which has happened to that country."

These concluding words to the opening chapter of *Little Mexico* set the pattern of Spratling's affectingly authentic account of the country's history, especially of the mythic and ceremonial memory lying beneath its contemporary presence. He showed little affinity with Lawrence's European sensibility, which often focused on the economic suppression of Indians, who, in order to live, must with a kind of wry amusement learn the tedious, meaningless, and exactitudinal tricks of the great white monkey who held the keys to the world. And though his primary subject was the "Little Mexicans," whose ancestors were Aztec and even the precursors of the Aztecs, Spratling rarely if ever was drawn to the dark sadistic power of that ancient religion which fascinated Lawrence and which he had used thematically in *The Plumed Serpent*. That work was written just before Lawrence's travel essays and had been excoriated in a review by Frances Toor in *Mexican Folkways*, where, supported by a devastating Covarrubias caricature of Lawrence, she accused him of being frightened of everything Mexican, showing only "the sinister and cruel," and not "the noble and lovable side of Mexican character."[11]

Spratling may well have shared Toor's easy allegorical interpretation of Lawrence's novel, but in his own attempt to picture what he seems to have felt was the least understood human element in the country's complex history, he made no effort to reconcile these two "sides" of the national character. Certainly he wished to subvert for his North American readership what he had called in one of the *Herald-Tribune* essays the false and misleading "tourist goods Mexican" image. In choosing to focus on the obscure and almost invisible "little" people, he created a kind of minor analogue to the scenes of ordinary life, humble tragedy, and revolutionary trauma which were even then being created in powerful plastic forms by the modern Mexican painters he so admired and had championed. It was, in fact, the analogy of painting that Diego Rivera used in his brief preface to Spratling's book: "You have made a portrait of Mexico composed of many small portraits of people and things."

11. Frances Toor, "Mexico Through Frightened Eyes," *Mexican Folkways* 8 (August-September 1926), 45–46.

Within the analogy Rivera seemed to praise in Spratling's writing some of the qualities in his own work that had always revered their artistic heritage: "Your portraits have the acuteness and grace of those painted by certain masters in my country who died before I was born." And, finally, he could also have been describing his own art, even the gigantic symbolic patterns in the public murals, where he noted in Spratling's little book its clarity and the mastery of design inherent in its mutually restraining tonal elements: "Those portraits were made with precision and tenderness and contain irony and love."

To be sure, the quality of restraint; that quality had always been present in Spratling's painting, drawing, and writing. In *Little Mexico* his descriptive stance is never altered toward one of superiority or derogatory judgment, whether the allusion is to the arrogant corruption of local politicians, the murderous brutality of the army, the terrible recollections of revolutionary chaos, or the innocent humor reflected in the social ceremonies with which village life is conducted. There is, for example, the account of the funeral of Tata Luis, whose ninety-year memory encompassed Carlota and Maximiliano, to say nothing of that ruffian outsider Díaz, who had no respect for the Church. Tata Luis was a *religioso*, the town bell-ringer, although no one was surprised when two o'clock was rung three times, or four o'clock thirteen. "His talk, like his life," wrote Spratling, "was full of simple and profound incident, without any glory or any particular plot." He was especially proud of the rain-bringing power of his favorite piece of statuary, the Child Jesus—Nuestro Señor—who resided not in the great *parroquia* but in the little church of the Holy True Cross. His fame was so great, Tata Luis recalled, that once over in Morelos, in Acuitlapán, during a drought the Acuitlapeños implored the loan of Nuestro Señor, and five or six men carried him there on a two-day journey. His arrival was miraculous, as the rain came down in torrents; in fact they wanted to keep him in their church, and our villagers had to fight their way out. But we were triumphant: no casualties, but three Acuitlapeños were killed and a *señora* got a black eye. After that *Nuestro Señor* was called "the Little General." You could always count on the Little General to bring just the right amount of rain. The Virgin of Guadalupe herself was often eccentric in this, once almost flooding the town with a cloudburst. "After that," he said, grinning, "we brought out the Child Jesus when we wanted rain. That was so he could show his holy mother a thing or two!"

Usually just a listener to stories such as this, Spratling could also be a silent participant in them. He had been off in the hills when he returned to find the funeral procession forming for Tata Luis. It took the same route through town that Spratling's own cortege would follow some thirty-five years later. The coffin, so elegant in its varnished red cedar that Spratling felt it contradictory to the poor shriveled body inside, was carried by friends of the deceased. Spratling's own funeral procession would be slightly more formal, perhaps, but no less deeply felt. To initiate Tata Luis's final journey, the village trio of flute, violin, and bass viol had selected from its repertoire of four tunes an air called "Sonny Boy." Thus the procession started, with Spratling in the line, and moved in stately fashion away from the plaza, stopping on its way to the Holy Field for the bearers to rest, both times as it happened, in front of a cantina where liquid refreshment was quickly sampled.

> At the burial ground, the coffin, shiny and resplendent in the light of the pine torches, was set down and opened, the slender little old body which only partly filled it was taken out and wrapped in an old sarape and lowered without further ceremony to its final rest. . . . The coffin, it seems, belonged to the sacristan, who keeps it there in the church for this purpose, renting it for two pesos a burial, providing it is returned the same day and in good condition.
>
> So we left Tata Luis, a servant of the church and of the old regime, one who had never presumed. He appeared no more formal in the wrappings of his old sarape than he had actually been in life.[12]

In all of this, the descriptive tone is one of benign gravity, which prevails throughout the book as Spratling's portraits suggest the unpretentious though quietly significant lives of little Mexico, whose racial experience had taught them long before Montezuma herded them to sacrifice that even events such as the revolution were like the earthquakes that shook their houses: one could do nothing about them. Tata Luis, said Spratling, though he could not read, "could have written an intimate history of Mexico since the days of the great liberator." The key word is "intimate," for the life of Tata Luis is one of several "voices" or "portraits" that "speak" to elements of the contradictory culture that Rivera in his introduction stated that Spratling because of his loving mutuality

12. Spratling, *A Small Mexican World*, 170.

with Mexico had a "right" to portray. And always lying beneath the contemporary, which may seem to an outside audience gently amusing, there is the strange, or the historic, or even the heroic: lest the funeral of Tata Luis seem only amusing, for example, Spratling, through his masterful selection of detail, is careful to note that old Timoteo, one of the casket bearers who weaves his way back to his burden from the last-stop cantina with a bottle of mezcal in his pocket, was the friend who years before in a daring coup had helped to save Tata Luis's life even as the Zapatistas had bound him to a burro and were carrying him off to certain execution.

It was not until Spratling settled in Taxco that the central idea and the design of a book on this subject took hold of his imagination. He recalls in the autobiography that the writing took three years; and he may have made a false start or two, perhaps pursuing the idea of a monograph devoted entirely to the *tierra caliente* region. The book's final version, however, actually subsumes in a highly concentrated manner all of his travels in the country and his observations of remote cultural happenings, many of which are mentioned in the *Herald-Tribune* essays and in his correspondence. He may have had available already some of the *tierra caliente* material, developed from at least two extensive trips there, one with Natalie Scott. He seems to have drawn off some of this, principally the description of a voyage along the Río Balsas, together with an account of his journey to Tierra Fría, to the north and west of Taxco, using these to "frame," as it were, the geographical and human focus of the book, which is Taxco itself and the impressionistic history recorded by the voices of his friends and acquaintances. He liked the *tierra caliente* section so much that he reprinted it verbatim in the later autobiography. But both are fine descriptive pieces, each recording, especially that on the mountainous unexplored *tierra fría* region, his archaeological interests. There are occasional allusions here and elsewhere in the various narratives calculated to make the remote less so for his outside audience: the green-toned, finely glazed pottery made in a poor village on the shores of the Balsas, a stately *incensario,* for instance, which would, Spratling affirmed, cause a sensation in a Fifth Avenue shop window, though it would sell for about eight cents in the market at Pungarabato. And his long descent into a *tierra fría* cave in search of artifacts is compared to that of Floyd Collins, who "would have had the time of his life here . . . if he had had the archaeological urge. . . . anyway, this is Mexico, not

Tennessee." Spratling got the wrong state of course; the cave-in that trapped and eventually took the life of young Collins and so sensationally mesmerized the United States occurred in Kentucky, not Tennessee, and in 1925, seven years before *Little Mexico* was finished and a year before Spratling made his first trip south. Yet the immediacy of the allusion to Spratling—perhaps he didn't in 1931 see how dated it was—suggests something of the autobiographical nature of the book, for it is indeed a climax and a seamless weaving together of all those careful notes and sketches he had made during his years of travel throughout areas of country that to him unconsciously retained in their microcosmic forms the life that was truly Mexican.

What makes *Little Mexico* such an original and unique complement to those histories then being written and published by his friends Stuart Chase, Ernest Gruening, and Carleton Beals, all of which defined and interpreted the political and social backgrounds of the contemporary scene, was Spratling's concentration on what was *unknown* about Mexico (unknown even, as he stated, to many Mexicans), this country where in the late twenties and thirties scores of new archaeological sites were being opened each year. To his romantic sensibility, quickened by his wide reading and his associations with such major antiquarians as Rivera and Covarrubias, he could identify the hot country southward as the "physical subconscious" of the nation: essentially unexplored in its wildness, but yet with vast untouched mineral wealth, the remainders of cities and pyramids of the continent's most ancient races, and appearing from a mountaintop vista in Guerrero or Oaxaca as "somehow unreal, fantastically impregnable like Indo-China, or Africa."

Spratling's descriptive excursions into these regions seem to record his early interest in the collection of pre-Conquest artifacts and suggest more than elsewhere in his writing his genuine capacity for assimilating anthropological scholarship. His descent into the cave that reminded him of Floyd Collins yielded a fine jar ("this is what we were looking for"), whose Aztec design not only suggested to him that the cultural stimulus of Montezuma's artisans far to the northeast in what would become Mexico City had reached these regions, but also led him to speculate on such questions that today's scholarship is still resolving: how far and in which directions the Aztec, Zapotec, and Tarascan civilizations had penetrated, and whether the Mayans had moved northward along the Mexican Pacific coast. His reflections on the race that hid their art in caves hundreds of years before he found some of it are not discursive to the design of the book but central to it, as is his account of the arduous journey to the mountaintop site of a pre-Conquest city, long since destroyed into ruins, where he saw inarticulately placed into the walls of a re-built stone hut temple fragments: carvings of idols, some upside down, and a section of a gigantic plumed serpent. And all of this history is somehow recorded in Taxco. The village's quiet isolation—far from the political center of the nation's belated attempt to enter the twentieth century—nurtured multiple memories of Mexico's past and provided a kind of verbal destination for the autobiographical journey in which Spratling had sought to integrate his own expatriate identity with that which is most indigenous and, perhaps, critical to the life of his adopted country.

It is with his friends and neighbors in the town that he explores these memories: with the *mestizo* shopkeepers, the *coloniales* (who advise him not to talk to the Indians because it is bad for his Spanish pronunciations), and, most importantly, with the little Mexicans themselves. They are descendants (one has only to look at the face of Tata Luis, for example, to know this, says Spratling) actually of one or more of the pre-Hispanic cultures whose migrations carried them to this region. But in their mythic memory, those who built the mountaintop city had no national identity; they were simply the "most-ancient-ones-who-have-gone-before." The historical—as opposed to the mythic—consciousness of those to whom Spratling listened always was centered, of course, on the revolutionary years when the Zapatista cavalry or the conscripted armies of Díaz could alter a town's history and disrupt its agrarian life in a single day. This recollection appears in the most masterfully written section of the book, that which reproduces the associational monologue of young Juanito, the gardener whose son was Spratling's first god-child.

> He loves to stop by and talk . . . and with a little encouragement will tell me the story of his life. He tells it like the narrations of an Aztec codex. There is nothing particularly heroic about it and he becomes strangely involved in place-facts and events, interspersed with encounters with wild animals and with witch-doctors. His dark face takes on an air of childlike absorption . . . and his voice is almost monotonous. These are the things the colonial ones think I am a fool to listen to:

> > That was now long ago. . . . But I had another sister and she was in service. She had been in service precisely in the house of Doña Petra.

And the Zapatistas took the cuadrilla of Tehuilotepec. They entered the town at night and being dark men and their clothes all white they quitted their rags and went into the town all naked. And there was little to rob and so they robbed the alcohol from the store of Don Mateos and burned it and then they took the women. When they arrived at our house it was two days later and first they wanted money and then they wanted my sister. And my mother said my sister was not there . . . . And the next night she hid my sister under the boxes where the hen is setting. And when the Zapatistas come they cannot find her. Nor do they find the *centavos* my mamá has. She has hid them behind a loose adobe in the wall and set the adobe in with the same mud. So they do not find her. But they take our covers from our bed and all our clothes and they leave us all naked. . . . But what I remember most from the Revolution is the hunger, because I was well little.[13]

In passages such as this, the *New York Times* reviewer observed, Spratling has "caught the simple fortitude shown by people who can go through wars without loss of courage." And side by side with the historic is always the mythic, to be witnessed, for example, in the dances performed at fiesta times in honor of the local patron saint: such as the Tiger Dance and that of the conflict between Moors and Christians, each enacting a plot buried long in the past, vaguely allegorical and defying logical exposition, with dialogue chanted in Aztec and the masks of hunters, Pilates, devils, Death and Time carved from the Zompantle—the Aztec Sacred Tree of the Dead—and painted with pure earthen colors. Perhaps older than the stories re-enacted in the ritual dances, older than the Conquest or even than the Catholic Church itself is the religious impulse that annually brings thousands of Little Mexicans to Taxco and to its special shrine of the Virgen de la Luz. This particular and very significant shrine is allegedly more potent in its miracles-work than the other ones in the town. Like those in countless other villages, it has no official connection to the Church; it is a kind of intimate private chapel, little more than a dark one-room windowless sanctuary in which a stained chromo print of the Virgin may be faintly perceived on the wall beyond where Doña Maria sits. Old, shrewd, cunning, she is intercessor, priestess, and manager-of-gifts, piously accepting oil and monetary offerings and painted *retablos* while obscurely promising marvelous protections

13. Ibid., 95–96, 103–104.

from illness, bandits, and snakebite. Nowhere does Spratling better illustrate a fusion of the known and unknown about Mexico than here in his account of this seedy yet sacred place, where the poor, the Little Mexicans, bring with them a faith in the miraculous power of the Virgin together with the Aztec ideology intricately woven into their daily lives. They kneel on the dirt floor amidst Doña Maria's chickens and cats, solemnly imploring the grace of the Holy Mother of Nuestro Señor, whose identity is subsumed in the more ancient presence of Tonantzin, goddess of fertility and Mother of the Gods.

But Taxco, of course, was vastly more to Spratling than the prototype village of the Little Mexican world where bourgeois and primitive, the imposed religion and mythic tradition were placidly incorporated. It was the place where he would make and lose his first fortune, the place where he would assume the identity for which all of his Mexican and New Orleans years had been a preparation. There he would no longer be the perceptive yet peripheral figure interpreting the creativity and cultural fusions of other times and other places but, rather, would come to reside at the center of his own artistic world.

8

"A Mexican Style of Our Times"

"Considering that we are living in Mexico and in the twentieth century—to employ the marvelous materials provided by our country . . . the resulting forms become apparent as something far removed from the influence of antiquated styles which have never had any reason to exist in our time. . . . I have assayed to produce a Mexican style of our times which the country's ancient civilization has not impeded and in which it may be perpetuated." These are not the words of William Spratling. They are, rather, those of his young architect friend, Carlos Obregón, one of the six "figures" of the Mexican Renaissance. Spratling had quoted them in his November 1931 appraisal of Obregón's work, whose spirit he saw as fully integrated with that pervading the artistic and social redemption of Mexico's ancient past. Yet the words might well have been Spratling's own, although when he quoted them, he could not then have known their application to his own creative future. Just how and when the last, longest, and most famous stage in Spratling's artistic career began are not entirely clear. That final stage, however, which would define the course of his life for the next thirty-five years, was less a dramatic departure from anything he had done before than it was a proper and logical, however unexpected, conclusion to it. This is not to say that the future Cellini of Taxco was inherent in the young Billy Spratling who in 1916 designed for his fellow graduates at Auburn High School their class ring. But by the early 1930s, when that identity began to take shape, Spratling as writer and architectural artist had, as we have seen, already in a long and steady continuum accomplished an impressive body of work that had interpreted the very cultural traditions from which his own "Mexican style of our times" would emerge.

Spratling's preparation for his career as designer of jewelry and wares both decorative and utilitarian is not truly analogous to the preparative journeys traveled by the Mexican Renaissance artists whom Spratling knew best and whose work he helped to interpret and publicize for a North American audience. Rivera, Siqueiros, and Carlos Mérida all completed European apprenticeships before returning to Mexico for the maturation of their art in native subjects. When for the first time Spratling's pencil was poised to initiate the process of creating a two-dimensional design that would penetrate and shape the white metal from the mines of Taxco, his considerable technical gifts had for years been enhanced through the thousands of drawings he had completed on three continents, ranging from the structures of the ante-bellum South to those of Gothic Normandy, Romanesque Italy, French Creole New Orleans, and New Spain. Perhaps, had the opportunity presented itself, he could have achieved through his assimilative energy in geographical and cultural sites other than Mexico the originality in design he accomplished there. But, of course, at least since 1928 he had committed himself to an absorption of the dual shapes of that country's artistic history and its contemporary legacy; and it seems impossible to separate the three-dimensional realities of his own artistic vision from that self-conscious act.

The concept of giving new life to the dormant silver-mining industry in Taxco by linking it directly to a design-manufacturing outlet in the same town was communicated to him, Spratling wrote, by Dwight Morrow, and was further supported by Moisés Sáenz and Diego Rivera. In fact, he dated modern silversmithing in Mexico from what he described as "the notable year of 1931," when he opened his first silver shop, calling it "Las Delicias": The Delights.[1] The idea does indeed seem to be characteristic of the visionary Morrow. However, the Morrows had departed the country and the ambassadorship in September of 1930, and had actually been away from Mexico for the first several months of 1930 at the London Naval Conference. He first, and then she, returned for a few weeks as he concluded unfinished diplomatic business, and Morrow may have passed along the silver idea during one of Spratling's social visits to Cuernavaca in late summer, when he also would have been discussing the Casa Mañana sketches with Elizabeth. But it seems more likely that the possibility of reviving the town's ancient industry emerged when the Morrows actually visited Taxco in October of 1929, staying at

1. William Spratling, "Twenty Five Years of Mexican Silversmithing," *Artes de Mexico*, December 1955, 87–90.

Spratling's rented lodgings during the tour he had arranged for them and seeing firsthand the contradiction between its still-evident colonial dignity and its economic poverty. At any rate, Spratling apparently took no initiative in the matter for several months or possibly for as long as two years.

Of course a life moves forward simultaneously on several fronts, however much our long retrospective attention may be attracted by the most prominent one. There is no allusion in Spratling's correspondence of the early thirties to his involvement in silver making. But as the Depression cut more deeply even into the inexpensive living he was maintaining in Taxco, he had much to keep him occupied, in his several writing projects, his attempts to market his own lithographs and the work of Mexican painters in the New York art scene, and his growing absorption with the collecting of pre-Columbian artifacts. There is a hint that in connection with the latter he was occasionally engaged in the all-too-common illegal exportation traffic. The Mexican government was becoming increasingly alarmed about the buying and selling of its excavated history, particularly, one assumes, by foreigners. In the midst of his frustration over the delayed publication of *Little Mexico* and his difficulties with the Murphys (to whom he had sold ceremonial masks), he wrote to Zigrosser:

> Last week I was inquisitioned about selling a valuable mask for ten thousand dollars, also charged with making innumerable excavations all over the state of Guerrero and of exporting idols in trucks. It was extremely nasty, with grand possibilities for international scandal. But I think I presented a very good case and I think they are convinced that it was a matter of dirty rumor and calumny. Apparently the matter is finished, but it certainly gave me a bad three weeks, and I found that a great many friends here are incapable of real friendship. Neither was there any sympathy from Ray.

And he noted in a marginal addition: "All this is confidential."[2]

During the same months of late 1931, he was also at least on the edge of the strident controversy centered in the attacks, both political and artistic, on Rivera by David Siqueiros and others, including Anita Brenner. Siqueiros had been living in Taxco since being exiled that year from Mexico City for participating in the Communist May 1 demonstration.

2. W.S. to Carl Zigrosser, November 22, 1931.

Spratling, whose portrait Siqueiros had painted during that year, had promoted the sale of his lithographs at the Weyhe Gallery and had even from his slender means loaned him money. In the same letter to Zigrosser describing the allegations about idol-selling, Spratling urged him to settle the gallery's account in its sale of the lithographs, stating that the "$65 difference would do Siqueiros a lot of good. At the moment he is very very ill. They took him off to Mexico last week. And they haven't a damned cent." The viciousness of the anti-Rivera polemics, however, was too much even for Spratling, who had at least a minor commercial stake in Siqueiros's work, and a month later he wrote that Rivera, then in New York for his show at MOMA, had always thrived on criticism: "All power to him. Practically all the rest, including Siqueiros, are incomplete, envious, poisonous people. Siqueiros is now attacking Diego, in the vilest fashion, in *Transition*, and I have renounced any friendship with him on account of it. One arrives at a point where there cannot be two ways about such things. Give Diego my love, also Frida.[3] The whole business was probably a strain on Spratling, since it additionally involved Orozco, whose art he had extensively praised in the *Herald-Tribune* essay of April 1929 and for whose work he also was an informal agent. Perhaps the best perspective on the matter, which would have been of more than passing interest to the colony of Guggenheim Fellows in Mexico City, was given by Frances Toor in a letter to Zigrosser in early 1932:

> How funny that who ever wants to come into the limelight as an artist, I mean from Mexico, feels that they must do so over the body of Diego. First it was Orozco and his followers against Diego and now it's Siqueiros, and now that Orozco doesn't speak to Anita Brenner, she's become a Siqueiro-site. S. had an exhibition here organized by Anita and the catalog from beginning to end was attacks, veiled and open, against Diego. Anita wrote that "esthetically and historically Siqueiros was the greatest Mexican artist." I like both Orozco and Siqueiros when their work is good—both are uneven—but I certainly do not think that either can come up to Diego.[4]

It was to the house of the most flamboyant of that Guggenheim group that Siqueiros, ill with malaria, traveled from Taxco, arriving with his wife and doctor in mid-November. Hart Crane was then living in the suburb of Mixcoac, not far from Katherine Anne Porter, and Sprat-

3. W.S. to Carl Zigrosser, December 26, 1931.
4. Frances Toor to Carl Zigrosser, February 16, 1932.

ling—in whose Taxco house Crane had met Siqueiros—may have helped to arrange for Siqueiros's temporary lodging there. Crane had arrived in Mexico to begin his Guggenheim Fellowship, and, as it happened, the last twelve months of his life, in April of 1931. Before the month was out he had met Spratling on his first visit to Taxco, being invited there by Moíses Sáenz who, along with Porter, was attempting to help Crane "quieten down" and not endanger further his fellowship following a scene of spectacular drunkenness, unpaid taxi and cafe bills, and the involvement of the Mexico City police, the American embassy, and the local representative of the foundation, Eyler Simpson. The scene was but one of several others throughout the year, one significantly involving Spratling, all harbingers of Crane's watery suicide in the Gulf Stream on his journey northward in April of 1932. Crane's was another of those lives, more famous of course than Spratling's own, that through its inter-section with his would further illuminate it for us.

Crane was only a few months older than Spratling, and the prospect of an American of his own age, especially one of Crane's rising stature, being drawn to the same qualities in Mexican life on which he himself had already reflected in his writing and drawings may have been part of the initial attraction. Early critical appraisals of "The Bridge" stressed its comprehensive power and technical brilliance but were less certain of Crane's vision of America set forth in the poem that was to remain his masterpiece. Allen Tate, for example, charged that in its praise of Whit-man the poem affirmed an idealistic view of America's obsession with industrialism. Crane at least felt that the poem's title metaphorically sug-gested a linkage between America's romantic past and the nation's ability to surmount for a yet unknown future the industrialism and materialistic values of its twentieth-century life, believing that, as he wrote in a mild but firm defense to Tate, "our age (at least our predicament) to be one of transition."[5] But Mexico! "Let us strip the desk for action—now we have a house in Mexico," he wrote in the first line of "Havana Rose," thus recording how, once he had changed his Guggenheim application from a French to a Mexican residency and began to absorb the literature about the Mexican ambience written by Anita Brenner, Carleton Beals, and others, his quick enthusiasms embraced, as Spratling's more deliberate

5. Hart Crane to Allen Tate, July 13, 1930, *The Letters of Hart Crane*, ed. Brom Weber (New York: Hermitage House, 1952), 352–54.

inspections had done, the creative possibilities of a cultural terrain far removed from the dizzy and potentially self-destructive pace of U.S. life in the twenties. "Humanity is so unmechanized here still, so immediate and really dignified (I'm speaking of the Indians . . . country people) that it is giving me an entirely fresh perspective. And whether immediately creative or not, more profound than Europe gave me. . . . This is truly 'another world'. . . . I still harbor the illusion that there is a soil, a mythology, a people and a spirit here that are capable of unique and magnificent utterance."

Even as this letter was written, Spratling was completing his own treatment of these very sentiments, not on the grand scale of the Cortez-Montezuma poem that Crane at one time vaguely projected, but in *Little Mexico*'s delineation of the baffling and illogical profundity of the "country people" of Taxco and its surroundings. And it was only a few months later that Crane, following his visit to the annual festival at Tepoztlán, perceived the defining strains in Mexican history that Rivera had painted on the walls at Cuernavaca, which Spratling had assessed in the religious architecture of New Spain, and which the literature of Mexico itself had never significantly addressed: "A drummer and a flute player standing facing the dark temple on the heights, alternated their barbaric service at ten minute intervals with loud ringing of all the church bells by the sextons of the church. Two voices, still in conflict here in Mexico, the idol's and the Cross."[6]

Spratling, of course, was not a mere sojourner, enclosed by the Guggenheim chronology, and had long ago set aside the sense of what Crane described as a "strange suspension." Nor had Spratling succumbed in any way to the intimidating side of Mexican life, the "rather lurking and suave dangers" that Crane could describe even at the end of his fellowship year and about which he had been warned by Waldo Frank who, along with Malcolm Cowley, had been the most influential in Crane's decision to go there: "I was afraid. I knew Mexico very well, and I knew how strong the death wish was in Mexico. I knew there was a dark side to all that had come out of the Aztec civilization. And I also knew what the climate did to Americans that weren't used to it.[7]

6. Hart Crane to Waldo Frank, June 13, 1931; Crane to William Wright, September 21, 1931; *Letters*, 371–72, 381.
7. Interview with Frank quoted by John Unterecker, *Voyager: A Life of Hart Crane* (New York: Farrar, Straus and Giroux, 1969), 650. The "suave dangers" allusion occurs

It may have been Spratling's apparently successful accommodation to all this that engaged the brief friendship, for Crane genuinely admired Spratling and his accomplishments, especially *Little Mexico,* which he had apparently read in page proofs: "You've never seen such beautiful arts and crafts as the Indian element here has perpetuated. Wm. Spratling's collection at Taxco is one of the best, and when his book comes out, called *Little Mexico* (Cape & Smith), for heaven's sake read it. Its illustrations are many and will give you more detail than I could squeeze into twenty letters." And during the fall of the year, one of the several non-poetic projects he considered was an extended review of *Little Mexico* in a discussion of how native materials of a foreign country can be utilized by the expatriate writer.[8]

But perhaps for the Spratling story, the Hart Crane interval with its embarrassing episode that saw Crane banished from Taxco residency is revealing in that it confronted Spratling with his own homosexual tendencies, which, from what evidence there is, had lain discreetly latent during the New Orleans years and during the early period of his Mexican apprenticeship. Crane's fully avowed homosexuality was well known among his friends and literary acquaintances. But when Spratling in October of that year wired Crane to invite Peggy Cowley to Taxco for a few days, he set in motion what would become in a few weeks a dramatic alteration in Crane's sense of self. Crane's attraction to Peggy Cowley during this period was, at the least, ironic, since it had been her husband, Malcolm Cowley, who had influenced Crane to come to Mexico. She was there to seek a divorce, and she and Crane intensely renewed their friendship of earlier years once she had moved to Taxco in December at the urging of Spratling and others, settling in a house owned by Natalie Scott. On the evening of the day that Crane arrived for an extended visit, Spratling observed the poignant scene reflecting what was to be their tragically brief happiness. He had brought Peggy's Christmas gift, "a pair of silver earrings, tiny baskets overflowing with flowers." She wrote, "The men insisted that I put them on immediately, so I went into my bedroom and changed into a dress that suited them. Hart whirled me

---

in a letter from Crane to Caresse Crosby on the date his Guggenheim Fellowship terminated, March 31, 1932, *Letters,* 405.

8. Hart Crane to Samuel Loveman, November 17, 1931, *Letters,* 388; Unterecker, *Voyager,* 703.

around and stepped back to get the full effect. "Isn't she wonderful, Bill?" he said."[9] And they had become lovers by the time Spratling wrote to Zigrosser on December 26: "Hope you had a swell Xmas. Things here were extremely quiet. I killed a duck and went over to eat it in Natalie's house with Malcolm Cowley's wife and Hart Crane." The alteration, as Peggy Cowley would later describe it, of Crane's "firm conviction that he was a homosexual and could be nothing else" may well have partially lessened his pervasive sense of guilt, and certainly it seemed to have influenced and framed the intense period of composition in which he wrote "The Broken Tower," his most significant poem begun and completed in Mexico.

Spratling seemed to regard Crane's rather sudden heterosexual transformation with some amusement. Both he and Crane's biographer, for example, record his recollection of Crane's entrance into Doña Berta's Taxco bar following his and Peggy's first love-making, shouting to everyone there: "Boys—I did it!" This was the day after Christmas. But Spratling was not amused a month later, when Crane, restless as always, was apprehended in an affair with an Indian boy. Spratling's version of the story is that it happened in his own house when Crane was staying there, that Crane told him about it the next morning, and that as a result Spratling affirmed that though they would remain friends Crane would no longer be welcome as an overnight guest. As usual in his retrospective treatment of central episodes from his apprenticeship years, Spratling seems to have re-cycled this one in the autobiographical file for his own purposes. The Indian boy apparently was employed by Spratling, and whether or not the actual affair occurred in Spratling's house, which doesn't seem likely, it was not at all a privately contained matter but was indeed scandalous. The facts are that the Taxco civil authorities placed Crane in jail overnight and it was they who imposed the stipulation that he be permanently banished from the town during the evening hours, as his telegram to Peggy Cowley on January 31 confirmed ("Can never enter Taxco again").[10]

Spratling's treatment of the Crane interval is as disjointed and inaccu-

9. The episode is described, with the quotation from Peggy Cowley's letter, in Unterecker, *Voyager,* 713. For some reason Spratling refers to her in the autobiography as "Mrs. X."

10. For the Peggy Cowley recollection and the chronology of the Taxco episodes, see Unterecker, *Voyager,* 712–24.

rate as some of the other items in the autobiographical file. He recalled, for example, that Henry Allen Moe, principal director of the Guggenheim Foundation, "Kindly extended Hart's fellowship for a second year." In fact, however, the fellowship had been dangerously close to termination during Crane's turbulent Mexican year, and the foundation administration undoubtedly breathed a collective sigh of relief when it was over, especially Eyler Simpson, who wrote to Moe that he had personally advanced Crane funds for travel expenses north so he could leave the country as soon as possible. And, further: "All I've got to say is that I'm going to take a good look at the new poet you are sending down here and if he doesn't present all the earmarks of what we sociologists would call a completely adjusted individual, I'm going to send him back to you on the next boat."[11] And in view of all the evidence to the contrary as to the meaningful and deeply felt passion—however brief—between Crane and Peggy Cowley, Spratling stated in the autobiography, specifically remembering "her skinny little nonvoluptuous, even boyish, person," that "love in its romantic sense" was not involved. She was to Crane "an ally rather than an amorous entanglement" as she gave him "instructions" in the other side of physical joys. As we shall see later, Spratling's judgment here, namely, that, at least in this case, Crane's affirmed homosexuality could not have been unified with an emotionally exhilarating heterosexual commitment, came some thirty-five years later, and after he had rejected such a possibility for himself. Crane's transgression, he wrote, "gave me something to think about. I have never been able to feel censorious about anyone's peccadillos as long as their acts do not create problems in other people's lives. But in this case, I confess I was somewhat shocked. In Mexico the saying goes that, "the smaller the town, the bigger the hell," and in a town as small as Taxco, I had to protect my own surroundings from any trace of scandal."

This suggestion about his own sexual orientation and conduct is no less oblique than that elsewhere in the autobiography, where in his offhand, apparently random, style he identifies authors whom he has especially enjoyed—most of them gay: Maugham, Tennessee Williams, Forster, Housman—and singles out the one story that "made a deep impression," Thomas Mann's *Death in Venice,* which concerns an older man's poignant and frustrated longing for a younger. Reflecting back

11. Simpson, quoted in Unterecker, *Voyager,* 753.

over his experience with Crane may, of course, simply have given Spratling another unforeseen opportunity afforded by the autobiography to say something important about himself and his life; and it was while *File on Spratling* was in preparation that in an interview with Faulkner's biographer he looked back even further than 1931, to August of 1925, identifying a homosexual encounter—omitted in the autobiographical account—that occurred during his European excursion with Faulkner when he was incarcerated overnight in the Genoa jail.[12] The whole Crane business, at any rate, must have been a close call for Spratling's reputation, especially at the moment when he was about to begin experimenting with a new commercial operation in the small town. Nevertheless, though the fact that he was gay was known and mildly accepted by his associates after he moved to Taxco-el-Viejo in the mid-forties, as it must have been also in the tolerant Vieux Carré community, he seems always, as he stated, to have effectively protected his "surroundings from any trace of scandal."

But Spratling did maintain his friendship with Crane, who, then returned to his rented house in Mexico City and living with Peggy Cowley, identified him as one of "a small group of quite interesting compatriots here which gathers occasionally at one or the other of our houses—most of whom are Guggenheim fellows like myself. Carleton Beals and his wife; Anita Brenner; Marsden Hartley, the painter, who has just arrived and who is wildly enthusiastic; Lesley Simpson (Univ. of California) and wife; Pierre and Caroline Durieux, head of General Motors here; Wm Spratling, whose book *Little Mexico* (just out) you ought to read, etc. Plenty of good company."[13]

The ready approval of *Little Mexico* and its unique interpretation of the Mexican scene by a group such as this, all of whom, though more or less temporary residents, in their writing and painting were also confronting what Lesley Simpson would call later "the New Land of Promise . . . a country that had solved the problem of living with itself," undoubtedly gave Spratling a new and permanent credibility. After all, neither he

12. See Chapter 2, above. The interview with Joseph Blotner is dated January 28, 1965. Faulkner almost certainly knew of the complete incident, and characteristically appropriated it for his fiction, as part of the raw material lying beneath such pieces as the unpublished *Elmer* and the story "Divorce in Naples"; see Joseph Blotner, *Faulkner: A Biography* (New York: Vintage Books, 1991), 162–64, 174–76.

13. Hart Crane to Solomon Grunberg, March 20, 1932; *Letters*, 404.

nor Frances Toor was planning to go back, and, before the others, each had breathed what Simpson went on to describe as "the invigorating air" that seemed to leave the Great Depression far to the north. But Simpson, writing his retrospective essay on the re-publication of *Little Mexico* in 1964 as *A Small Mexican World,* remembered that Spratling was generally absent from those gatherings, centered in Mexico City, of painters, scholars, and writers—all especially awed by the "towering figure of Diego Rivera," since "you rarely came to the city in those days, being fully occupied with your dream of reviving the ancient art of the silversmiths in Taxco."

How much Spratling was working in that direction, if at all, in the spring and summer of 1932 cannot be determined from his correspondence, since he makes no allusion whatsoever to this new possibility. Certainly there was no income from such a source: his August letter to Zigrosser, already quoted, stated that about all the money he could earn was from renting his horses to tourists. By then he had finally recovered from Cape and Smith his Rivera drawings, selling them rather quickly in Taxco. By January his predicament was so severe that, as he wrote to Zigrosser, "they've cut off the lights and there's no milk these days for the coffee—that's a nuisance." His reason for the letter was one more desperate attempt at income. He sent thanks for the "most welcome" check for six dollars, probably from a lithograph sale, and begged the favor of Zigrosser to send down any of the remaining Mexican art work that he had earlier sent to the Weyhe on commission. "Please mail me— preferably today—any Rivera watercolors which may be still with you. I can sell them here and it's almost ready cash. . . . [T]he Diegos—though I hate like the devil to let them go—can be sold here and probably better than in N.Y."

That he was right about this is substantiated by a brief correspondence between Frances Toor and Zigrosser about the salability of works, for example, by Rivera. Although Toor complained that tourists in Mexico City were scarce, she had managed some sales—a Rivera lithograph for twenty dollars—but she was disturbed by the rumor from New York that prices there had been lowered below those in her own gallery: "You must realize that we cannot ask higher prices here than those you are selling at in New York, especially these days when the dollar is up again to $3.50 (Mex.)." Zigrosser replied: "I am afraid that misinformation travels faster than correct information. The price of Orozco, Siqueiros, and

Rivera lithographs are just where they were. We tried an experiment for a short time of selling the lithograph by Rivera, Nude with Long Hair, and one by Orozco, The Family, for ten dollars but they did not sell any more at that price than at the regular price. Consequently, we returned them to the original price."[14]

While all of this illustrates the dismal state of sales in the center of the U.S. art world, it is also suggestive of the promising market for such things that was moving southward through Mexico City along the newly constructed highway connecting the capital with Taxco and Acapulco. Toor's observation that "no one in Mexico ever buys art" had been preceded by Spratling's in one of the 1931 Herald-Tribune pieces that "there is almost no such thing as a buying public in this country." Ah, but the tourists! They were finding their way to Taxco in increasing numbers, renting Spratling's horses for one thing, but also involving themselves in this "undiscovered" place with its expanding art colony. "Taxco unfortunately," Natalie Scott had written in the previous spring, "has lost one of its qualities which so much appealed to me, that of a snug remoteness. There are visitors, visitors these days, and a social-bohemian strain creeping in which is most sad. Many of the visitors are individually very interesting, but as a 'conjunto' they're saddening." It was undoubtedly the advent of a potential buying population such as this that for Spratling quickened the idea of the silver enterprise. His writing prospects had disappeared, the collapse of Cape and Smith had resulted in the paltriest of sales for Little Mexico, and he had long since spent the income from his Casa Mañana drawings. The psychological effects of the Depression may have been the same for Spratling, at least temporarily, as they were for Natalie—a kind of paralysis caused by what she called the "quivers." It would not be long before her generous and energetic spirit would find a new life in her care for the poor and crippled children of Taxco, just as her friend Bill would find another also. But now, having "received one of those random taps from the hammer of depression," as her letter continued, she had been forced to sell the Taxco house she had bought less than a year earlier (and had rented to Peggy Cowley) and "to which I had devoted myself ardently for several months, with the happiest results."[15]

14. W.S. to Carl Zigrosser, January 10, 1933; Frances Toor–Carl Zigrosser correspondence: December 24, 1932, February 14, 21, 1933.

15. Natalie Scott to Carl Zigrosser, May 3, 1932.

In addition to his financial woes, Spratling's health was poor toward the end of the year. By January of 1933, he was seriously ill, writing to Elizabeth Morrow about additional drawings she had requested: "I've been in bed with malaria 15 days & there's no immediate change to be hoped for—I'm alright in the mornings—except for a dizziness & weakness which make it impossible to do serious work . . . things are as well as can be expected—seem to have unlimited quantities of quinine." But within a week, he had worsened and had turned once more to her for help. In the last months she had experienced the death of her husband, felt the horror of the kidnapping and murder of her first Lindbergh grandchild, and watched the deteriorating health of her daughter Elisabeth. But, as always, she was generously responsive to Spratling. "I think you must be," he wrote,

> one of the kindest people in the whole world. It was terribly good of you to send the money. I hated having to ask you to do it. The malaria is finished but there resulted a funny business with the liver which necessitates an operation. When I wired the doctor had just advised me I'd have to enter hospital immediately & then on a second exam said I wouldn't have to go for a week or two. . . . The hospital is going to be a darn nuisance. However, if it weren't for you, I couldn't even have raised the wherewithal. You're a sweet and lovely person.

A notation in this letter suggests that Spratling was also trying to secure income from sales of artifacts, perhaps to some of Mrs. Morrow's friends: "Katherine Sullivan [her secretary] was awfully nice and wrote that there had been a bite concerning the masks. I'm wondering if the people were serious. If you see them you might tell them that if they like those things it's a good opportunity. It's really a pretty swell collection."[16]

It seems to have been here in 1933, forced to borrow money for his own health care, and at the lowest ebb of his fortunes and future outlook since moving to Mexico, that Spratling made his final and most oracular connection with the indigenous culture of his adopted country. Although in the autobiography and in the truly magisterial essay he published in 1956 on the history of modern silversmithing in Mexico, he alludes to 1931 as the initiating year of Las Delicias, what evidence there is suggests

16. W.S. to Elizabeth Morrow, January 3, 10, 1933.

he was not consistently engaged in the design and manufacture of silver objects at least until two years later. In an earlier and less comprehensive essay published in 1938, Spratling specifically states that the new Taxco industry "has actually come to life within the past five years," and that "five years ago the only work given to silversmiths was the occasional making of a string of gold beads, some silver trimmings for a saddle, or perhaps spoons were made for some old lady who happened to have a little silver in her possession and had no other use for it." In his personal correspondence with Uncle Leck and Aunt Miriam he made clear that 1933 was the initiating year of the Taller de las Delicias, writing, for example, in the January 1937 letter: "This shop which I started less than 4 years ago, with six workers & $160 pesos cash, now employs 80 people & is selling about $160,000 a year."[17] And four years later, still within the flush of the meteoric financial success of the new enterprise, he sent a copy of the 1938 article together with an informal account of his career to Aunt Miriam (who was preparing a talk for the Woman's Study Club of Lafayette, Alabama) in which he referred to the development of "the silver industry in Taxco since I started it in 1933." By then, the "Taller de las Delicias" had become "Spratling y Artesanos," and in a revised price list published in the next year, 1942, Spratling confirmed yet again the accurate date by re-printing the 1938 *Mexican Life* essay and blithely inserting in it a new paragraph: "The silversmiths in Taxco celebrate June 27 as their annual fiesta, 'El Dia de la Plata de Taxco.' This date also marks the founding of the Taller de las Delicias in 1933."[18]

The confused chronology here seems to be only a function of Spratling's uncertain memory—with only a slight touch of his re-invention tendency—as he tried in the 1956 essay and ten years later in the autobiography to recall events from a long perspective. Actually, however, his focus there on the importance of 1931 as the beginning period of something important in his creative life is accurate. As his other sources of

17. William Spratling, "Modern Mexican Silversmithing," *Mexican Art and Life* 3 (July 1938), 1–4; W.S. to Dr. and Mrs. L. W. Spratling, January 11, 1937.

18. W.S. to Mrs. L. W. Spratling, November 29, 1941; *Lista Plata Fina, Revised List, Fine Mexican Silver by Spratling*. The imprint date is March 10, 1942, and the name of the firm is given as "Spratling y Artesanos, S.A." The letter to Aunt Miriam in the previous year is written on stationery with the firm's name thus. This corrects yet another error in the posthumously arranged chronology in the autobiography, which gives 1945 as the date that "Taller de las Delicias" became "Spratling y Artesanos."

income were then disappearing, he began to experiment almost on the most rudimentary basis, using of course local artisans, in the organized manufacture of native crafts, but of furniture and of both decorative and functional objects made of tin, not silver. The silver impetus came later, although Spratling reverses the sequence in the autobiography, giving the impression that the Morrow-inspired industry was an immediate commercial success and that he, Spratling, only initiated the experiment with the expectation that it might well become self-supporting, thus allowing him the freedom to pursue his real vocation of writing. It is difficult to see how he might have felt then that he could write anything more definitive than *Little Mexico* regarding his own "inside observer" perspective; and he had essentially exhausted his sequence of essays with illustrative renderings of Colonial architecture. There was the possibility that he could compete, or at least share, in the scholarly interpretation of pre-Columbian artifacts already being undertaken by major academicians from the United States, but there was little profit in that direction.

But clarifying the chronology of his entrepreneurial movement into design and manufacturing actually gives proper credit to Spratling's independent perception and ingenious vision, stimulated as they no doubt were by the bleakness of his financial situation. The slow but modest economic promise of his designs in wood and in the traditional material of tin, which he described in the autobiography as "intensely Mexican" and the "poor man's silver," were natural links to a parallel experiment with silver, although Morrow's connection with the venture is not mentioned in any of Spratling's correspondence or early writing on the subject, and apparently appeared for the first time in the long essay on Mexican silver he published some twenty-five years later. According to a series of articles written for the *Mexico Magazine* and published in 1938, the configuration of Spratling initiatives and the town's rising eminence began with Spratling's rental of a small building, remote from the Plaza de la Borda, which initially housed a workshop area for six employees: three carpenters and three tinsmiths. This was prior to the 1932 publication of *Little Mexico*. The workers turned out designs by Spratling, and, as the account continues, for an original investment of thirty-five dollars and after a year or so of very tough going, the new products were sufficiently attracting the attention of "discerning" Mexicans as well as the *turistas* so as to justify expansion.

In 1933 Bill was ready to move into larger quarters. . . . So he arranged a lease on a low rambling building of eighteen rooms a block from the plaza facing Borda's pink cathedral. . . . Having worked in cramped quarters for so long, the spaciousness of the new quarters gave Bill several inspirations. There was ample room now for weavers to make serapes and why not silversmiths as well as tinsmiths and carpenters? Weren't there three alive silver mines on the outskirts of Taxco producing as fine a grade of silver as any other place in the world? The designs he would attend to himself. That was the part of the business he loved most.[19]

The account was written by Kim Schee, a friend of Spratling's and a frequent visitor-resident of the Taxco scene, and although it contains something of the easy-success story that Hollywood's *The Man from New Orleans* would emphasize a few years later, its specific details and close proximity to the events it describes give it a certain credibility. Moreover, it confirms Spratling's own chronology, published in the same year, in his first essay on the Taxco silver industry. And, too, it helps to explain the almost astonishing disparity between the mournful conditions of his finances as recorded in the early 1933 correspondence with Elizabeth Morrow and a singular allusion to him in a late 1934 number of the *Literary Digest*. In an article describing such places as Carmel, California, and Santa Fe, New Mexico, which were beginning to attract colonies of American writers and artists, and subsequently great numbers of tourists, Taxco is mentioned as just such a site in Mexico. And its principal artist-resident is Spratling. Not only is he identified, as quoted already, as "America's ambassador extraordinary of the arts," but also as painter, writer, and "the town's leading businessman . . . [who] has revived the native handicrafts in his *taller* where he employs sixty Indians."[20]

This high-profile allusion, accompanied by a photo and caption of a street scene in Taxco "where William Spratling sketches and writes," confirms on the one hand that the first half of his public persona was now complete. It had been achieved in about six years of Mexican residency and was based not only on *Little Mexico* and his *Herald-Tribune*

19. Kim Schee, "A Hollywood Scenarist Looks at Taxco's William Spratling," *Mexico Magazine,* October 1938, p. 6.

20. "Tourists Follow Artists to Nature's Hideouts," *Literary Digest,* December 15, 1934, p. 24.

pieces, but also on his having sustained in publication after publication the writer–architectural artist mode of antiquarian interpretation he had brought southward from New Orleans. In addition, his "ambassadorship" had been enhanced through his significant involvements in the artistic traffic between the Mexican Renaissance and the U.S. gallery and exhibition milieu. Though this first "half" of his identity would be less enduring than the other, now just emerging, the one was nevertheless a critical preparation for the second. In his essay on Spratling and Taxco, Schee notes that Spratling's only collateral for his initial investment in the furniture and tin shop was "a few orders Bill had picked up from friends living in Cuernavaca." These were probably friends of the Morrows, and perhaps the Morrows themselves who in 1930–1931 were still intensely interested in furnishing their beloved Casa Mañana with authentic Mexicana, perhaps even then planning to retain it once the ambassadorship was over. Indeed, the story about Morrow's advice may have taken the original form of his suggesting to Spratling the development of a general native crafts experiment, which, properly organized, could be commercially successful and would benefit the woeful economy of Taxco. And it was Spratling, as Schee maintained, who concluded that the difficult experiment with silver might be attempted following the little shop's success with the more readily workable materials of wood and tin.

However this may have been, the years 1933 and 1934 formed an intensely committed and dramatically successful period for Spratling, as for the first time he began to combine the discipline of his architectural pencil with his rich impressions of Mexican history and artistic motifs. His correspondence in January 1933 is written on plain unlined paper, but at least by the end of 1934 he was using an elaborate letterhead advertising the four products of the new shop, whose display and salesroom, together with a workroom of about the same size, were now located in his own house:

PLATERIA CON PLATA TAXQUEÑA, SARAPES DE PURA LANA, HOJALATA
MEXICANA, EBANISTERIA CON MADERAS DE LA TIERRA CALIENTE

WILLIAM SPRATLING
TALLER DE LAS DELICIAS
CALLE DE LAS DELICIAS 26
TAXCO, GUERRERO
MEXICO

The two endpapers of *File on Spratling* are reproductions of the "maps"
that Spratling had drawn, respectively, of his house at 23 Calle de las
Delicias (*"la casa de Guillermo Spratling y tambien de sus amigos"*) and
of the "Rancho y Talleres de Spratling" at Taxco-el-Viejo. From the scale
of the first drawing, probably executed in 1933 or 1934, there appears
to be room for about twelve or so workstations in the *taller*. In the 1938
essay, the Taller de las Delicias is referred to as being "formerly located"
on that street and employing almost one hundred workers; thus most of
the native-crafts manufacturing must by 1935 or so have been located in
La Aduana ("The Customs House"), the large building rented in 1933,
which was itself subsequently called "Las Delicias." What Natalie described, below, in her 1935 letter as the "elegant" display-sales room
may have remained for a time in Spratling's house on Calle de las Delicias, which was not far from La Aduana.

And a letter written by Natalie Scott to a New Orleans friend early in
1935 on this very stationery seems to confirm that Spratling in a very
short time had indeed become "the town's leading businessman," that
the nearly completed Mexican National Highway was making picturesque and unspoiled Taxco readily accessible to a stream of international
tourists, and that the success of Las Delicias was already creating its imi-
tators:

> At the moment, I am keeping Bill Spratling's shop for him, while he has
> gone off on a trip of some sort, as sudden as the kind I like to take. He
> looked a bit weary and fagged these past couple of weeks, so I was glad to
> see him have a change; but the life of a salesgirl is monotonous. The shop
> is very elegant—I think that you would like a lot of the things, very interest-
> ing designs in silver and in tin, and some really stunning sarapes.
>
>   The customers vary greatly, little eager, rat-faced tourists sometimes,
> would-be aesthetes, hard-boiled business men, and so on. Had an awfully
> amusing time with a couple from Switzerland who tried to set me down on
> prices; whereupon I sent a little boy from the shop with them to show them
> the work of other silversmiths in the town. They came back and bought
> extravagantly for their home in Switzerland, and the old boy eventually
> told me that this was the only place in Mexico where he had bought any-
> thing![21]

21. Natalie Scott to Mrs. Samuel G. Robinson, January 8, 1935, Natalie Scott Papers,
Manuscripts Department, Tulane University Library.

The last five years of the thirties were probably the happiest of Spratling's life, and certainly among the most prosperous, in that his personal and artistic gifts had finally found their proper setting. In 1935 the organizational dimensions of Las Delicias—with perhaps fifty employees— were such that they could be monitored effectively by a single *patrón,* and the shop showed no tendency toward the disastrous over-expansion and decentralized authority that would bring about its demise in the next decade. It was, of course, Spratling's first experience since leaving his teaching post at Tulane with an uninterrupted income. Even after Christmas, business was so brisk that Natalie could hardly handle the sales alone: "Keeping Bill's shop is a job, all day, and heavy going at times. Awfully nice shop, with really fine workmanship and materials. You may imagine how busy it is when I tell you that I've been three days trying to write this."[22]

There must have been for Spratling a certain exhilaration about it all, not the least of which would have been his awareness that his efforts were doing something positive for the economy of Taxco and for its future too, since the majority of the shop's employees were young people, apprentices who would learn a new trade that was yet an old one, coming to life again under the guidance of Don Guillermo. And he seemed especially to enjoy his new eminence as ambassador-of-the-arts to those groups now regularly arriving in the quaint colonial town:

> I first encountered William Spratling in the spring of 1935 as a member of a painting class brought to Taxco by the New York artist Wayman Adams. Spratling was a gregarious individual with great personal charm and once he found out we were there he invited Adams and the rest of us to a reception at his home where we were introduced to other American residents. His home was on the Calle de las Delicias which ascends from the main plaza at a steep incline. We arrived somewhat breathless and very thirsty after the climb and immediately began to drink from a large bowl what we judged to be the best lemonade we had ever tasted. It was *tequila con limonada* and some of the older members of the class were unable to leave the party on schedule because they could not hold a steady course down the hill.[23]

22. Natalie Scott to "Pam" (daughter of Mrs. Samuel G. Robinson), January 8, 1935; Natalie Scott Papers.

23. Maltby Sykes, unpublished notes for an essay on Spratling's designs, in possession of the author.

Where in the early thirties Spratling usually did not have the money for travel to the United States, his frequent trips now to New York, New Orleans, and elsewhere—especially his notable flight on the *Hindenburg* to Berlin in 1936, which he memorably recalled in the autobiography— form an image of his rising prosperity. A comprehensive view of the good state of his business affairs at this time may be seen in a long letter he sent to Uncle Leck and Aunt Miriam on January 11, 1937. The letter, first, is important in recording the organizational evolution of Las Delicias. "In spite of myself," I have, Spratling wrote,

> . . . become the complete business man. . . . I have just completed the shop's incorporation as a Ltd. (*Sociedad Anónima*) and all the stock is my own, and its internal organization, entirely my own solution, is practically finished & complete. There are 4 departments, with heads, subheads, etc., & about 12 people in the office & sales. We are making the best things in Mexico, particularly in silver. The thing has acquired an amazing amount of fame in so short a time. Of course I am not rich—have saved very little. It has almost all, apart from what I fling away, gone into the creation and completion of the shop. But I own my house and car & some danes & a dachsund, keep an apt. in Mexico City & manage to have a small dollar acct in N.Y.

The "four departments" were probably those organized to fashion the products advertised in the shop's printed literature: furniture, textiles, tinwork, and, of course, silvercraft. The arrangement as described by Spratling in 1937 as almost complete was implicit almost from the beginning of the new venture with the "heads, subheads, etc." being especially evident in the most sophisticated and complex of the four disciplines, as illustrated in the 1934 photograph of the pre–Las Delicias organization, El Taller de Platería al Señor Guillermo Spratling. Here the hierarchical structure of the *taller* is already in place and would remain essentially the same even though it would expand horizontally as the scale of production increased in response to sales. At the center, or "top," of the structure of course was the creative figure, the designer—Spratling himself. At the next two tiers appear the principal production and managerial staff of the *taller,* who in their early stages would have shared the responsibility for quality control with Spratling. Although "*jefe*" and "*sub-jefe*" are the organizational names given to the two highest members, they are in fact a "maestro," and assistant maestro, or master silversmiths skilled in all dimensions of the craft and responsible for the final fabrication of Spratling's designs. Two apprentice maestros, working their way toward the level of independent artistry, complete the group, and it is they who most closely supervise the "etc" in Spratling's letter: the six original "*ayudantes*," or assistants to the apprentice maestros, and the eight *aprendizes:* fetchers, pounders, polishers—but most of all, learners through their participation in a series of reflective exercises designed by Spratling to teach them the connection between the part and the whole.

The photograph, while not illustrating the genius of Spratling as designer, pictorially suggests the interwoven qualities that made Las Delicias the brilliant creation which would become the model for those later and even larger *talleres* in Taxco that would flourish long after the decline of the original. The analogy with his silvercraft is not exact, but Spratling as an occasional practicing architect was experienced in directing skilled labor toward the completion of a three-dimensional design. And though the vertical organization of his first *taller* may seem obvious enough for bringing a visual concept into a production capability, there was little, if any, precedent for it within the wide and ancient spectrum of Mexican native crafts. The structural hierarchy of Las Delicias was itself, however, a direct response to Spratling's initiation for the industry of the essential role of entrepreneur, creating a commercial connection between production and a clearly identified market. As he wrote to Aunt Miriam and Uncle Leck, he owned *all* the stock in the little corporation and the "solution" to production was *entirely* his. What he didn't specify in the dramatic success story was his unique capacity for a shrewd market analysis. As one who had been an "outsider" but was now an "insider," he possessed the ironic perspective to see that those very *turistas* whose occasional condescension and superficiality he had satirized in *Little Mexico* were the only buying public he could count on. Certainly, as he had long known from his first experience with the exhibition-sale of Impressionist art in Mexico City, there was none to be found among Mexicans, especially in economically depressed Taxco. Within a few short years, his silver designs in jewelry and tableware would be purchased by distinguished diplomats and movie stars, and he would eventually receive such international commissions as that of Emperor Haile Selassie for four dozen table settings. But now, for those U.S. and European Depression-era travelers who could afford the trip in the first place, he would offer things distinctly Mexican, of high quality, and at a modest price. "We are making the *best* things in Mexico, particularly in silver."[24]

Entrepreneurial vision, location, proper organization—all these, together with an inexpensive workforce, would have been enough for commercial success. But in addition to bringing all this together, there was a further Spratling touch that was essential for the imprinting of his name on the artistic and economic history of twentieth-century Mexico. This was his active encouragement among the young apprentices within the *taller* of that innate sense of form and line which years ago he had been taught by Rivera, Frances Toor, and Dr. Atl to observe in the drawings, painting, and sculpture of Mexican children. What seems unmistakably clear from the new enterprise's organizational coherence and, also, from occasional incidents released from their mnemonic repose into the printed file is that to Spratling the Mexican silversmiths and apprentices in his employ were actually his colleagues in his efforts and responsibility as a designer to, in his word, "dignify" the native materials—silver, tin, wood, fabrics—from which his art was formed. He was engaged with them in sustaining a folk-art, an art of handwork by a people "happily unburdened with instruction whose imagination could be freely translated into their products." And this art was in strong contrast to what he regarded as the "abnormal" style of mass production in the United States, where people "no longer respect those who work with their hands."

For the *ayudante* lucky enough to be chosen to work in Don Guillermo's *taller de platería,* there was, suddenly, a chance for a professional future—a chance to find a place in a promising economic structure unknown in this remote village since the eighteenth century. And if there is something of that hope and confidence mirrored in their large serious eyes as, uniformly non-smiling, they gaze at us now from this photograph of some sixty-odd years ago, it was well-founded indeed. For by the end of the decade, some of the original fourteen apprentices—Antonio Pineda and one of the Castillo brothers among them—would work their way toward a maestro identity for themselves and would de-

24. W.S. to Dr. and Mrs. L. W. Spratling, January 11, 1937. The detail of the forty-eight place settings for Haile Selassie is recorded in a letter from Spratling to his brother David, May 22, 1955, Collection of Mrs. Paula Wester. The letter is now in the Auburn University Archives.

part with Spratling's blessing from Las Delicias, taking with them what they had learned there into creative lives of their own, their splendid designs helping to ensure the Taxco continuum initiated by Spratling.[25]

That continuum eventually would enclose literally thousands of workshops, many of them of the "cottage" variety, in which an individual artisan would fabricate under contract design variations from the various *talleres* that would be sold in the scores of shops surrounding the plaza or located on the hilly streets. Given the small scale of the first year or two of Las Delicias, however, there was undoubtedly within the organization a camaraderie and agile coherence that reflected the enthusiasm and quick intelligence of its leader. Even though the number of workers had increased dramatically by 1937, with the silver department no longer located in Spratling's home, this feeling seemed still to be present, as suggested in Spratling's recollection in the autobiography of how, once in that year he had reached the Mexican coast during his long sailing voyage from California to Acapulco, he wired the Taxco shop to draw lots for two of the smiths to fly over to Mazatlán for the rest of the trip. Their decision, instead, was a symbolic gesture of organizational identity, as by acclamation they sent over the senior maestro and the youngest apprentice to share with the boss his adventure. A delegation from the shop met the boat in Acapulco, as recorded by Kim Schee, with a gift good-humoredly fashioned just for him: a silver medal showing a *conquistador* figure, engraved "Nuestro intrépido Marinero."

That senior maestro, Alfonso Mondragon, appears as the "*jefe*" in the 1934 photograph, and his continuance with the *taller* at least until 1937 suggests that for several years the original administrative-production personnel remained in place. However, while Spratling makes clear that the innovative organization grew sequentially within the entrepreneurial vision, he is not particularly helpful on the evolution of his own essential role as designer, especially of decorative artwork in silver. Some assistance in this direction is provided by the recollections of the "*sub-jefe*" in the 1934 photograph, Artemio Navarrete, who outside of Spratling himself seems to be the person most closely linked to the initiation of

25. For an analysis of the production dynamics within the silver industry from the late thirties to the late fifties, with some attention to the Spratling and Castillo brothers' *talleres,* see Gobi Stromberg, "The Marketing and Production of Innovation: The Taxco Silver Industry" (Ph.D. dissertation, University of California, Berkeley, 1976).

the silver enterprise. If the photograph is a contemporary likeness, he appears to be much younger than Spratling. Even so, he was probably well into his seventies when he was interviewed about the pre–Las Delicias period, and his memory here and there may be no more reliable than Spratling's—he recalls, for example, first meeting Don Guillermo "around 1925," before, of course, Spratling's first visit to Mexico and probably at least two years before Spratling got as far south as Iguala, Navarrete's home. Still, his remembered details of their early relationship are more specific than Spratling's generalized recollection and, moreover, harmonize well with the reasonable thesis that the whole commercial experiment with silvercraft, visionary as it may have been, was less spontaneous and more carefully planned and tested than one might assume from Spratling's account.[26]

In the autobiography, Spratling mentions only that, with what had become by then the Morrow-inspired idea of the silver enterprise in his mind, he persuaded "two boys who were good goldsmiths" to move in 1931 to Taxco from Iguala, long a site for fine work in gold jewelry, but not in the much less respected metal of silver. In the long and definitive 1956 essay on the history of Mexican silversmithing, he specifically names Navarrete as "a young silversmith from Iguala" who moved to Taxco "to work for a small silver shop, founded with the germ of an idea," and was the "nucleus" who began "to form silversmiths." In his own account, Navarrete confirms that he did move to Taxco on Spratling's invitation but only after Spratling on several occasions had sought him out in Iguala: "Don Guillermo visited my small workshop in Iguala and ordered a silver ring which I was to make following his design and using a stone he provided. Later, he placed other orders that I made following his designs, ornamenting the articles with Grecian frets and using the stones, generally jade or onyx, which were then found in that area. It was difficult for me to follow his instructions because I could neither read nor write and, in addition, spoke no English." Don Guillermo was very pleased with the contractual relationship; the two became friends, and Navarrete recalls that, on arriving in Taxco, it was Siqueiros, in 1931 still living in his Taxco exile, who elaborated to him Spratling's idea of a

26. See Lucia Garcia-Noriega Nieto, "Mexican Silver and the Taxco Style," trans. Ahmed Simeon, *Journal of Decorative and Popular Arts* (fall, 1988), 42–53. Quotations from an interview with Navarrete appear on p. 44.

workshop "right here in his home." Navarrete began to work at his little table "all by myself," with Spratling's weekend visitors beginning to "buy everything I made."

According to Navarrete's version, which seems reasonable enough, it was he who began to invite neighborhood children to help wash, beat, and polish the silver, for which Spratling was willing to pay. And it was probably when the number of boys began to expand the limits of the workstation space available in the large room shown in Spratling's "map" of 23 Calle de las Delicias, that the second of the "two boys" was invited from Iguala, the more senior artisan Mondragon, who, like Navarrete, was not only fully skilled in ornamentation and fabrication, but also possessed the essential maestro ability to translate a design concept into finished product. Thus was the *platería* initiated, moving over a three-year period from a one-man operation, which was commercially tested in miniature against the market that Spratling's network of friends and acquaintances external to Taxco was uniquely capable of creating, toward the organizational pattern illustrated in the 1934 photograph.

Of the four craft-manufacturing processes at Las Delicias, the most complex by far in its treatment of the basic raw material was that of artwork in silver. The mineral wealth in the mountainous terrain surrounding Taxco had, of course, been mined long before the Spaniards arrived. But as early as 1524, following the conquest of Montezuma and the city of Tenochtitlán, Cortéz, desperate for metals critical for weaponry casting, wrote to the Emperor Charles V that he had been informed "by the grace of God, who has ever been swift to supply us with what we lack" that deposits of both tin and iron were readily available "in the province of Tazco some seven and twenty leagues from this city."[27] The subsequent discovery in the area of rich veins of silver hastened the advent of organized mining by the Spaniards. It was thus Taxco silver that was among the very first precious metals to be mined and exported throughout the sixteenth century from New Spain, finding its way to such remote places as Corunna in Portugal, where the paymasters of El Rey, Philip II, were supervising the construction of the Invincible Armada. And it was from Taxco four centuries later that the first silver art objects were exported to Europe from the Western Hemisphere. Sprat-

27. Hernan Cortes, *Five Letters, 1519–1526*, trans. J. Bayard Morris (New York: Norton, 1928), 274–5.

ling may have known from his very first design for a Navarrete fabrication that he was potentially resurrecting an art with an ancient tradition of ornamental distinction. In pre-Conquest Mexico, as he expressed it later in his review of the silver industry, silver was rarer than gold and, being more difficult to work, was highly prized. His further observation that, among discoveries of pre-Columbian jewelry, the number of gold pieces far outnumbered those of silver would seem to be illustrated by evidence in the remarkable archaeological excavations beginning in 1925 at the famous Tomb 7 at Monte Albán in Oaxaca. There the gold ornamental pieces were not only more numerous but, in contrast to the relatively simple designs of the silver ones, more elaborate and delicately carved in their workmanship.[28]

Economic historians would find it difficult to quarrel with Spratling's further observation that the phenomenal development of the silver industry in Taxco is without a modern parallel in its rapidity and distinctive quality. All the more remarkable for this small, poverty-stricken town was that within the relatively short period of the thirties decade it emerged as the "Florence of Mexico" and was on the verge of international reputation—this from a native craft nurtured from the beginning under almost primitive conditions and dependent for its commercial survival on sales to a tourist trade inhibited by the Depression and the threat of World War II. And, incontrovertibly, Spratling was at the center of everything. The financial risk he took was not great, on a matter of scale; he had almost no money to invest. But the venture was, as we have seen, almost a last shot at independence and economic survival. Yet as critical to him as the experiment was, it seems impossible to dissociate the personal from his anticipation that he was potentially forming a partnership with "Little Mexico" itself, whose character he had defined and praised in the manuscript he was just completing when he made his first investigative trips to Iguala. That he seemed especially preoccupied in the early going, when he was also weakened by his bouts with malaria, is indicated by the observations of Natalie, the person who knew him best. In her May 1932 letter to Zigrosser in which she laments her own financial problems, she wrote that during her recent visit to New Orleans, "Bill was more than usually high-handed in my affairs while I was gone, so

28. See Alfonso Caso, "Monte Albán, Richest Archaeological Find in America," *National Geographic,* October 1932, 487–512.

relations are a bit strained there." Had he, without telling, borrowed from her for the new enterprise? Perhaps. But it's "such a waste of effort to resent Bill," she went on, suggesting his obliviousness to everything beyond the range of his focused concentration, "as he is genuinely quite color-blind in imaginative comprehension to the rights of others. And generous and well-intentioned as far as his vision does go." Probably at no time in his career was his capacity for disciplined intensity so crucial.

Still, without Spratling's most original contribution to the Mexican Renaissance, all that he was organizationally bringing together would have produced a *taller* with a dubious future, unimaginatively replicating colonial images as native artisans had been doing for a hundred years. His genius as a designer and his seminal influence on the silversmithing art in their own distinctive ways formed a cultural parallel to the great public creativity of his friends Rivera, Orozco, and Siqueiros. For that resurrected art form incorporated, as he himself would write in his retrospective review of the Taxco miracle, "a new understanding of an entire racial background and sense of plastic, including pre-Columbian."

During the last several decades, as the reputation of his art and, of course, the commercial value of his work have enormously accelerated, descriptions of the Spratling style have properly and uniformly emphasized its elegant simplicity; the quality of its finish; its striking fusion of pre-Hispanic folk symbols and Aztec and Mayan design motifs with both the sweeping curves of Art Deco and the restraint of Cubist patterns; and its combination in both ornamental and utilitarian tableware and serving pieces of silver with rosewood, ebony, and such semi-precious stones— all available in Guerrero—as jade, onyx, amethyst, and turquoise. Such descriptions typically encompass the full range of Spratling's design career, one of the most significant portions occurring long after Spratling y Artesanos had disappeared: his experience, commissioned in the mid-forties by the U.S. Department of the Interior, with Alaskan Eskimo culture, which profoundly affected his work and is reflected most dramatically in his North Star jewelry series. Both his early and late work, however, in its international character, its ancient motifs and sophisticated modernity, is "unmistakable," a description—with which Spratling naturally concurred—used in the first scholarly treatment of the history of Mexican jewelry.[29]

29. Mary L. Davis and Greta Pack, *Mexican Jewelry* (Austin: University of Texas Press, 1963), 179.

Spratling's observations on his own design style are infrequent and unspecific. However, in a fine critical passage on the concept of style itself, he makes clear that his was a slow growth:

> STYLE is that elusive and precious element which is usually a result of years of searching and attempting and designing with all the strength of one's personal convictions. After many half-successes and not a few outright failures, it is possible, if luck is with you, to begin to show a certain recognizeable trend in your work, and then at long last, if people want to be nice about it, they will begin to mention so-and-so's style. In other words, style is not acquired overnight, no matter how good a draftsman you are (or have employed), or by simply deciding to adopt a style, starting from scratch with an "original drawing" or something seen in Ladies Home Companion. It is built as you build a house, with one brick and then another fitted to it, at the same time maintaining an original concept and an objective, which becomes a growth.[30]

A slow growth indeed, for—as implied throughout this study—Spratling's early life and steady accumulation of diverse artistic experiences were all an unknowing preparation for the unexpected opportunity awaiting in Taxco his transforming hand. In the autobiography he recalled that in the matter of his collecting pre-Columbian art, his interest was not essentially to secure archaeological information but with "the sensing of three-dimensional form. . . . Collecting sculpture has to do with one's sensitivities in an intimate way. One feeds on it. If I have acquired any archaeological knowledge, it has been by osmosis." One could proceed further and affirm that one of the most characteristic elements of the Spratling style, his imaginative use of ancient religious and folklore symbols, was also acquired by osmosis, by his travels throughout Little Mexico, his immersion in its culture, and his verbal and visual re-incarnations of it before he ever conceived of Las Delicias. Educated as an architect and trained to think three-dimensionally, translating two-dimensional designs on paper into three-dimensional forms of a prescribed material, he seemed to think of his silver designs as small sculptures, as created analogues to the miniature lapidary artifacts which he found in the mountainous regions of Guerrero and which, as we have seen through allusions in his turn-of-the-decade correspondence, he was already "swappin' " with Rivera and others.

30. Spratling, "Twenty Five Years of Mexican Silversmithing, 89.

Spratling's principles of design and his concepts of drawing were already established before he came to Mexico. His reliance on what he clearly identified in the autobiography as his "background" allowed him "to take up where other people left off and achieve a certain amount of improvement in the silver, the tin, the furniture and the weavings, since an architect is primarily concerned with materials and their possibilities, particularly in design." This presupposes, of course, that to a designer changes in scale have little effect on the principles involved in resolving a given problem, whether it be a new hotel on the Mississippi Gulf coast or a pair of earrings. And though it may be an over-simplification, Spratling, to begin designing silver, essentially had only to familiarize himself with the working properties of the metal and to adjust his designs to the specialized techniques employed by the *jefes* who would execute the pieces.

Born precisely at the turn of the century, Spratling in his professional education and in his associations with faculty colleagues at Auburn and Tulane would have been influenced by the significant transition from the imitative and revivalist design principles of the nineteenth century to those of the twentieth, which found their earliest expression in the integrations of form and function in the work of architects Louis Sullivan and, later, Frank Lloyd Wright. Spratling's architectural training provided him with an understanding of function, construction, and ornament, a combination well-suited to the design of tourist items such as tableware, housewares, furniture, and even jewelry—which, as with utilitarian objects, also has an essential function, that of adornment, which can be expressed in the design of its varied forms. He had taught engineering drawing as well as graphics, and every review of his own pre-Mexico artwork emphasized and praised the discipline of his images and the control of his rendering hand. Even his writing, the essays and *Little Mexico*, exhibit what the *Times-Picayune* reviewer of the latter called the "precision" of his style. There the selection of detail, the use of quotation and anecdote—the ornamentations of the narrative line—are fully integrated with the intended function: to draw, as it were, or to sculpt, an indigenous and isolated society living in the twentieth century but whose view of the world was marked by racial memories of oppression and ancient ritual.

Spratling did, of course, bring much more to his ultimate vocation than architectural perception, a precise pencil, and a sense of modern design principles. Indeed, his preparatory years, as we have seen, contained an experience not without a limited parallel to those of the great Mexican muralists of the twenties and thirties, or even to that of Faulkner, all of whom had either painted or written themselves through the artistic environments of Europe—and also, of course, in Faulkner's case, New Orleans—assimilating such experiences into new beginnings as their artistic visions confronted and were shaped by the revolutionary and mythic history of their native traditions. Spratling's achievement was, at the least, distinctive in that his fusion of modernity was with a tradition not native to him, one that he had to learn, by "osmosis" surely, but also by disciplined study.

Being free from indigenous claims on his art undoubtedly helped Spratling to avoid the repetitiveness and apathy that had gradually encompassed much of Mexican designs in silver jewelry and household objects. And though the stunning discoveries of Mixtec and Zapotec motifs in the wide range of ornamental pieces found at Monte Albán in 1932 would have quickened the imagination of any designer working in Mexico, Spratling for years in his thousands of published and unpublished drawings during his travels throughout Mexico had seen and sketched the animals, fish, fruit, serpents, and other symbols as they appeared on Indian pottery and in the cheerful subversions wrought by native craftsmen beneath the great domes of Colonial religious architecture. Perhaps the most original accomplishment of his art was to produce designs with an unmistakably inherent Indian feeling but whose origins are subsumed in the whole history of Mexico's ancient iconography.[31]

Like many American artists in the early years of the century who had no recourse in their apprenticeship to a highly developed tradition in their own country of painting, sculpture, and design, Spratling's outlook was enriched by his exposure to the European influences whose standards were then the measure of acceptance and quality in American art. The first and most important of such exposures was that which augmented his self-taught and self-imposed drawing program and which he recorded so enthusiastically in his teenage correspondence to his brother: the eight-week experience in the summer of 1919 at the Beaux Arts School and Art Students League in New York. In addition to the intensive periods each day in sculpture, drawing, and watercolor rendering,

31. See Davis and Pack, *Mexican Jewelry*, 14 for commentary on a specific design.

he would have learned much from his observation of other classes; the League was democratic in character and the teaching methods as varied as the teachers themselves, who were selected from the most distinguished artists working in New York at the time. That it was, as he wrote to David in the letter, already quoted, "immensely" enjoyable and made him "chock-full of ideas" may be correlated with his initiation at this time of the sketchbook and portfolio of memorabilia that he would retain for the rest of his life and that covered the period between the New York weeks of study and his first trip, on the SS *Oskaloosa,* to Europe in the summer of 1921, entries ceasing once he began to publish his renderings of the New Orleans scene. The contents of the sketchbook partially illustrate the range of Spratling's drawing experiences during these formative pre-professional years, together with those he executed for editions of the college yearbook, the prize-winning medallion designs for architecture classes, and his sketches for the plastic molds to be cast in bronze bas-relief portraits. While some of the New York sketches are routine figure assignments, many are those beyond what he could engage in Alabama: nineteenth-century public statuary groups, monumental archways and pedestals with classical ornamentation, large-scale structural perspectives such as Grand Central Station interiors and the skylines from St. Johns and Hoboken, and numerous museum furniture, sculpture, and decorative holdings. The best drawings in the book are those of Renaissance filigree metalwork at the Metropolitan, the one continuous form he would study and draw extensively for *The Wrought Iron Work of Old New Orleans,* and would also see on gateway and window ornamentation throughout Mexico, and whose complex sinuous curves would be expressed in his jewelry designs.

These youthful and buoyant confrontations with the urban shapes of America's greatest city and the enclosure in its public monuments and museum possessions of European influences in design occurred at a time when Billy Spratling was successfully resolving his family stresses and sense of self-worth. This would shortly evolve into the truly cosmopolitan portion of his artistic education as he sketched and sketched and sketched the architectural forms and ornamentations of Gothic and Romanesque in Normandy, Belgium, France, and Italy (where Faulkner talked continuously of love and death); and subsequently those of the Spanish-French inheritance in the Vieux Carré, those of the Old South, and, finally, those of New Spain. This rich texture of experience, together with his antiquarian sensibility and his verbal descriptions of these icons of the past within a polyform of space, architectural time, and human history, all contributed to the substructure of the international style in design that was slowly evolving when in January of 1937 he wrote his confident letter to Aunt Miriam and Uncle Leck that the organization of his enterprise was "almost complete."

9

"Tell Them I'll Be There"

With its retrospective content, the 1937 letter to Alabama is also important, along with the essay Spratling wrote a few months later for *Mexican Art and Life*, in that together they may serve as convenient signals to mark the close of his apprenticeship period. "Convenient" rather than precise. But at least by the end of 1937 the work produced by Las Delicias had gained throughout Mexico a reputation for originality and superior quality. If the total internal organization was not yet complete, it was fully engaged in multi-crafts production, with forty-six of the almost one hundred craftsmen working in silver. Every article of the latter was still meticulously handcrafted, assuming its final identity from its inception as a two-dimensional design through a three-dimensional modeling, modification, and fabrication-finishing under the maestro's supervision. By 1937, of course, the primitive conditions of five years earlier as described in Navarrete's one-man operation—the melting down of one-peso coins to secure the malleable silver ("in a brazier, without a blow-torch because we had no electricity"), the physical polishing of the final article against the forearm—had been replaced by some mechanized processes. Also, silver was being purchased in ingots directly from the mines and purified by metallurgists at the shop, and tools and molds designed by Spratling were facilitating the manufacturing process. And Spratling had by then himself designed and supervised the construction of a commodious hotel, thus enhancing the natural tourist attractions of Taxco as well as extending his own sales market.

It was time for some perspective, both personal and professional. The letter home, affectionate and reminiscent in tone, seems to look back to so much of Spratling's early life. It began with his apology for not writing or visiting Alabama, but "you mustn't think that I don't think of you all and of the plantation and Opelika." He wanted to be remembered to all the family, to Aunt Mary Willie, Maude, and Corinne: "Tell them that I will eventually be there & that I expect a barbeque at least. I'll bring some tequila and the firecrackers. Give all my best when you see them— Cousin Leila & good old Prof. Biggin—and for you & Uncle Leck much love and a warm embrace." Much of the letter described a meeting with David, whose Coast Guard vessel had put into Acapulco on the first of January, with Spratling flying down for a short visit. They re-read their letters from Alabama and "talked at length of you all with a great deal of affection." It was "even a pleasanter meeting than I had hoped for—& I think we were both made very happy by it. Just going up and down the coast in the car—a good dinner with lobsters—a launch out to island and swimming & then an awful lot of beer and reminiscing that evening (until 2 a.m.)—a regular sailor's holiday." David, who, like himself, had graying hair, appeared to him "maturer," and he was pleased to see that the men on the boat seemed to like him and respect him.

He noted in the same letter that he had kept up with his New Orleans roommate of ten years before, writing that "I have just finished a book of translations & really should go to NY about it. And coming back I want to go by California where I am supposed to stay awhile with Wm Faulkner and perhaps I'll buy a sloop and sail it back to Acapulco." Within a few months he would realize both of these projections, describing in another fine passage in the autobiography how he sailed the boat he purchased in California, a twenty-four-footer, from Santa Monica to Acapulco. If that account from its thirty-year perspective may have been slightly embroidered in the narrator's favor, the voyage, which took over a month with Spratling having little if any sailing experience, was still a memorable achievement, illustrating in another mode the kind of plural capability that marked Spratling's career. The visit to Faulkner occurred in April of 1937, when Spratling "unexpectedly," according to Faulkner's biographer, turned up. The old friendship was re-kindled for a few days, with Spratling borrowing Faulkner's car and the two doing what Spratling recalled in "Chronicle of a Friendship" some "quiet drinking" together. But his visit coincided with one of the unhappiest and most alcoholic of Faulkner's Hollywood periods. Both Estelle and Jill Faulkner were present at the meal Spratling shared with the family, as recorded both in *File on Spratling* and in the Faulkner biography, where he witnessed the extent of Faulkner's drinking—from which he passed out, with Spratling visiting him next day at the hospital.[1]

---

1. Spratling's recollection is corroborated by Joseph Blotner, *Faulkner: A Biography*

Like much of Spratling's correspondence, the letter is an important validation of strains in his personal life that rarely emerge in the public persona, which, even then in 1937, was developing toward the almost legendary status it would assume by the time of his death. Here, of course, is illustrated again his continuing affection and loyalty to his Alabama family, who, along with his college years, seemed to form a retrospective image of stability as he gradually grew more isolated from them. "I assure you I'm still most anxious to get back to Alabama," he wrote in a later letter to Aunt Miriam, "from time to time I feel a real nostalgia for those days on the plantation and for a life at cousin Leila's and with the ΠKA bunch. In the back of my brain though there's an inescapable conviction that those sorts of things cannot be revived."[2] And his allusion to Faulkner, who somehow he then knew was writing for the movies in Hollywood, perhaps reinforced his understanding of how important the whole New Orleans experience had been to him, how fortunate he'd been to come to know Faulkner when each was unknown, and how good it would be to see him again now that both their careers had assumed a similar trajectory of accomplishment. That experience, of course, was not an isolated one: Spratling frequently re-visited New Orleans, and Natalie was permanently in Taxco, as was Elizabeth Anderson by 1937, fully involved in her new career as fashion designer; and Caroline Durieux was a frequent visitor too. His promise that he would return to Alabama—bringing with him a bit of Mexican holiday—would not, of course, be realized for another twenty-five years. Now, however, his nostalgic boyhood, family, and college memories from Gold Hill and Auburn had no less a validity than those associations from New Orleans. He had transcended each place, but all had become coherently linked, would always be permanently "there," in the personal chronology that had brought him to Taxco.

The essay he wrote during those months for a forthcoming *Mexican Art and Life* number is a quick survey of the silver industry's growth during the thirties, but it expresses for the first time in published form Spratling's sense of what he had achieved. He is generous in his praise of his young maestros Mondragon and Navarrete, of the elder and influen-

---

(New York: Vintage, 1991), 379. Why Spratling chose to record this painful Faulkner episode cannot, of course, be determined, although his remembrance in the last year of his life of Faulkner's alcoholic behavior coincided with his own pattern of heavy drinking during this period.

2. W.S. to Mrs. L. W. Spratling, November 29, 1941.

tial Iguala silversmith Don Wenceslao Herrera, and of the symbiotic relationship between Taxco and Iguala: what was now coming to life in the one, and in the other its long tradition of fine work in gold and filigree. He is very much aware of the high quality of silverwork being produced in the designs of two major houses in Mexico City, Casa Sanborn and that of his—and of the Morrows'—friend of several years, Frederick Davis, whose "good taste" and "certain business ability" he admires, but he notes that neither manufacture their own articles but send them out on contract. There is undoubtedly a feeling here of satisfaction that he alone had brought it all together: the art, the craft, the production, the marketing, all at the source of the silver itself. The imitation and pilfering that inevitably beset commercial success of almost any kind—and he estimates that over half the design forms being used in the small shops of Mexico City originated at Las Delicias—Spratling here seems to regard as a stimulus to experimentation and as separating distinctive work from the ordinary. He is not especially illuminating on the evolution of his own art of design, but others in the Las Delicias silver group were by then obviously following his lead and contributing to the development of the several new designs he states were being produced each week, these displacing others less successful. And certainly it was a mark of his disciplinary genius that each piece making its way through the horizontally expanding hierarchy of the *taller* would continue to reflect the unmistakable Spratling style: "Don't make it prettier, he used to tell us," recalled one of the first and most brilliant of the Spratling *ayudantes*; "I want you to do it exactly as you see here in the design."[3]

Lying behind this remembered voice of authority is the force of Spratling's disciplinary genius as well as the compressed history of experimentation and resolution within the Las Delicias *taller* that had been successfully completed by the end of 1937. To be sure, the elegant silver and rosewood serving sets and what Spratling described as "cocktail cups like Aztec chalices" then being produced had emerged, as he wrote, from the influential shapes of "things" done on the ranches and from those of traditional Indian motifs. One remembers, however, Navarrete's recollection that Spratling's earliest designs, which he brought to Iguala for three-dimensional translation, were ornamented with "*Grecian* frets"

3. Antonio Castillo, as quoted by Larry Rohter, "In Mexico, Spratling Means Silver," *New York Times*, December 17, 1987, C14.

and that the earrings, probably fabricated by Navarrete, which he presented to Peggy Cowley on Christmas Eve, 1931, were apparently a modification of a standard cornucopia-like design, "a basket overflowing with flowers." It was not until he committed himself to a native presence in all of his work, "a style," in one of his best phrases, "which had a right to exist in Mexico," that the permanent identity of Spratling designs would emerge.

That something new and truly distinctive had been created from the successful integration of this controlling principle with the rich texture of Spratling's mnemonic experience and the hospitality of his orderly pencil to the Art Deco, Cubist, and even surrealist lines of twentieth-century European design was significantly confirmed toward the end of 1937. It was then that Spratling was invited to show his work for the first time in a major exhibition outside of Mexico. The invitation letter was from the Brooklyn Museum for an "Exhibition of Contemporary Industrial and Handwrought Silver," scheduled to open on November 19:

> We are most anxious to have your work represented as we wish to include something of Mexican design executed by a distinguished craftsman. We thought at once of asking you for a contribution and shall have no other Mexican silver in the Exhibit. . . .
>
> I am looking forward to the arrival of your work which is so much liked by . . . everyone familiar with Mexico. We are delighted to have silver so fresh and so different in treatment from our traditional English and Colonial styles. The combination of silver with mahogany and the exotic Mexican woods will give such a note of variety and color to this large Exhibition of Silver. We truly appreciate your cooperation in representing Mexican Silver at its finest.[4]

Spratling, of course, was delighted and replied immediately, writing that he would send at once, by courier, "articles of silver which I consider most representative of the work being done here."

> It gives me great pleasure to observe the definite appreciation which you have for our work. You do us much honor.
>
> Hoping that the things which I send you will be to your taste and that you will not fail to mark them not as "Taxco Silver" but as the work of William Spratling in his shop, Las Delicias in Taxco, Mexico—if that is not too much to ask.

4. Louise W. Chase to W.S., October 13, 1937, ARS.

Thanking you very much for your great kindness in including our work in such an important exposition, I remain . . .⁵

Until the catalog was published, Spratling may not have known just how comprehensive the exhibition was. Over forty of the most eminent designers and manufacturers of American silver were represented, together with museum-quality examples of eighteenth-century English and American silver whose designs and decorative patterns had been historically important. The catalog foreword stated: "While the exhibition is almost entirely of American work, it includes some Danish and some Mexican silver, as these have had a strong influence on American silversmiths." It was a significant moment of recognition for Spratling, a transitional moment one might say, for now he had assumed the stature of a significant artist whose work was influencing the design of the decorative arts in his native country—what would eventually be called the "American School." Almost fifty years later, for example, the term would be used in the title of a major historical exhibit in New York City during the summer of 1985: "Mexican Silver Jewelry: The American School, 1930–1960." A review emphasized the character of the Spratling style, "now in revival," whose seminal designs are "probably as abundant in the nation's jewelry boxes as Tiffany lamps once were in attics across the land." The research behind the exhibit and its name had confirmed, of course, that it was Spratling's pioneering and innovative work that had "influenced a generation of Mexican and American designers."⁶

Clearly, by 1937, the second major stage of Spratling's life and career had begun. That relatively short stage, which would be framed by the immediate pre-war and post-war years, would be marked by extraordinary affluence and the elastic expansion of Spratling's reputation—which he was so anxious to have clearly identified in his first response to the Brooklyn Museum—throughout Europe and the Americas. Both of these were much furthered by the exhibition, which brought his work to the attention of wealthy collectors and manufacturers. There were several requests for price lists for the nineteen pieces Spratling had contributed, and the exhibit's curator wrote to him shortly after the opening: "The case containing your silver is one of the most admired in the Exhibition.

5. W.S. to Louise W. Chase, October 22, 1937, ARS. Spratling donated his nineteen pieces to the museum following the close of the exhibit.
6. Rita Reif, "A Genius of Mexican Jewelry," *New York Times,* June 2, 1985, II, 31.

The jewelry is shown against a dark red woollen background which tones in with the wood handles of the flatware. As your silver is the only example of Mexican craftsmanship in the Exhibit, it has received a great deal of attention and admiration."[7]

That much seemed to Spratling to be coming together here as 1937 drew to a close—both remembrance and prospect, a significant ending and a promising beginning—is indicated late in the year as he commemorated his new prosperity and eminence with a valuable gift sent to Professor Biggin for the Architecture Library at Auburn, a 1747 edition of drawings by the British architect James Gibbs. The newspaper account of the gift included a laudatory review of Spratling's career.[8] His ascending reputation and the good financial times must have been, at the least, exhilarating. Now, in his continuing relationship with the Morrow family, it was he who could afford to be the generous one; and there is an air of confident intimacy in his correspondence not present in the earlier letters, although Elizabeth is still "Mrs. Morrow":

> I'm presuming to enclose with this the new catalogue for silver, not very well printed but complete, and the map of Taxco may amuse you. If there is anything you ever want to order (for Christmas presents or otherwise) all you have to do, as they say here, is to command me and they will go to you directly by mail without delay. This is just an idea.
>
> My affectionate regards to your family, and please tell Aubrey that when he is ready to reduce, to come down and I will take him tiger hunting. Also please congratulate Anne for me on a beautiful job. It's a grand book, and I suppose I don't have to tell you that.
>
> I'm looking forward to your visit in March and remember, you mustn't bring a lot of people.[9]

And, a few months later, apparently in response to her request that he play his now-perfected role of host for some of her visiting friends:

> Thank you for both of your letters and you may be sure I'll do what I can for anybody that you send along.

7. Louise W. Chase to W.S., December 1, 1937, ARS.

8. "Valued Addition to Library at Auburn Noted by Biggin," *Montgomery Advertiser,* November 13, 1937.

9. W.S. to Elizabeth Morrow, November 1, 1938. Aubrey Morgan had married Elisabeth Morrow and, following her death in 1934, subsequently married her sister Constance. The book was *Listen! The Wind,* published in 1938 and the second of Anne Morrow Lindbergh's stories of intercontinental flights with her husband in the early 30s.

I am delighted to hear about Connie and that all is well with her. Please give her and Aubrey my love and I am hoping that you all show up as planned for in September. Maybe you will come to Acapulco with me. I am building a little house there, which is way out on a wooded point and isolated from everybody.[10]

If he had any apprehension that the spreading conflict in Europe would adversely affect his new prosperity, such would be unfounded. The war actually closed European sources of manufacture, which led to an enormous increase in sales throughout North and South America, Spratling y Artesanos doing an annual business at the astonishing level of some $380,000 in the year the United States entered the war. In that year Spratling was eulogized in a full-page article in *Time*. Written in the journal's usual style of breezy compression, and accompanied by a photograph of Spratling and a hillside perspective of Taxco, the essay was still sufficiently accurate to establish for the first time for a wide popular readership, probably the widest in America, the basis of the Spratling legend, which continues to blend romantic inaccuracy—some induced by Spratling himself—with his authentic artistic and cultural legacy. In the context of the annual silver fiesta in June, commemorating the origin of the Taller de las Delicias, he is pictured as "good-looking William Philip Spratling of New Orleans" and Taxco as "Mexico's Florence." With his entrepreneurial vision he is the town's "First Citizen" of the twentieth century, and his name is thus associated with five centuries of the ebb and flow of Taxco's silver fortunes; and with Cortez, de la Borda, Díaz, the revolutions. In his career as "an artist of considerable merit," Spratling is also associated with Faulkner (still "Falkner" to *Time* in 1941), with Rivera, Orozco, and Siqueiros. And, the essay concludes, as Spratling thinks about his connections to Taxco's prosperity and architectural preservation, he must in the town's idyllic setting feel "pretty good" as he sits "on the balcony of Paco's saloon after work, watching the setting sun lighting the tops of the Indian elms in the little plaza, and experimenting with pinks and roses on the twin filigreed towers of the *parroquia*."[11]

Pretty good indeed! But that feeling was already inherent four years

10. W.S. to Elizabeth Morrow, May 24, 1939.
11. "Fiesta at Taxco," *Time,* July 7, 1941, p. 16.

earlier in the enthusiastic letter he had written home to Alabama, a symbolic closure of his artistic apprenticeship in his knowledge that Las Delicias was doing the best work in Mexico. While in that year of 1937 he could not have imagined the international attention that the *Time* article would bring to his reputation, he probably knew from the results of the Brooklyn Museum exhibition that it was only a matter of short time before his designs would find their way into the windows of the finest stores in metropolitan America: Lord and Taylor's, Marshall Field, Macy's, Neiman-Marcus, Tiffany and Company. Ah, Tiffany's! The supreme image of style and elegance! He must have thought many times during these years of the irony of that connection. For it called up one of the turning points in his early life, one that would accommodate the initiation of the long journey from Alabama to Mexico. In May of 1921 he had written to the prominent Chicago sculptor Lorado Taft, asking him for a recommendation to the Tiffany Foundation, which Louis Comfort Tiffany had established in 1918, as an apprentice in sculpture and design. But in response to a request for evidence of his artwork, he could furnish only a newspaper photo of the President Thach piece, having sent everything else he had directly to the foundation. "The enclosed is about all I have to show you. You will pardon the headline. The tablet is now in bronze, erected, and the size is 16 × 21 inches. The cut is rotten, and I'm sorry I haven't another photograph to send. Nevertheless, I am hoping this will suffice as a sample of my work. Thanking you again for your interest, and assuring you of my gratitude if you will address a letter for me to the Tiffany Foundation, I remain . . ." (May 6, 1921).

A few weeks later, in July, exactly twenty years to the month prior to the article in *Time,* he was notified in a letter from his cousin, Judge William Thomas of Montgomery, that his application for admission had been rejected. The rejection was but another frustration that increased the lonely dilemma of his early life: somehow to establish for himself a meaningful future within the claims of his still undirected artistic interests. The letter with its disappointing news was somewhat chiding; Judge Thomas was acquainted with a Foundation trustee, the eminent sculptor Daniel Chester French, and perhaps if Billy had sought Judge Thomas's advice on recommendation procedures earlier, the application might have been successful. Yet the idea of apprenticeship in sculpture was possibly a good one, he continued, and he would be willing to help if Billy would go to New York and present himself "along the line of one who is poor but ambitious, needing encouragement and instruction."[12]

Much, as we have seen, lay within this twenty-year frame, marked here by the Tiffany disappointment. He kept the letter of rejection for the rest of his life in the scrapbook-portfolio chronicle, writing across the top of the page in the mature hand of his later years the single reflective word: "Opportunities!" This was not the only one that would fail to materialize, of course, in the long process of "encouragement and instruction" that began, after another uncertain academic year at Auburn, with the offer from Tulane. If he was fortunate in experiencing the heightened cultural moments that were New Orleans and Mexico in the twenties and thirties, and in the people that he came to know there, it must be said that with his ambition—not without an element of self-promotion—and his assimilative genius, he did make the most of the opportunities that fell in his direction, resolving all that he encountered into an extraordinary apprenticeship. But, again, that apprenticeship took no clear direction toward a preconceived purpose. Indeed, his greatest achievements were almost unexpected, and perhaps even he, at the age of thirty-seven, was surprised that in the hard work and intensity of making the color of silver become his color and creating new lives of opportunity for hundreds of young men who also needed encouragement and instruction, he himself had become a master.

12. William H. Thomas to W.S., July 1, 1921, ARS. Tiffany had stated that the purpose of his foundation was to "help young artists of our Country to appreciate more the study of Nature, and to assist them in establishing themselves in the art world." For a history of the foundation, see Hugh F. McKean, *The "Lost" Treasures of Louis Comfort Tiffany* (New York: Doubleday, 1980), 265–69.

10

"Capitalization of a Personal Act"

"After all these months, I thought you might like to know how things are going. Briefly, having quietly vegetated for more than four years and living as you saw me when you were here, even since September 48 I have been extremely busy. There's been no money to speak of, but two important things are now about to click; I have designed a complete new line of Spratling Silver which is now in production with Conquistador, S.A. (the largest silver manufacturers in Mexico City, of which I am also a Director) and the new things look very good indeed and though they have not been shown and will not be until November, orders are already coming."

The long and discursive story that was concluded with Spratling's initial artistic and entrepreneurial triumphs seems almost obscure when compared to the familiar emergence in the last thirty years of his life of the public persona. It was then, of course, that the Spratling name began to find its way into all the guidebooks and the elegant brilliance of his designs brought him into contact with a wealthy and influential society both in Mexico and the United States. The basis of that public image was already established and, indeed, irretrievably set in motion by the end of the thirties decade, when he was on the verge of becoming one of the most prominent American expatriates living in Mexico. As we have seen, however, lying behind this emergence was a personal drama of maturation, marked by frustration—even, at times, desperation—as well as courage and genius. It is no less true of his later career, despite the general familiarity of its outline, that it too contains a relevant drama of personal experience. In fact, this part of his career might be considered as two separate "stories." The first of these, that of the sudden economic prosperity and widening reputation of Spratling y Artesanos during his middle years is brief and, in its disastrous decline toward the close of World War II, ultimately stressful, coming to its conclusion as Spratling de-

parted Taxco and made his final journey southward, a few miles down
the mountain to his newly acquired property, where in the valley by the
Río de Taxco–el-Viejo he would establish Rancho Spratling. Although he
could not have foreseen the fiscal decline of the business itself, his very
purchase of the property with profits from the early forties suggests that
he eventually would have departed the Taxco environment anyway, with
its constant copying and thievery of his designs and the emergence of
rival shops, most of which were operated by former *ayudantes* he had
trained, and with a few notable exceptions, were turning out imitative
pieces that subverted the high standards of craftsmanship established by
Spratling y Artesanos. There is some indication also, as Elizabeth Anderson recalled in her own memoir, that Spratling's prosperity and eminence
produced from some quarters a calculated and vindictive nativism, which
in short-lived scandal sheets attacked his personal life and alleged his
participation in the illegal pre-Columbian-artifact traffic.[1] The transitional movement to Rancho Spratling and to the last "story," or chapter
in his life, seems to be caught in the words above, from a letter he wrote
to his sister Lucile on October 11, 1949.

Each of these stories is played out against quite a different kind of
background from that of Spratling's personal and artistic maturation.
The full content of both must, perhaps, await a further telling, accommodating in the process the complex issue of World War II and its effect on
the economic and political climate of Mexico, as well as the problematic
matter of the traffic and appraisals of legitimacy in the world of pre-
Columbian art. Yet even a review of that content available to us, buried
as usual in the slim body of Spratling's correspondence, will suggest further the wholeness of the Spratling story: the connection between the
private man and the public figure of undoubted intercultural significance.
Such a review reveals on the one hand less the story of an individual
assimilating a culture other than his own and imposing his identity upon
it than an account of that same individual gradually finding himself a
prisoner within the unfamiliar forms of corporate management he, ironically, had helped to create. The second is partly a tale of recovery from
that disaster and of new achievements. And while both illustrate the
Spratling energy and uncommon power of renewal, each is also marked

1. Elizabeth Anderson and Gerald R. Kelly, *Miss Elizabeth: A Memoir* (Boston: Little,
Brown, 1969), 268–75.

by unhappy judgments, the accumulation of oppressive financial obligations, rueful reappraisals, and, finally, with the encroachment of age, as his interests became concentrated on the stone images from Mexico's ancient past, perhaps a certain pride, if not arrogance, in his accurate perception that no private act or condition could subvert the public legend.

If the telescoped drama of high financial times for Spratling y Artesanos and the gradual managerial confinement of its founder is framed in its conclusion by the 1949 letter to Lucile with its news of "vegetation" and recovery, a prologue to that story would be the anxious telegram sent in the late summer of 1940 by Spratling to Elizabeth Morrow: "Financial tourist situation suddenly extremely difficult here. Would save shop if you find possible lend me 2000 dollars payable September first. Your bank depositing my account Park Ave branch National City." The telegram was sent first to Northampton, Massachusetts, where, since the fall term of 1939, Elizabeth had been serving as interim president of her beloved Smith College. Perhaps no single element in all of Spratling's private or public lives testifies to the finest qualities in his character, transcending all those less admirable, than his capacity to inspire the friendship and trust of this quietly remarkable woman. In the midst of her busy administrative efforts to unify the college and the personal stresses on the whole family brought by the criticism of her famous son-in-law's position on American's neutrality and unpreparedness for war, she quickly and generously responded: "Depositing today $2000 in Park Ave. Branch Nat. City Bank. Glad to do it."[2]

Clearly, the financial evolution of the business, which had seemed so promising at the close of 1937, had been deterred. The "tourist situation," on which much of the optimism had been based, had obviously been affected by the war in Europe and such consequences in Mexico as the country's nationalization of its oil interests and the devaluation of the peso, this plus some minor but highly publicized revolutionary activity against the government in the province being described in one of Natalie Scott's perceptive and richly detailed letters to New Orleans in the spring of 1938: "There is still the difficulty about the instability of the exchange, which is working a hardship on business in general. Poor

2. The contents of the telegram, which is dated only as "1940," and its response are contained in a handwritten transcription in the Smith College archives.

Charles Pickard hasn't sold a car in two months. The peso is going slowly lower. There will have to be some readjustment made. . . . The road has never been closed at all, that is, the highway, and cars have come over it daily, with never a mishap. . . . The other day, several car-loads of tourists coming from Texas turned back because they saw soldiers on the road!"[3] Though the efficient administration of President Cárdenas could put down in good order a provincial revolution, for at least two years, from 1939 to 1940, the volatile international situation proved commercially chaotic for a business such as Spratling's. "I don't envy you running the plantation (about which of course I know nothing)," he wrote during this period to Aunt Miriam. "I have my own hands full here with more than one hundred workers, and the tourist season so bad, due to politics, that for the first time since being in business I actually have financial worries. Enough to mention, I think, that my Company at the moment owes me personally over 70,000 pesos. Whether pesos or dollars, that's quite a lot of money." And only a few days before, he had already been forced to write an apologetic letter to Elizabeth Morrow:

> I'm really very embarrassed about the financial shape of things here and I'm writing you before the first of September to advise that on that date I'll not be able to cover your loan. I'm selling the house in Acapulco, which cost $42,000 pesos (and which should be very easy to dispose of) though I only have an offer at the moment for $25,000. . . . I promise you that if by the first of November it isn't sold for a more decent price, I'll let it go for whatever I can get for it and immediately cover the $2,000 dollars which I owe you.

> Yesterday I balanced my books in the shop as from the first of April and in the smallest department alone there has been a loss of more than 50%. Political happenings are really taking us for a buggy ride this time. . . . Really I'm terribly embarrassed in a strictly financial sense, this being the first time since going into business that I have not been able to meet my obligations on the dot. I seem to have plenty of security to offer, but there just isn't any cash when three-fourths of one's selling season has been wiped out. . . .[4]

3. Natalie Scott to Mrs. Samuel G. Robinson, May 23, 1938, Natalie Scott Papers, Tulane University Archives.

4. W.S. to Mrs. L. W. Spratling, August 27, 1940; W.S. to Elizabeth Morrow, August 17, 1940.

The crisis produced its most lasting response, however, in Spratling's decision to break up the organic unity of the *taller*. As he wrote further in the letter to Alabama:

> I've made a contract licensing a firm in New York to reproduce a great deal of my silver jewelry up there. It is a good firm and they sell to about one thousand of the best stores in America. The line is being produced at this moment and should be distributed within a month from now. It may or may not be really business. As a matter of fact it may produce enough to make it possible for me to sustain this shop through thick and thin.
>
> Bonwit Teller, I understand is going to give the things a window, and probably you'll see the announcement in Vogue.

It was a significant moment, perhaps even irretrievable. Profits from the new arrangement did indeed help substantially to save the "shop," but the business would not survive the "thick and thin" of the next five years. Spratling's movement toward this New York connection, though prompted by financial pressure produced by the war, was consonant, of course, with the relocation from Europe to New York City of the international world of painting and design, as Paris succumbed to Nazi occupation, London to siege, and all Continental capitals to the stresses of fascist or communist domination. All of this new commercial and creative centrality in America conversely was hospitable to the further visibility of the Spratling style. The economic recovery of Spratling y Artesanos was swift and dramatic, and within two years Spratling, no longer on the brink of ruin, could write quite a different kind of letter to Elizabeth Morrow, this one in the summer of 1942 describing the sensational success of his design of a series of silver buttons depicting patriotic symbols of the Allied cause:

> Thank you so much for your letter of the other day, also for Katherine Sullivan's request for buttons which came this morning. I am mailing you direct to North Haven two of each type we make and hope you will accept them as a present. I am sure that to any one to whom you may give them will certainly cause wonderful propaganda for us, that is, if they like them.
>
> The thing is going exceedingly well here in Mexico and there has been a mass of publicity and every one is wearing the button. They are selling in 32 stores in Mexico City, also in Monterrey, Guadalajara, Oaxaca and Laredo. In Laredo a man wants 10,000 buttons, but I have to find out

about his credit first. We have even had orders already from Venezuela, Buenos Aires, Havana and from several American cities. . . .

P.S. Jane Chamberlain, head buyer at Macy's is someone you should know. Macy's is giving a whole window to the button.[5]

In the chatty reconciliations and reinterpretations of the past that permeate the autobiographical file, Spratling devotes, as usual, minimal attention to the principal disappointments of his career. He allocates almost as much space to descriptions of his boat, the *Pez de Plata,* with its stylish Covarrubias murals, as he does to the two and one-half pages given to the dizzying rise and fall of the company. The purchase of the yacht is a convenient symbol of the flush times obviously implicit in the 1942 letter to Elizabeth Morrow. By then capital investment in the stock formerly owned entirely by Spratling and the consequent impersonalization of the organization were well under way. The intensely rapid expansion of production to meet the enormous post–Pearl Harbor demand from the United States and other countries for luxury goods secured a level of profit by 1943–1944 well beyond that mentioned in the 1941 *Time* article. A company statement prepared for stockholders for that period, for example, indicated that the Taxco shop during 1943 alone sold over 200,000 pesos' worth of silver articles and that the company's total profits for 1943 increased by one million pesos over those for 1942.[6]

This statistic for the small company of Spratling y Artesanos was but a parallel to what was occurring within the larger economy of Mexico during these same years: almost a tripling of the national income, from 6.4 billion pesos in 1940 to 18.6 billion in 1945, with a corresponding increase in per capita income. The displacement of agrarian reform by a new commitment to industrialization as central to the future of the nation had already been initiated by the administration of new president Avila Camacho even prior to Mexico's 1942 entry into the war. But the war itself, with Mexico's immediate support of the Allied war effort through its supplies of strategic raw materials, contributed substantially to the country's economic development, especially as it became clear that the nation must produce its own share of manufactured goods to offset

5. W.S. to Elizabeth Morrow, July 24, 1942.
6. The reports are dated December 31, 1943, and February 7, 1944, ARS.

the wartime shortages of its customary imports as well as to increase its exports to other Latin American countries.[7]

Although the parallel is not exact, the changes initiated by Spratling y Artesanos to meet the demands of a new and profitable market are a microcosm of this larger scene. Certainly the company, by increasing production through the incorporation of some mechanized processes, contributed in a small way to the social goals of the new industrial consciousness by enhancing the worth of the national product and expanding employment opportunities for a growing and needy population. And though Spratling could observe, within the multi-year perspective of the file, that the company's ultimate failure as manipulated by "unscrupulous 'Yanqui' investors may, in part, explain Mexico's uncertainty about the wisdom of allowing foreign capital to come into the country," the Mexican Congress actually, in 1944, as the new U.S.-Mexican cooperation during the war was removing many of the old suspicions and animosities, passed legislation permitting foreign investments in the industrialization initiative.

The internal affairs of Spratling y Artesanos during this five-year period that would lead to betrayals of trust and deliberate short-term profit taking by major stockholders, primarily by Russell Maguire, the principal Americano investor, are inherent in much of the extant legal-financial documents of the company. To some extent this process was on the one hand a textbook example of questionable management and risky expansion against a volatile market controlled by political conditions. After it was over, such could be perceived even by a long-distance, though sympathetic, observer such as Spratling's brother-in-law: "I find it difficult to describe my feelings about the demise of Spratling y Artesanos. Your words "It's all very sad"—a gross misunderstatement. I feel as though something of my very own had died—for I have watched this baby grow since 1939. . . . What the basic causes were I can only speculate about—overexpansion, internal friction, conflicting policies, mechanization, short-sighted financing has been repeated over and over again in the States. . . . I hope you'll tell me someday."[8]

7. See Michael Meyer and William Sherman, *The Course of Mexican History*, 5th ed. (New York: Oxford University Press, 1995), 627–37.

8. Dr. Edward Bleir to W.S., undated, but written sometime in 1947, identifiable by a reference to his and Lucile's N.Y. conversation with Frances Toor "just arrived with the copy of her new book," which would have been *A Treasury of Mexican Folkways* (New York: Crown, 1947), in which she "has mentioned you gracefully," ARS.

But the tangled series of events was more than the economic "death of a small company," in one of Spratling's best autobiographical compressions. For all of his pleasure in the commercial rewards of the business and for all his ready accommodation to the unexpected bonanza wrought by the international situation, to Spratling the demise of the business was the corruption of what can accurately be called an ideal, a reciprocal partnership between himself and Little Mexico. And it was his name, his creative reputation, that had been used in the process.

In fact, the financial report already cited emphasized that the dramatic success of the business and its high visibility in both Mexico and the United States had been absolutely dependent on these very things. In spite of the glowing optimism of the report, however, which also noted that employee morale was excellent and that the effects of such local competition as the Los Castillos shop were negligible, other observations proved ominous: the span of management responsibility was becoming increasingly uncertain—it was now too wide for the sole Spratling control; the finest silverwork of the company was still done by hand, but there was a need for more capital to increase machine operations; and a large new contract with Montgomery Ward promised higher profits yet. Spratling's dissatisfactions with management practices and capitalization measures for the physical relocation of the company to the large La Florida site just outside of Taxco were not fully manifest until 1944–1945. Even then, one of the American stockholders could write with genial concern for Spratling's good offices that the "creaks and groans of the new financial frame for Spratling y Artesanos will, I hope, soon be eliminated" and that "I want to tell you again that I think the plant is going to be a notable and deserved monument to what you have accomplished in the silver industry in Mexico."[9] And Spratling himself sent personal handwritten holiday greetings for 1944–1945 to friends and special clients inscribed on an aerial photo of the site bearing his current hallmark "desde muestra nueva planta en la Antigua Hacienda de la Florida."

The scale of operation there and the issue of quality control are indicated in a brief correspondence with Montgomery Ward a few months later, which actually occurred shortly after a frustrated Spratling, his advice consistently ignored, resigned from all management responsibility with the company, this coming only a year after he had agreed, in March

9. Meredith Parker to W.S., April 19, 1944, ARS.

of 1944, to a contract as salaried employee with the title of "director-manager" in charge of production, artistic direction, and sales.[10] The Montgomery Ward exchange was a reminder that the U.S. Federal Trade Commission had filed in 1944 a complaint that Spratling jewelry was not $980/1000$ (i.e., only 2 percent copper) chemically pure as advertised; tests showed the complaint accurate, "a very serious situation" that should be corrected. The reply, from Manolo Jiménez, the manager who had succeeded Spratling, stated that "technical difficulties" in the several melting and rolling processes of sheets originally 98.0 percent pure allowed certain impurities to intrude and that this, along with the inability to separate all cuttings and filings from hollowware silver from those used for jewelry, had led to the deletion of the "980" stamp "that had been used by Spratling y Artesanos for many years." He concluded that Montgomery Ward should have been advised of this earlier. "Technical difficulties," to be sure, but the incident illustrated the obvious, that the large-scale operation had eroded yet another of the qualitative elements of which Spratling had properly been so proud and had widely advertised from the inception of the Las Delicias experiment. The level of production is indicated by the fact that the Montgomery Ward tests were made on six bracelets out of an order of fifteen thousand; another indication of quality control problems was the return in the previous month, about the time of Spratling's administrative resignation, by Montgomery Ward of 863 bracelets for repair: either too short or the last link too lightweight.[11]

In his speculative letter to Spratling about the death of the company, Ed Bleir had put it well: "the capitalization of a personal act." That the organizational and creative identity of Spratling y Artesanos had been bought and sold in the depersonalized capitalist mode was verbalized twice by Spratling after it seemed clear to him that the company's survival was dubious. In a letter to one of his fellow stockholders and longtime friend, gallery owner Alberto Misrachi of Mexico City, Spratling outlined in great detail what he perceived to be a managerial disaster, including such problems as confused costs and pricing calculations, com-

10. "Contrato de Trabajo que celebran 'SPRATLING Y ARTESANOS, S.A.' como patrón, y WILLIAM SPRATLING, como trabajador," March 20, 1944, ARS.

11. Paul K. Bonebrake (manager, Jewelry Department, Montgomery Ward) to W.S., May 19, 1945; Manolo Jiménez to Bonebrake, May 29, 1945, ARS. The detail about the returned bracelets is in a letter from Jiménez to Spratling, April 25, 1945, ARS.

plaints by the U.S. Treasury Department that tariff codes had been violated, absenteeism and lack of direction by senior management in Taxco, serious delays in production of new models, outdated catalogues. But to Spratling the most devastating condition, indeed the disheartening "capitalization" of what he had personally developed, was the erosion of morale among the workers, who

> formerly employed in an atmosphere which was friendly and conducive to good craftsmanship, are now syndicalized and the former confidence between Company and the individual worker has disappeared. There is no longer to be found the same frankness on the part of the worker, and even among the workers themselves comradeship has been replaced by a suspicious attitude toward each other. All sense of cooperation or of individual responsibility has been replaced by a vague feeling of discontent, several of the best workers have gone to work with other firms and even the "trabajadores de confianza" are discouraged and are looking for work elsewhere. . . .
>
> So, dear Alberto, I have to tell you that, though the plan may not be a bonanza for the financier Maguire, for us it is utterly fruitless, and worse. Our money is working for Maguire and this includes approximately $200,000.00 of my own. You certainly must have noted in my above remarks a few salient facts; the Company's selling bases and our established market itself have been disrupted, earning capacity has been systematically decreased, the principal reforms sought by the investors who dealt with Maguire have been delayed or side-stepped, and that intangible but priceless element, frank cooperation between the Company and its individual components, has been sacrificed.[12]

Spratling sent a copy to an official of the Bank of Mexico (Don Eduardo Villaseñor) stating that the contents of the letter ("Alberto says its dinamite") not only justify his earlier communication concerning the poor choice of Jimínez as manager but also suggest that Maguire's methods illustrate the worst features of "present industry capitalization in Mexico."

Spratling's most intimate expression about the decline of his fortunes, however, had already a few months earlier been communicated, perhaps not so surprisingly, to Elizabeth Morrow. He had been to New York for "a business conversation, the object of the trip"—presumably to meet

12. W.S. to Don Alberto Misrachi, January 17, 1946, ARS.

with Maguire—had visited with Covarrubias and d'Harnoncourt, but had been unable to reach her by phone.

> You must know that the apparent neglect was not due to lack of affection. The company control is being taken over by bigger shareholders & I have been gently (not so) set aside. It's a long story and the other people have behaved rather badly—having been able to snatch themselves a bargain. What they cannot understand is that my prime interest is the future of the company & not increased income for myself.
>
> The long and short of it is that the new investor (Maguire Industries) would have gladly put the $200,000 as necessary for our production plans (he admits)—but the other shareholders (without consulting me) closed with him for 50,000—which gives him (Maguire) complete control & does not solve our problem. Maguire is naturally delighted—& Spratling is out. . . .
>
> Forgive me if I seem to burden you with all this—but five months of fighting their apathy & the bad faith of them & now, having resigned from the company (as a measure) have made me feel that I have to explain to someone—there are only two people in my confidence here & naturally I can't share these things with the workers, though they are my best friends.
>
> What amazes me, who have never thought of myself as a businessman, is what perfectly stupid businessmen these financial people are—and how they manage to sacrifice personal relations, good faith, etc.—the only really irreplaceable capital—in order to make a column of figures show a bigger margin. I won't bother you with any more of it.[13]

Perhaps Spratling should have much earlier realized what he later seemed to understand, that Maguire Industries was cleverly manipulating (in the autobiography Maguire is "Mr. Manipulator") Spratling y Artesanos as a write-off for U.S. income tax purposes. Perhaps Spratling should have also realized that while the company's expansion had been in part a function of its superb designs and craftsmanship, the economic conditions wrought by the war had been significant, conditions that certainly by 1944 could be predicted as coming to a close. "Billy never was one to handle finances," as his Alabama family could reminisce, and in his own words he had never thought of himself as "a businessman." He had enjoyed, to be sure, the wealth and high times of the early incorporation, but there seems no reason to disbelieve his confessional to Elizabeth

13. W.S. to Elizabeth Morrow, July 8, 1945.

about the relative importance of his own personal gain. He had "to *explain* to someone" that what had been squandered was the *human* capital of the enterprise—and potentially its good name, its achievement of creating new designs from an old tradition, a "Mexican style of our times."

11

"A Man as Free as the Wind": The Last Years at Taxco-el-Viejo

This first of the two stories inherent in the rest of Spratling's life was completed in only five years or so. The second, however, his final years at Taxco-el-Viejo, was sustained for over twenty. Yet the first story clearly penetrated and permanently marked the second. In addition to the frustration expressed in the private communication to Elizabeth Morrow, there is also a note of weariness, the emotion that seemed to characterize his departure for the "vegetating" period he recalled for Lucile some four years later.

And another note may have been sounded also, though we can be less certain of its meaning to Spratling. From what we can tell, his fondest relationships with women outside the family bond had been, with one notable exception, those with women significantly older than he, and certainly his feelings for Natalie Scott, Elizabeth Anderson, and Elizabeth Morrow had been marked by respect, trust, and even a certain kind of dependence. He had quite a different kind of attachment, perhaps his only romantic one, for Mary Anita Loos, niece of the famous Anita, whom he and Faulkner had known in New Orleans. Some ten or twelve years younger than Spratling, she was a writer and an actress, as beautiful, witty, and intelligent as Spratling was dashing and adventurous. They had first met in the late thirties and had been occasional companions for years by the time Spratling moved to the ranch. She had seen him off on his sensational one-man voyage from Santa Monica to Acapulco, and he recalled in the autobiography that it was to her that he sent the first message after arriving safely: "Voyage completed *sin novedad*. My love to you."

In her affectionate, poignant, and admiring tribute to Spratling, published in the memorial volume from a 1987 Mexico City symposium on Spratling's career, Mary Anita recalled how she had been "dazzled by his vitality, his imagination and talent and by the quality of his brown eyes as he spoke of archaeology or art." From their correspondence, their voyages on the *Pez de Plata*, their visits in New York and Mexico, she recalled he "had been for me like a master-teacher of many marvelous things," and though their friendship had flourished, it was only "a romance of the spirit." Their relationship had, however, at least for her, held the promise of much more than that. She was in love with Spratling, as affirmed by members of the Rosa and Miguel Covarrubias circle, to which both she and Spratling were socially connected.[1] To her, and perhaps briefly for Spratling, marriage had been a distinct possibility. But he could not bring himself to that point, although it is not clear whether it was because of sexual orientation or his preference for an isolated life whose extensions he alone could determine. Perhaps no single letter in the Spratling correspondence is more unexpectedly revealing of a central personal experience in Spratling's life—indeed of a side of his character we could have learned about from no other source—than hers to him once she had received his decision. Although the letter is dated only as "Monday, Sept. 11th," its contents suggest that it was probably written in 1946 or 1947, soon after Spratling had begun his artistic and psychological recovery from the Spratling y Artesanos failure:

> Bill, dearest,
>
> This may surprise you—but I can't tell you how relieved I was to get your letter. From your wire I was in grave fear that I had lost you as a human being,—that you didn't want me to come to Taxco,—that would have been an irreparable loss to me.
>
> Darling, with all my heart I understand your letter, and I admire you for your honesty, which to me is the keynote of your character.
>
> You wrote to me that if it made sense, you'd ask me to marry you. I wrote back in a burst of affection for you that it would make sense. Neither was a declaration or a promise, but both, I think, manifestations of the deep fondness and admiration we have for each other. . . .
>
> I am happy to know that you are still a sanctuary,—and soon I shall be rewarded for long hours of work by seeing your smiling face. And your new "Las Delicias," and the ahuehuete trees, and a meal shared with Elizabeth, and a feeling of warmth and comfort between us. . . .

1. Mary Anita Loos, "Recuerdos de William Spratling," in *William Spratling* (Mexico City: Centro Cultural Arte Contemporaneo, 1987), 19–25; see Adriana Williams, *Covarrubias* (Austin: University of Texas Press, 1994), 141.

It is the moment, and the goodness of two people together which means more than anything to me, as time goes on. . . . I felt terribly apart from you when I got your wire for I thought you had drawn a limit to life,— which surprised me in you,—a man as free as the wind, and why not? Your life belongs solely to you and you've made a wonderful thing of it. Marriage for the sake of marriage means absolutely nothing to me, as you must gather from the fact I'm thirty four and still single. It would only make sense with anyone if I wanted terribly to belong to that person whether we were apart or together, and if he in turn wanted me just as fervently. Actually, darling, you and I don't know each other. How could we even dream of such decisions? I would be just as frightened as you are if I felt bound to anything except what had always been between us, which is something pretty damned wonderful and rare. Let's not tamper with it!

If I felt coming to Taxco would limit you or me in any way, I wouldn't come. So, free of such thought from your very clear letter, and with my mind at ease, I'm coming happily. . . . I'll probably stay at the Reforma the night we get in. I'll try to reach you by phone. If not possible, I'll get a car and drive down. And it'll be wonderful to see you. Give my warmest love to Elizabeth, and explain to her that I'm coming happily, without any complication,

> Como siempre,
> Maria[2]

No loop was closed off here in this gentle and touching accommodation. It was one only expanded, for Spratling and she would remain the closest of friends throughout her own marriage and divorce and for the rest of his life. Mary Anita, along with brother David and Elizabeth Anderson, would be named as Spratling's heirs, and she would help to resolve his posthumous affairs prior to the resurrection of his name in the "Sucesores de William Spratling" creation.

The period from 1945 to 1948 may have been for Spratling passive in one sense, a restoration of energy for the creative renewal he described in the same letter to Lucile. But it was a hard time economically. Not as difficult as fifteen years earlier, when the power had been cut off, there was no milk for coffee, and his hospital care had depended on an Elizabeth Morrow loan. Still, with his investment losses in the company and the value of the stock rapidly declining, he had been decimated financially. And, despite his bravura account in the reconstructed autobio-

---

2. Mary Anita Loos to W.S., ARS.

graphical file of his intimidating ultimatum to expose Maguire and his unethical conduct to the U.S. banks with which Maguire Industries did business, there was actually nothing that he, now a minor stockholder, could do as the company continued to market his own name ("Spratling Silver") to the advantage of Maguire.

The beleaguered conditions inherent in the "vegetating" period just prior to September 1948, when, as he wrote to Lucile, he had become "extremely busy" and "two important things" were "about to click," are indicated by his legal problems in securing a mortgage on the Las Delicias house. This was calculated to repay yet another loan from Elizabeth Morrow, this one the largest yet, $7,000, and was probably the basis that allowed him to start up a small *taller* at the ranch. His obligations were politely but firmly set forth by the Morrows' longtime secretary, Arthur Springer:

> I need not tell you that Mrs. Morrow was impelled solely by her personal regard for you to make the loan which you requested of her, and for business reasons only she would never make loans of any sort in Mexico because they are not of the type of investment in which her financial advisors deal. She feels, however, that as a matter of general principle, she must follow the advice of her lawyers and ask you to cancel the present mortgage upon your Taxco home which is characterized as a "fictitious" one, execute a new "just" mortgage and to the satisfaction of Basham, Ringe & Correa, and deliver it to them for her account. I conclude that this will put you to a little additional trouble . . . but you will recognize as a further gesture of Mrs. Morrow's friendship, her willingness to forego all interest, and even to assume out of her own pocket, the burden of paying an income tax to Mexico upon this interest as computed under Mexican law even though not received by her.[3]

It was all yet again a case of Spratling's good intentions exceeding his financial grasp. He wrote to Elizabeth in May, somewhat inaccurately, that "Believe me, it is the first time in my life that I have ever had to apologize for my circumstances." He continued: "I hardly know which way to turn. But I have to confess how ashamed I am that so much time has passed & I have not been able to execute the security of my house to cover my debt to you. I feel this very deeply. . . . Ringe and Basham have

3. Arthur Springer to W.S., February 17, 1948, Elizabeth Morrow Papers, Smith College Archives.

written urging that I provide them with the mortgage as promised and I have lain awake nights seeking a solution. . . . the bank will not let go the house separately which is only one of three properties of mine attached by them." He sent along "some papers, fruits of 20 yrs. collecting, which I beg you to accept, either as collateral or for sale to liquidate what I owe you." Or, if this were insufficient as a bookseller might handle it, he made the equally unlikely offer to transfer to her name title to the *Pez de Plata,* then up for sale ("practically the only property I own which so far is not encumbered"). He concluded with "I think you know that I have always been able to fulfill my moral and economic obligations. I have kept my face to the light. . . . Again, I beg you to forgive my aparent [*sic*] negligence—I do feel so ashamed."[4]

Yet Spratling continued on the friendliest of terms with the Morrow family, visiting with them on their periodic trips to Cuernavaca. And, somehow, he managed to initiate a slow financial recovery, although there is some indication, the usual confused chronology in the autobiography notwithstanding, that the initial Mexico City business arrangement for the new designs that he had enthusiastically mentioned to Lucile did not work out. The second thing about to "click" was his securing from the U.S. Department of the Interior the long-awaited contract to energize the native arts of Alaska on the Las Delicias model of manual production. The project had been first encouraged by René d'Harnoncourt and proposed by Governor Ernest Gruening, whose highly regarded history, *Mexico and its Heritage,* had been published in 1928 and who had admired all that Spratling had accomplished. The long-term fiscal and organizational plan for developing the kind of cultural interchange calculated, in Spratling's phrase, "to show the natives of Alaska how to produce things that belong to Alaska and which will ultimately enjoy a great demand outside the territory" did not materialize. Yet his involvement is a splendid illustration of his visionary capacity to assimilate the artistic culture of a society isolated from his own experience and to translate that perception into creative forms both "old" and "new."

What he felt was imminent in the 1949 letter to Lucile was approval of the final contract for the larger project he had begun to develop as early as 1945, a project to be expedited by his ability to pilot his beloved Ercoupe, *El Niño.* He had learned to fly during the early flush times of

4. W.S. to Elizabeth Morrow, May 15, 1948.

Spratling y Artesanos to facilitate his regular delivery of silver designs to Mexico City. He estimated in the autobiography that he made over two thousand such flights over the sixteen years that he owned *El Niño* before it was destroyed in a crash landing during a storm on the last of these trips. In an exploratory mission, he made a remarkable one-man flight to Alaska and, as Interior Secretary Stewart Udall later recalled, "flew his own plane into all remote sections of Alaska, where he visited hundreds of communities, seeking out both native materials and native talents. The result was one of the most detailed studies ever conducted of this nature."[5] It was only after completing this comprehensive report that Spratling altered his conception of the design possibilities inherent in the project, which he originally felt could be executed in a month or two and, as he wrote to Jimínez, would "strengthen" the production of Spratling y Artesanos.[6] The design and fabrication of the two hundred models contracted to Spratling actually were not completed until 1949, a process that involved the unlikely Taxco residence of a small group of Eskimo artisans, where they worked side by side under Spratling's directions with their Mexican counterparts. The models—jewelry, functional tableware, small decorative objects—were sent by diplomatic pouch to the U.S. Interior Department, accompanied by a detailed letter from Spratling describing the artistic process and encouraging the project's commercial possibilities for the Alaskan economy.

What finally happened to the plan within the department's bureaucracy is uncertain—Gruening later, as senator from Alaska, described it as "lack of funds and sufficient interest of the Department of the Interior"[7]—but the immediate reception of the artwork was enthusiastic, Assistant Secretary William Warner speaking of Spratling's "remarkable abilities," praising some of the pieces as "exquisite," and all of them exhibiting "a surprising and somewhat striking modern art form."

> I have suggested that it all be photographed and that it be exhibited to jewelers here and in New York before being sent to Alaska. I suspect that you will want to have some of the pieces in a traveling exhibit that you or one of your men will take around to the principal native centers.
>
> I think this is a ten-strike![8]

5. Secretary Stewart Udall to Board of Trustees, Auburn University, November 22, 1961, Auburn University Archives.

6. W.S. to Manolo Jimínez, August 15, 1945, ARS.

7. Senator Ernest Gruening to Board of Trustees, Auburn University, July 25, 1961, Auburn University Archives.

8. William E. Warner to Don C. Foster, Alaska Native Service, May 17, 1949, ARS.

Even a cursory review of the list of meticulously described models supplied by Spratling shows that in the Alaska activity he essentially replicated on a smaller scale something of the Las Delicias achievement, here integrating the traditional Eskimo craft of fossil ivory and whalebone (baleen) carvings with the working of fine metals and jade. Northern images of walrus, mammoth, and polar bear, and Tlingit Indian ceremonial masks and hunting motifs incorporating spear and arrow, the four winds, the north star itself—all find their places among the cups, pendants, crosses, knives and forks, earrings, and candlesticks which, when exhibited during the fall in Juneau, made what Assistant Secretary Warner called "a sensational debut." But aside from the intrinsic artistic and potentially significant economic values of the Alaska project—and Secretary Udall affirmed that this "contribution of Mr. Spratling . . . will continue to better the lives of thousands of Eskimos"—for the Spratling story, it was all obviously a renewal of his creative life. Some "vegetating" it was! For during the entire four- or five-year period of the transitional and symbolic relocation to Old Taxco, in the midst of personal disillusionment, weariness, and financial chaos, he was hard at work, finding a new direction, one undoubtedly inherent in the "new line" of designs he described to Lucile that he was introducing in 1949. It was a new direction that would continue to influence his art.

The recovery was slow but steady. By 1951 Natalie could report that "Bill seems very content on his 'rancho.' He has some twenty-five silversmiths there and is turning out some very interesting things. . . . [He] has not been very well. He should really go for a thorough check-up, but he has had a great many expenses and is rather hard-up at present, so refuses to go. An attitude which I can understand, tho I deplore it." And as she briefly described her own slender means and her busy but satisfying life with the day nursery, she found, as always, the good phrase, this one reflecting both her and Spratling's situation: "Things are different now, but still lovely."[9]

However, by 1953 Spratling could write to Elizabeth Morrow that "Things here have improved a little. (I have just this week begun advertising the house in Taxco for sale). I've had a little catalogue printed (on credit) in an effort to make sales independent of the Taxco-Mexico competition. . . . I suppose it will be a month or so before this shop will feel the effects." The tone of the correspondence now was clearly

9. Natalie Scott to Carl Zigrosser, September 20, 1951.

optimistic. He was obviously pleased to report to her about his "favorite son" designation and "do you know I am now a street (Calle Guillermo Spratling)"? These new honors had made it "impossible to evade lots of civic details." His preservationist sympathies, brought with him from New Orleans, had long since seen the connection between Taxco's unique colonial appearance and the economic success of Spratling y Artesanos. And though the town had been protected by law since the late twenties against such as plate-glass windows, public garages, and irregular signage, Spratling had for years been the leader of the informal preservation review committee. Now, in the post-war years, given the town's growth and the enormous increase in tourists—over 400,000 from the United States visited Mexico in 1952 alone—his role in maintaining Taxco's architectural integrity and controlled environmental conditions were more important than ever. Thus he could write further to Elizabeth Morrow that he was coming up from the ranch almost every weekday for meetings of his "junta,—which has its hands full," but through its efforts, "Taxco with a new *Ley de Conservación* is going to be much cleaner and sweeter."

He had offered "to exchange silver with Charles Lindbergh" for an inscribed copy of the newly published *Spirit of St. Louis*, and when the book came he responded to Elizabeth with gratitude and with a sense of nostalgia: "For me it is a document that is significant of an epoch—our epoch, an experience to have read and something that gives me a deep satisfaction to possess." There may have been also a note of relief that the recent financial embarrassments were reconciled: "But I must confess to you that your brief note saying '. . . dear Bill' did me even greater good, it was so heartwarming to know that you think of me with affection. You know, of course, that I have always loved you." He wished her "a wonderful Xmas," and if she should come down after the holidays, he would be able to make her comfortable at the ranch, as "things are better now" and he could "perhaps make up for that awful dinner of two years ago. Please choose yourself a handsome Xmas present from my catalog & let me send it—please!" The letter closes with "My love to you, as ever, Bill"[10]

These unusually intimate expressions of affection reflected certainly the emotions of gratitude, relief, and optimism. But also nostalgic recol-

10. W.S. to Elizabeth Morrow, September 16, 1953; November 20, 1953.

lection: "*our* epoch"! The Lindbergh flight, of course, had metaphorically inscribed for so many Americans between the wars a sense of freedom and cultural achievement; and for a verbal moment it seemed to document for Spratling his own exploratory experience during that period, when his apprenticeship had first linked his life with that of the Morrows. Now, some twenty-five years later, he could at least recall the heightened awareness of living through an epoch such as that. And he was beginning to put things together again, though clearly his fortunes would not again attain their earlier promise. In his fine comprehensive essay on Mexican silver published in 1956, he was perceptive enough to see, despite the sad experience of his own enterprise in the forties, that the artistic and commercial Taxco scene he had essentially created had actually been enhanced by the war. The competition produced by an unprecedented seller's market had intensified the quality of design, and the pre-war reputation of Taxco silver (originated, of course, in the work of Las Delicias) had allowed the industry to survive the sudden market withdrawal as well as some ill-conceived export duties imposed by the government. In the early fifties, his Rancho Spratling operation was one of almost three hundred large and small talleres in the Taxco region. But he would not make the same mistake again, observing in the same essay, "The best work, it has always seemed, has been produced by relatively simple methods and in *talleres* of not more than 50 artisans. Since silversmithing is an intricate affair, consisting entirely of personally attended detail, large organizations seem to lose touch with quality and feeling and invention."

Making silver again under such a controlled environment of scale and renewing—probably strengthening—his ties with the premier jewelry houses in New York, Chicago, and San Francisco did not mean, however, a return to flush times. In the same year of the "silversmithing" essay, for example, Spratling was still carrying a considerable debt from a loan made by a friend from college days, probably secured along with that from Elizabeth Morrow, as a means of "starting up" again. As security, he had mortgaged the Taxco house, which he had not sold after all, and he and Elizabeth Anderson in February of 1956 were working out an arrangement whereby she would liquidate the debt through monthly payments in return for, as she expressed it, "the use of the house for the rest of my life. . . . Since our wills are mutually in each other's favor (we being each the sole beneficiary of the other), I suggest that any immediate transfer of the property is not urgent."[11] In the next year, he clarified his financial situation further in his response to what he called a "magnificent proposition" from a New York firm—apparently to replicate for a year in Cambodia the design techniques with native crafts on the Mexico and Alaska pattern. "A few years ago, to make the story short, I was literally wiped out economically. I began all over again some six years ago and, with only my name and $8000 pesos capital, 1) in two years paid off some $250,000 pesos debt, and 2) today my small talleres (here in the country below Taxco) are barely regaining something like a solid business and artistic standing."[12] He expressed reservations that he could work it out, since he had no bank resources or residential management with which to entrust his Rancho Spratling operation.

Just what Spratling's level of income was, or how much it fluctuated, during the last ten years of his life is unclear, which is apparently the way he wanted it. As late as 1960, he could remark to a visiting friend from college days that "people don't know whether I'm a millionaire or broke."[13] Certainly the former was never true, and in the last two or three years there was even an inclination toward the latter. His public reputation, however, begun before the war, ironically began to crystallize at the time of the Spratling y Artesanos disaster with the *Reader's Digest* publication in 1945 of "Silver Bill, Practical Good Neighbor." Probably more widely read than the 1941 *Time* piece, the article is often factually inaccurate and, obviously based largely on interviews with Spratling, contains several fanciful reconstructions, some of which found their way into *File on Spratling*. Here for the first time in print, for example, is the story of the alleged financial negotiations between Morrow, Rivera, and Spratling concerning the Cuernavaca murals as well as that of Morrow's role in the initiation of the Las Delicias enterprise. In its informal, slightly overwritten style the piece is a telescoped success story typical of the journal's contents. It conceives of Spratling during the genuinely hard times of the early Taxco years as living "happily . . . in elegant simplicity," and at present, in 1945, when in his own epistolary words he was

11. Elizabeth Prall Anderson to W.S., February 10, 1956, ARS. The college friend was Herbert L. Hahn, a Birmingham, Alabama, businessman who had been a member of Spratling's college class of 1921. Both Hahn and his brother Fred (class of 1924) wrote letters in support of the honorary degree.

12. W.S. to Russell Wright, February 8, 1957, ARS.

13. W.S. quoted by W. Kelly Mosley, interview by author, June 15, 1992.

being "literally wiped out economically" as pursuing "a dream life in a story book town." And the first artisan for Spratling's designs, the talented young Artemio Navarrete, actually already known to Spratling by reputation for his fine gold and silver work in Iguala, becomes, for the *Reader's Digest* audience, an old man who was found by Spratling, in his search throughout the countryside for just one silversmith, "hidden away in a small Indian village"; he had almost forgotten his craft, the story goes, and "had to be retrained before he could make a few simple pieces I designed for him."[14]

All this, to be sure, was stuff for Hollywood, and in one of its first short films printed in color Warner Brothers in 1948 released *The Man from New Orleans,* which was based largely on the *Reader's Digest* essay, even to the point of repeating the extended old silversmith episode, invented entirely by Spratling. With Spratling portrayed by a Mexican actor, the film was fully as idyllic in tone as its source. However, it did capture pictorially the linkage between Spratling's New Orleans career and the Taxco scene, including his preservationist influence, and though Spratling may not have cared for the "Good Neighbor" label any more than he did for "Silver Bill," he fully endorsed the film's content with all its romanticized exaggerations. After all, focusing as it did on the human dimension of the Spratling achievement, it carried to hundreds of thousands of moviegoers an image of a *norteamericano* who had made a significant cultural difference in the life of another country. And who could argue with the essential accuracy of the *Reader's Digest* conclusion: that Spratling "had come to live in this little Mexican town because he loved it and remained to protect its beauty and help make it prosperous and happy"? With such as this, Spratling's popular reputation had become unassailable, and "legend" was the term henceforth increasingly associated with his life. Indeed, in a widely publicized 1952 episode when he was feared lost at sea during a flight from Havana to Nassau to attend the wedding of prominent socialite Nancy Oakes, one newspaper account described it thus: "When his life ends, as all men's must, it will be difficult to speak of Spratling in the past tense. Taxco and its silver industry will continue as proof of his ability to merge past, present, and future." As Natalie Scott put it later in a letter to New Orleans, Spratling

14. J. P. McEvoy, " 'Silver Bill,' Practical Good Neighbor," *Reader's Digest,* September 1945, 19–22.

turned up as "a lively corpse," reaching Nassau after a one-day forced landing on Andros Island because of bad weather. But the event, which involved searches by U.S. Navy and Coast Guard planes along with those of the Cuban Air Force, verified what was by then clearly his celebrity status, the affair being reported by wire services throughout the United States and in many foreign countries.[15]

The sixties were the years of public adulation for Spratling and were marked by such relevant events as the re-publication of both *Little Mexico* (in 1964 as *A Small Mexican World*) and *Sherwood Anderson and Other Famous Creoles* (in 1966, University of Texas Press); a celebration of his work, "Homage to William Spratling," sponsored in 1965 by the Mexican-American Institute in Mexico City; an exhibition, mostly of his pre-Columbian collection of artifacts, called "The World of William Spratling," which traveled to several museums in the United States; and a multi-page photographic-essay publication in the *Architectural Digest* (1966) of the same figures but photographed in the gallery designed for them at Rancho Spratling. The latter described the private collection as one of the largest of its kind in the world, and Spratling as a "noted American known as the father of the Mexican silver industry," and as "an extraordinary man . . . whose books, lectures, and his great contributions to the art world have made him the number one cultural ambassador between this country and Mexico."

The last decade of Spratling's life, however, began with three events that may well have recalled for him the "epoch" of struggle, early triumph, and the passing of his youth: the deaths in 1957 of Natalie Scott, Diego Rivera, and Miguel Covarrubias. If Spratling was "The Man—," then surely Natalie Scott was "The Woman from New Orleans." After settling in Taxco, she had maintained her wide New Orleans network of family and literary connections, and for over twenty-five years she had been for Spratling his closest bond with his pre-Mexico experience. In one of his *Herald-Tribune* "Mexican Letters," Spratling remembered that Sherwood Anderson had called her "the best newspaper-woman in America," and during her Mexican residency her loquacious style contin-

15. "Planes Scour Ocean Area for Craft of Ex-Orleanian," *New Orleans Times-Picayune,* December 30, 1952; the quotation is from an unidentified news clipping (Artists Files, HNOC), which recorded on December 31 that the "safe arrival of William Spratling in Nassau is cause for rejoicing"; Natalie Scott to Martha Gilmore Robinson, March 29, 1953.

ued to find numerous expressions in the long, superbly written letters back home, blending family trivia, splendid evocations of life in Taxco, and perceptive commentary on world events and Mexican and Louisiana politics. Her hospitality to a constant stream of visitors, including, as she wrote, "all sorts of people whom I've never heard of who turn up from N.O.," may have exceeded even that of Spratling, but her active, outgoing social life belied the quiet heroism of her overseas Red Cross duty in both world wars, for which she was awarded the Croix de Guerre for dragging wounded soldiers to safety from a bombed hospital in May of 1918. As the obituary notices in the New Orleans press affirmed, her lasting human legacy was her founding in her adopted town the Pro-Infancia, which operated a day nursery for the needy children of working mothers, and her continuous trips, as recorded in her letters, of bringing crippled children from Guerrero to Mexico City and arranging there for their free medical attention. An account of the long funeral procession attended by hundreds of "visibly affected" Mexicans was published in the *Times-Picayune*: "You can imagine the uncontrolled emotion displayed by the little children and the many poor whom Natalie had helped throughout her life in Taxco."[16]

Natalie Scott's career, of course, in achieving its own form of distinction following her transition from New Orleans to Mexico had been a parallel to that of Spratling, and her Taxco residency had been for him a continuous image of remembrance and of no-nonsense companionship. During the earlier part of that period, when Spratling in his twenties was affirming a definite, if directionless, commitment to an apprenticeship in another culture, it had been the work and voice of Rivera that had instructed him in the mythic power of Mexican history. Spratling had been able actually to observe the foremost painter of his generation at work on some of his greatest achievements—and had indeed been intimately involved in initiating one of them. Although never associated with the strident political pledges that affected the artistic careers of Rivera and some of the other Mexican Renaissance painters, Spratling had nevertheless defended Rivera against the jealous snipings arising from within that circle. Rivera had written an introductory note for *Little Mexico* praising the "acuteness and grace," the "irony and love" of its portraits, and there

16. "Miss Scott Final Rites in Mexico," *New Orleans Item*, November 19, 1957, p. 1; "Memorial Rites Set for Writer," *New Orleans Times-Picayune*, December 15, 1957, p. 3.

is no reason to doubt Spratling's statement in the long silversmithing essay that Rivera had been most encouraging in the origins of Las Delicias. Indeed, there may be no better testimony to Spratling's talent for cultural assimilation and to the originality of his creative spirit than his friendships with Rivera, the dominant figure of the Mexican Renaissance, and with Covarrubias, who was to Spratling its finest historical scholar. The three had, of course, been a triumvirate of *cambalacheros*—traders or exchangers—in pre-Hispanic artifacts, in fact among the very first such explorers. Spratling could not match Rivera's comprehensive knowledge of the history of Mexican art and had not the expert eye of Covarrubias for an object's archaeological authenticity and provenance. Indeed, it seems likely that the impressive collection he eventually developed may have owed much to his shrewd bartering technique, likened by one observer to Spratling's knowledge of the subtle art of horse-trading in the southern United States.[17]

Yet Spratling's capacity for intense concentrated study should not be underestimated in this regard, nor should his power of absorbing what he saw and discussed in his travels throughout Little Mexico, especially in the state of Guerrero and the *tierra caliente* region, whose stone idols he made his own special collecting province. As early as 1930, as we have seen, he was already a perceptive collector of folk art, contributing several eighteenth- and nineteenth-century pieces to the Carnegie Exposition organized by d'Harnoncourt. And records at the Brooklyn Museum from the mid to late thirties show that he was both donating and selling antiquities, including some pre-Columbian pieces, to that institution. There are, moreover, a number of references in his correspondence to a friendly relationship with the distinguished Harvard archaeologist Joseph Spinden, including a request in 1937 that Spinden be told "that I already have made all the tracings of my collection of stamps and that within a week I shall send him a set of photostats as promised."[18]

He remained a professed amateur, and if his reputation as a collector was somewhat marred in his last years by his occasional traffic in the widespread fakery of pre-Columbian art, the high quality of his ability to appraise and collect authentic examples of that art is manifest in his

17. Gerald Kelly, "William Spratling: Arquitecto-Diseñador," in *William Spratling* (Mexico City: Centro Cultural Arte Contemporaneo, 1987).

18. W.S. to Louise W. Chase, October 22, 1937, ARS.

most impressive publication, *More Human than Divine* (1960), a presentation with superb photographs of his collection of *remojadas,* small ceramic clay sculptures from central Vera Cruz. Spratling's short interpretive essay on the collection, much of which he donated to the National University of Mexico, makes no attempt at archaeological analysis, but emphasizes what always seemed to attract him about this ancient art: its human qualities and how in the calmness and restraint of its stylized form it offered a welcome antithesis to the pace of life he had left behind in New Orleans. In some of his finest writing, he described those artisans in this culture who had created, a thousand years before Columbus, the pervasive smiling faces of their sculptures: "A sheer delight in everything that concerned daily living possessed and motivated them. That, and a childlike conception of what life is good for. Nowhere in the world has a sculptured record been left by a people so warmly and so obviously concerned with the personable, the pleasant human creature, something worthy of meditation in the present age of increasingly complicated living."[19] The volume was dedicated to Covarrubias, "the man with the most informed and clearest vision of his country's artistic past," and one who "had for thirty years most constantly shared and stimulated" the author's love for the ancient sculpture of America. The dedication to Covarrubias, like the death of Natalie Scott, completed another of those long loops of enclosure that so often marked Spratling's life. For it had been more than thirty years since the two young men in the French Quarter, Spratling and Faulkner, had first encountered what was then the stylish and clever work of Covarrubias, using it as the model for *Sherwood Anderson and Other Famous Creoles.*

More Human than Divine was a splendid affirmation of Spratling's long and notable involvement in the cultural and economic life of Mexico, and *Time,* in selecting the book for a complimentary review, identified him as he who "in time became a sort of legend as the man who revived in Taxco the proud craftmanship of the past."[20] But his best work was behind him. By the mid-sixties some of his friends felt that he was losing his eye for silvercraft design and for collecting. In fact, he seemed to have lost interest in the design process, and the self-discipline that had

19. William Spratling, *More Human than Divine,* preface by Gordon F. Ekholm (Mexico City: Universidad Nacional Autonama de Mexico, 1960), 11.
20. "A Legacy of Laughter," *Time,* June 20, 1960, p. 62.

sustained his art, indeed had made it possible through hard times and a
long apprenticeship, was now transferred to a strictly regimented life on
the ranch. The regimen was centered on a structure that may—like the
hours of drawing in his college rooms fifty years earlier—have served to
counter an observable tendency toward depression, this time alcohol-
related. Spratling's pre-occupation with the trading and acquisition of
artifacts and his almost daily reception of visitors literally from far and
wide—assorted celebrities, Alabama and New Orleans friends, and occasionally relatives—with meals and the ritual of cocktails, always precisely timed. Whether he had overnight guests or not, when he retired he
threw the master generator switch, leaving the ranch in total darkness.
And his own compulsion with punctuality could be offensively extended
to his guests, one Alabama relative and her companion recalling that
unavoidable transportation problems from Mexico City had made them
late for dinner at the ranch. "Bill was furious when we finally arrived
and the meal was not a pleasant experience at all. But he was sorry about
it, and next day when we arrived in Acapulco, the red carpet was really
rolled out for us because he had called ahead, a kind of apology, I
guess."[21]

Alberto Ulrich, Spratling's young friend from those days who shared
with him an interest in pre-Hispanic art and who, following Spratling's
death, purchased the ranch and silver enterprise, recalled that on his first
visit to Taxco-el-Viejo he witnessed Spratling supervising the unloading
of a truck filled with stone ornaments which a group of Indians had
brought for his review. What is "real" and what is "fake" in such appraisals became increasingly problematic after World War II, as both
scholarly and popular interest in pre-Columbian civilizations enormously increased the value of their art among museum and individual
collectors alike. How discerning Spratling was about all this and whether
or not he significantly participated in transactions allowing ancient art
objects to leave the country cannot be clearly determined, although, as
already indicated, he had been accused of such, much to his distress, as
early as 1931. However, the perverseness that so often accompanies the
kind of isolated egocentricity and occasional misogyny that Spratling
seemed to affect in his last years sometimes expressed itself in his absorp-

21. Mrs. Kenneth Spratling Kirkwood (Alice), interview by author, September 19,
1993.

tion with collecting. For example, the distinguished archaeologist Gillett Griffin recalled his visit in the year of Spratling's death to Taxco-el-Viejo. Following breakfast the two were seated on the porch when a young man appeared with a carton of four stone objects which he wanted to sell. "They were obviously bad. But Spratling took me aside and asked me earnestly whether he should buy them. I didn't know if he was testing me or setting me up. I said I wouldn't buy them. . . . He was brought to my house for a party after an opening. He showed me photographs of a relief from Chalcatzingo. I learned afterwards that he was trying to sell it at my house." Though Griffin could laugh about the episode later, "I was somewhat angry" at the time, he remembered, that a guest in his house was attempting to sell something that should have remained in Mexico. "We all thought the Chalcatzingo monument was a fake, but it was real. . . . Some of his friends are convinced that he really was losing his sensitivity and eye—but I really wonder."[22] Perversity, shrewdness, misplaced commercialism, vanity. All these, perhaps. But there is every indication that in some of his dealings of this sort Spratling over-reached himself, made poor judgments, and, whether he knew what he was passing off was not real but fake, lost the trust of several wealthy friends and clients. This, along with the attenuation of the silver enterprise, had reduced his personal finances to a low ebb in the last two years of his life.[23] This may indeed have been a period of loneliness for him. Possibly he had become tired of being in himself something of a tourist attraction, and his angry ambivalence as he grew older about what he may have perceived as the public meaning of his career found repeated expressions in conversations, for example, with such visitors from his earlier life as Alabama relatives and college friends whom he genuinely welcomed to Taxco-el-Viejo. At least one reconciling interval that vividly linked the indirection of his early life with the established eminence of the later was the long-anticipated return to Alabama. The occasion was the unanticipated awarding in 1962 of an honorary doctorate by his alma mater.

There are a few brief allusions to the visit in the autobiography: lunch with old friends, the nostalgic walk down College Street, lecture to a faculty-student convocation in art and architecture wherein he was intro-

22. Gillett Griffin, letter to the author, November 23, 1993; Gillett Griffin, interview by Ann Waldron, February 7, 1994, Princeton, N.J.

23. Alberto Ulrich, interview by author, August 17, 1995 (Rancho Spratling).

duced by his old friend from the mid-thirties in Mexico, Maltby Sykes, who had worked with Rivera as mural assistant on the Hotel Reforma murals in Mexico City. And, of course, the memorable evening party at Roamer's Roost, the Spratling plantation in Gold Hill, which was a roaring success once—as he fails to record—his hostess made clear that his clumping rancho manners and touch of self-important rudeness wouldn't do. But none of these associations touched the depth of feeling that the honorary degree possibility seemed to hold for Spratling. Years before, he had written somewhat wistfully to David who, following his retirement, had returned to college and earned his degree: "It makes me feel good to know you've finally got the sheepskin. I myself wouldn't know what to do with it unless I were going to go back to teaching—which doesn't seem very attractive any more now that I'm in my 60th year." While the award was under consideration, he wrote to a longtime friend: "I cannot deny that an honorary degree to be conferred by Auburn would be a sort of vindication of my life objectives and a deep satisfaction to me after all these years."[24]

Clearly, another loop in the personal drama of his life would be closed. And with the courtesy of expression he always used in writing to the older members of his father's family, he expressed his desire in the forthcoming visit to experience briefly the daily privacy of his boarding-house undergraduate years of 1920–1921. "Whatever happens," he wrote to the daughter of his elderly cousin, who was even then still the owner of Terrell's Boardinghouse, a longtime Auburn landmark, "I hope to stay in my old room with Cousin Leila the 13th—thanks for your letter that came today and tell Cousin Leila that my private joy in returning to Auburn will be her, seeing her in person, and not the doctorate." The day he arrived back in Taxco, he wrote again: "I think the most heartwarming contact in my 40-year-return was seeing you and to be able to give my dear Cousin Leila a little hug and a kiss. I want you to know how very grateful I am for your hospitality and helpfulness."[25] He added that the taxi just made it to the Columbus, Georgia, airport on

24. W.S. to David Spratling, October 11, 1959, courtesy Mrs. Paula Wester. The friend was Ralph Hammond of Arab, Alabama, who had been instrumental in bringing the matter to the attention of the university trustees. The letter is dated July 5, 1961.

25. W.S. to Annie Terrell Basore, November 22, 1962; W.S. to Prof. and Mrs. Basore and Leila Terrell, December 18, 1962.

time, but didn't mention, as witnesses later affirmed, that as part of his traveling apparel he had donned his recently acquired long black academic gown which, with its attached college hood, fluttered about his thin shoulders as he entered the plane for the trip back to Mexico.

Despite the fact that during this last half-decade the Spratling legend was being further enhanced, there may have been some bitterness in his realization that the self-fashioning that had contributed to that legend had long since been completed—although the unexpected possibility of putting together *File on Spratling* offered him in one of the final acts of his life the confirmation of that process. The autobiographical prospect was apparently suggested to him by his editors at Little, Brown following the re-publication in 1964 of *Little Mexico.* However, most, if not all, of the book seems to have been prepared in 1966 and early 1967, following the publication in 1966—to which Spratling refers—of the facsimile edition of his early collaboration with Faulkner on *Sherwood Anderson and Other Famous Creoles,* together with his own recollections of the Faulkner friendship. Reconstructing this portion of his New Orleans experience, descriptions of which appear in the autobiography, may well have stimulated Spratling to think further about the shape of his total career.

The book seems oddly dedicated to James Thurber, whom Spratling undoubtedly knew but who is not mentioned elsewhere in the text and who in his own work made no apparent reference to Spratling. But thinking back to the book he had created with Faulkner, who had supplied the text and he the drawings, may have reminded Spratling of the text-cartoon pattern of much of Thurber's work and reminded him further of the title of one of Thurber's principal collections, which had been published first in the forties but re-issued in the sixties. It was that title which Spratling quoted in the dedication: "To James Thurber, also a draftsman, who wrote *My World, and Welcome to It,* alas, what a title!" Whatever affinity he may have felt for Thurber as a "draftsman" is less clear than that Thurber's title recalled that of the widely traveled exhibit of Spratling's own lifework which had been organized in the previous year as "The World of William Spratling"; and it may have recalled also the revised title of *Little Mexico, A Small Mexican World,* which Spratling seemed to regard as his principal work of cultural interpretation.

One has every right to anticipate finding in an autobiography the embedded image of a life created by the author in the form he or she who lived that life wished it to be remembered. Set down before the final defining moment, it is potentially a way to challenge or even subvert the inevitable obituary, to create a fiction that will reveal the self in terms of the content selected from the life being remembered and in the arranging and shaping of those remembrances for the gaze of readers more strange than familiar. As Spratling began for the first time to recollect images of his life for an anonymous readership, these several fusions of remembrance and ambiguous identity seemed to have influenced the nature of his self-projection. For what he constructs is, in fact, as his title suggests, a "file"—but not so much on his life but on his "world." In a sense, the contents of that file almost make its author unknown: his world, indeed, seems to succeed his life. There are few private disclosures. *File on Spratling* will not illuminate for us, for example, what we have already seen: a transformation of the restless, self-conscious young student from Alabama within a year or two into the gregarious and confident figure who successfully infiltrated the ambitious literary and artistic society of the Vieux Carré. But what the file will show us is a world at once both unpredictable and yet promising, a world which the "I" named William Spratling always views ironically, including his own flamboyant—sometimes egocentric—but always grateful participation in it. It is above all, for the author, a world of Mexican ambience and rhythm, one in which he allowed himself to be absorbed while at the same time coming to terms with it in his art and with the integrity of what has been called his "accomplishments in living."[26]

It would be overstating the case to suggest that an unconscious purpose of *File on Spratling* was to modify for an American readership a Spratling identity that was principally popular and commercial, replacing it with a rather enigmatic persona that had attained its form and distinction in a cultural environment foreign to those readers. Yet despite the apparently discursive, almost aimless pattern and the indication that at least portions of the book were dictated with another hand being involved in the compilation, we should not assume too quickly that it was casually dashed off in the few months preceding his death. There would

26. For an extended discussion of the nature of autobiography and of "Autobiography and America," see James M. Cox, *Recovering Literature's Lost Ground: Essays in American Biography* (Baton Rouge: Louisiana State University Press, 1989), esp. 11–32.

seem to be no credence, either, in the theory that Spratling died before he was able to make editorial revisions. As indicated in a letter written to Alabama in November of 1966, he had the manuscript in his possession for a period at least nine months before his fatal accident. He wrote that he himself had sent it off to its publisher—thus the book was actually in press prior to his death. He referred to the manuscript as "my autobiography" and that "Little, Brown will be publishing this in March or August," but indicated his sense of its incompleteness and occasional inflated stories by adding: "Just pay no attention if you discover a few little lies."[27] If much of the content of *File on Spratling* was initially in the form of oral transmission, that content still was reviewed and confirmed—rearranged, extended, re-written perhaps—by Spratling himself at a time when the legacy of his life and the meaning of that legacy were very much on his mind. If in the alteration of an oral to a written form he missed a revision or two, there is still no reason to believe that in the last year or so of his life he would have abandoned the pride and discipline he had always shown in his writing. Moreover, he put his name, and his alone, on the title page. Many of his recollections, as we have seen, are absolutely on the mark in their evocative accuracy, but, as we have seen also, there are also omissions, for whatever reason, that were critical in the private and public evolution of his career.[28]

References to *File on Spratling* have consistently regarded its content as legitimately autobiographical, the two most recent pictorial volumes on Spratling's silver designs, for example, in citing *File* for episodes in Spratling's life, refer to what he "wrote" in the book. However, the file is eclectic in content, loosely developed on a chronological frame, with occasional excursions either into sections taken from Spratling's other writings or into what appear to be anecdotal recollections that meandered into his memory. All of this encloses those several passages of undoubted veracity, the whole volume being strangely an image of what might be called the Spratling environment during his last years at the ranch.

27. W.S. to "Alice" (Mrs. Kenneth Spratling Kirkwood), November 2, 1966.
28. The additional "hand" in *File on Spratling* was probably that of Gerald Kelly. Ulrich, interview. Kelly assisted Elizabeth Anderson in her book about herself; his fine recollective essay on Spratling in the 1987 Mexico City symposium volume has already been cited.

> We were cordially ushered into a room so astounding that my image of it has never faded. . . . It was a museum, art gallery, and home—a fascinating jumble, a happily conceived disarray rather than a self-conscious display.
>
> Sculptures in every conceivable material . . . posed, pranced, perched, smiled, glowered, or simply gazed blandly from every corner, shelf, niche, and beam. Masks glowered at coiled serpents. A self-portrait of Diego Rivera stared straight through the only anachronism in the room, an airplane propeller standing on tip near the doorway to the patio. Yet it too belonged, as valid a part of Bill Spratling as his congregation of friends from a far more remote past.[29]

This atmosphere was indeed what another visitor in the mid-sixties identified as the "vivid world of William Spratling, where his full flavor lies . . . surrounded by redolent symbols, masks and ivory brought home from Alaska . . . a profusion of well-read books, manuscripts and portfolios, all dusty, from which fall letters from Rivera, sketches by Covarrubias, and notes for new silver designs on odd scraps of paper." And at the center of this disarranged but magnetic world was "an incredible person . . . an egoist of the first water. One can talk of nothing but William Spratling, and his personality is an intense, enveloping one. [We] had a very odd dinner served on a dirty red tablecloth . . . and I sitting in the old leather chair where John F. Kennedy lunched with Bill Spratling."[30]

This is the environment from which *File on Spratling* emerged. The book is itself a "happily conceived disarray," a file of remembrances *on* a life named "Spratling" that we can reconstruct only as far as the contents of the file and our inferences about them will permit. To be sure,

---

29. Robert David Duncan, "William Spratling's Mexican World," *Texas Quarterly* 9 (spring 1966), 98. The two pictorial volumes, both valuable in extending our knowledge of Spratling silver, are Sandraline Cederwall and Hal Riney, *Spratling Silver* (San Francisco: Chronicle Books, 1990), and Penny C. Morrill and Carole A. Berk, *Mexican Silver* (Atglen, Pa.: Schiffer Publishing, 1994). Both seem oriented toward collectors and specialists in Mexican silver, especially the latter book, which contains a price index for vintage pieces. The Cederwall-Riney offers a definitive illustrated history of Spratling hallmarks, and the Morrill-Berk, in addition to its splendid color photographs, contains informative essays on Spratling and his contemporary designers, many of whom Spratling influenced.

30. The description is from a letter, dated January 29, 1965, to a friend (identified only as "Emerson") by John P. Leeper, the museum curator who organized the exhibit of Spratling's work and collection of pre-Columbian art. From papers of the Marion Koogler McNay Art Institute, San Antonio, in the Spratling collection, Auburn University Archives.

the file contains many fragments and disconnections—as would the file on any life—which seem not to find a reasonable place even within an organization of calculated disarray. And though there are also exaggerated accounts of this or that adventure, more often than not the detail is less important than the structure of the autobiography's disarray it helps to illustrate. The fine and exciting account of Spratling's 4,300-mile sailboat voyage from Santa Monica to Acapulco ("this made sailing history"), which ended in a "hero's breakfast," is juxtaposed to an account of another voyage he took in the same year—on the *Hindenburg*—to Germany. And our public remembrance of the hovering fiery horror at Lakehurst at the end of the return voyage to America encloses the ominous details of Spratling's recollections: the spatial immensity, the elegance and tranquillity within the enormous craft, and how, over Ireland, "the great searchlight in the middle of the ship's belly would bring into daylight brilliance the farms and yards and chickens and housewives as they rushed about trying to make us out there just above them." He is reminded of these details after thirty years, he says, by a letter from Mary Anita Loos (who herself would remember, in her appreciation of Spratling after his death, that she had tried to help him clarify some of his recollections for the book). In her letter she had remarked about the very singularity of his *Hindenburg* trip and the oddness of its being safer than the sailboat voyage. She had been with him, he recalls, in Santa Monica before he cast off, and her letter reminds him further of her Aunt Anita, "who used to charm Bill Faulkner and me in New Orleans back in the twenties."

Almost every episode in *File on Spratling* contains associational memories like these, sometimes only illustrating the range and recognizable density of the world he has lived in, others broaching feelings he declined to place directly into the file. The several allusions to Sherwood Anderson, for example (whom he still "can't forget"), recall his New Orleans period of beginning maturation and achievement but also its connection to the present in his continuing friendship with Elizabeth, whom he now frequently visited in Taxco, just as she visited him at the ranch, bringing news from the town. He had helped her financially during the war, and once her debt was paid off, she wrote to him just before his initial Alaska trip, with her usual "Dearest Bill" salutation: "I needn't tell you how grateful I am for your forbearance all this time. I'd feel very low at the thought of your going so far away for so long except that I'm delighted to think of what a good and timely thing it is for you." Within a year of these Spratling autobiographical reflections she, along with Anita Loos, would become one of his heirs and would subsequently write in her own autobiography that "I miss Bill Spratling so very much more than I ever missed Sherwood Anderson."[31]

To be sure, *File on Spratling* is an odd book, revealing in its abrupt and unexpected connections the reconstruction of a life that was perhaps irregular but also richly episodic in its structure. When extended, however—indeed authenticated—by the revelations of Spratling's private correspondence, the volume assists us toward achieving a sense of the wholeness of his life, a linkage between creative genius and human being.

Shortly before his death, Spratling, together with Jaime Castrejón, mayor of Taxco, reviewed and approved the documents for his final gesture linking past and present—plans for the Museo de Taxco, which would house his collection of Guerrero pre-Hispanic antiquities being left in his will to the city. This act of generosity receives scant attention in the autobiographical file, but Spratling's one comment suggests that he had some perception of a larger legacy of which his own creative work was but a part. He wished to contribute to the people of Mexico what he described as "a sense of the worth and dignity of the high culture which preceded our own." His words were "*our* own," for the Spratling being re-created through his remembrances and, for us, further through his other writings, had indeed entered another culture, helping to reclaim and dignify for it a civilization older and perhaps more mysterious than any which lay embedded in the great continent remainder lying to the north. The extensive account in the *New York Times* of the museum conception and of Spratling's career began thus: "Although Santa Prisca is the patron saint of this city, her icon is encountered less frequently around town than the stock photograph of a white-haired, bespectacled North American, the late William Spratling. All but a second patron saint by popular acclamation, Mr. Spratling . . . is now going to be memorialized if not quite canonized, by a museum adjacent to Santa Prisca's cathedral." The *Times* account predicted, accurately as it turned out,

---

31. Elizabeth Anderson and Gerald R. Kelly, *Miss Elizabeth: A Memoir* (Boston: Little, Brown, 1969), 304. Elizabeth's letter to Spratling is dated only "Sunday," though its content ("They'll probably want to give you the company when you get back") identifies the year as 1945. One of her continuing handwritten accounts of what she owed, "Memorandum of debt to William Spratling," was sent to him, signed and dated May 13, 1943, ARS.

that the museum when completed would inevitably bear Spratling's name despite his rejection of such as the planning was completed; "it would make me feel dead," he said.[32]

Just four days after making this statement, Spratling died as a result of the auto accident on the same Iguala road that, some thirty-six years ago, with designs for a revolutionary art form in his pocket, he had traveled in search of a young silversmith, thus initiating that portion of his life which would make him famous and, indeed, would make what preceded it a proper story for us to know. To those several friends who had known him during his Mexican years, as they recalled his personal character in press interviews the day after his death, he was "a strange dichotomy":

> He was generous but very aware of money. . . . A brilliant salesman, he could also be rude. . . . People loved him and disliked him. . . . The Spratling charm? When he turned it on, you couldn't get away from it. . . . He had an excellent feeling for the table, probably part of his Southern inheritance. . . . He was sort of an exhibitionist and enjoyed the tourists who came to his shop. But I think he was a lonely man and so went to nature. He retreated into the countryside and met people only when he wanted to. . . . He had the habit of calling friends three or four times a day just to chat, because he was lonely. . . . He lived alone but he wanted people. He had an antenna for them—he knew how you lived inside yourself. Yet he couldn't live with people. . . . He had a great capacity for friendship, and was a loveable man. . . . He liked people to wonder about him. . . . Although an eccentric character, he was a wonderful friend. . . . He had no political views, was not dedicated to anything special. He believed in humanity. He was an ardent American, but had a great love for the Mexican people. His silversmiths respected him. They knew he knew his job. They understood him because he thought in their ways. He was kind to them but always in a gruff manner. They knew they could rely on him. And he never expected thanks for what he did. . . . He had no fears except one, a long lingering illness. . . . He just couldn't squeeze enough out of life. . . . He was a legend in his own time. He was a citizen of the world, at home everywhere in his own personal way.[33]

32. John Canaday, "Spratling's Spirit Hovers over Touristy Taxco," *New York Times*, December 25, 1967.

33. "The Many Sides of William Spratling," *Mexico City News*, August 20, 1967, pp. 13a–15c. Among those quoted were Helen Escobedo, director of the Museum of Arts and Sciences at the National University; John Brown, cultural attaché at the U.S. embassy; and Howard Phillips, former editor of *Mexican Life*.

In his letter to Alabama with which this account of Spratling's life began, David, following the account of his brother's funeral, wrote that "Bill was a great American." In using that term, now so casually bestowed in our informal discourse, David had no doubt been overwhelmed by the public mournings of thousands of Taxqueños, making visible what he could not possibly have understood before: the unprecedented loyalty, respect, and gratitude his brother's image would always hold in this place he had essentially re-created. The assignment of greatness must always, of course, find its own criteria, but at least we should consider how fortunate we are to come upon a life like Spratling's! On the one hand, a portion of its retrospective fullness seems to remind us of recurring elements of the artistic life in America during the early decades of the century: the coming-of-age story told in his youthful correspondence; his disciplinary commitment to creative longings that would lead he knew not where but that may well have thwarted the potential for depression inherent in his continuing sense of lonely displacement; the obligatory European voyages to confront and assimilate the cultural forms of the older civilization; the emergence of the characteristic features of his expressive technique, which, as he wrote and drew his way across the decade of the New Orleans twenties, extended our record of an important American time and place; and finally, of course, against a background of disappointment and contention with the Great Depression, the maturing and triumph of his artistic statement.

That statement, however, found its mythic shapes and hard metallic color in another America. Spratling was different from most of the artistic expatriates between the wars in that he never returned, and his art by its very nature could not serve as one of those verbal or plastic records of a "foreign" experience that created for some of the best-known writers and painters of that period an ironic relationship between themselves and the values of their native country. At the center of the Spratling legacy is, of course, a minor art form, but one that, augmented by the brilliant entrepreneurial vigor of its creator, transformed an economy. If his designs do not reflect the personal drama lying behind them, they capture nevertheless the most observable qualities that he brought southward from his long apprenticeship: the discipline and order of his architectural training and his romantic inclination toward the iconographic forms of cultures isolated or suppressed by forces more powerful in their modernity.

The cobwebby disarray at Rancho Spratling so artfully sustained by its founder has long since disappeared, being displaced by the easy ambience yet efficient quality control of Los Sucesores de William Spratling. Under that aegis the Spratling name is more than ever still a synonym for excellence, as the master's designs are being produced and marketed throughout the Western world, supervised at the rancho's *taller,* as of this writing, by the last maestro trained by Spratling himself. The wider parameters of the Spratling legacy, however, transcending the art itself, are suggested by some of the comments offered in support of the honorary degree awarded five years before his death. With none of the effusiveness often inherent in such matters, the judgments are brief and direct, as though self-evident. Nelson Rockefeller stated that Spratling "has made a very real contribution to the cultural life of this hemisphere"; and to Lyndon Johnson, he was "an American of genuine distinction whose vision and success . . . has played a direct role in furthering relations" between Mexico and the United States. But it was René d'Harnoncourt, then director of the Museum of Modern Art and one of Spratling's first friends in the early Mexican days, who gave specific substance to these affirmations. Spratling's "extraordinary understanding of Mexico," his active and perceptive intervention on behalf of the major modern Mexican painters in bringing them to the attention of the U.S. public, and his own creative initiation in Taxco of "a true renaissance of Mexican folk art in modern context"—all this has "created a climate of understanding" which has been a major contribution to the confirmation and acceptance of the arts of Mexico, both ancient and modern. Then, with casual authority, perhaps the rarest compliment and indeed the unassailable element of the Spratling legend: "I know of no one person who has so deeply influenced the artistic orientation of a country not his own." Few Americans have left behind them a claim such as this.

In the same wide context of commentary on a life that gave much more than it took, another of Spratling's oldest friends from the halcyon twenties, Lesley Byrd Simpson, observed that possibly of the greatest significance was the "relationship between our two peoples" that Spratling's career had created in "the love and respect that all classes of Mexicans have for him. He understands their personality as few Americans do. They are proud of him; they trust him; and they look upon him, quite properly, as a lifelong friend."[34] And there can be no doubt that his affection and friendship for the country he had made his own were equally genuine. When the optimistic possibility of the Alaska project first emerged, he had written to Elizabeth Morrow, even after just enduring the collapse of Spratling y Artesanos, that "I cannot bring myself to face leaving Mexico." But when he finally did so, the description of his solitary northern flight and of his return—this time a journey down the other side of the long continent—might serve as an image in itself of the reciprocity between the life of this curious genius and the southern place which somehow had made possible his splendid endowment to the future:

> At 4:14 the *Niño* was at last circling the blue sky above Taxco. I watched the plane's shadow pass over the red roofs and green laurels. I chopped the engine for the 3,000 foot drop to the ranch by the river, then on to land at Iguala. Back in the green hills of southern Mexico, I had left the violent winds, dark skies and cold drizzle of the northland and was back in the sun once more.[35]

34. The letters are all addressed to the Auburn University Board of Trustees: that of Rockefeller, August 7, 1961; of Johnson, July 22, 1961; of d'Harnoncourt, August 30, 1961; and of Simpson, July 18, 1961; Auburn University Archives.

35. W.S. to Mrs. Morrow, July 8, 1945. Spratling's account of the Alaska journey was published as "Flight to the North Star," *Flying,* March 1950, pp. 32–33, 51–52.

Selected Bibliography

Writings by William Spratling

Curtis, N. C. and William Spratling. "Architectural Tradition in New Orleans."
Journal of the American Institute of Architects 13 (August 1925): 279–96.

———. *The Wrought Iron Work of Old New Orleans.* New York: Press of the
American Institute of Architects, 1925.

Faulkner, William, and William Spratling. *Sherwood Anderson and Other Famous Creoles: A Gallery of Contemporary New Orleans.* New Orleans: Pelican Book Shop, 1926.

Spratling, William. "The Architectural Heritage of New Orleans." *Architectural Forum* 46 (May 1927): 409.

———. "Cane River Portraits." *Scribner's Magazine* 83 (April 1928): 411–18.

———. "Chronicle of a Friendship: William Faulkner in New Orleans." *Texas Quarterly* 9 (spring 1966): 34–40.

———. "Diego Rivera." *Mexican Folkways* 6 (1930): 162–96.

———. "The Expressive Pencil." *Pencil Points* (June 1929): 365–72.

———. "Figures in a Mexican Renaissance." *Scribner's Magazine* 85 (January 1929): 14–21.

———. *File on Spratling.* Boston: Little, Brown, 1967.

———. "Flight to the North Star." *Flying* (March 1950), 32–33, 51–52.

———. "The Friendly Capital of Rebel Mexico." *Travel* (September 1929): 35–36.

———. "Guanajuato, the Most Mexican City." *Architectural Forum* 48 (February 1928): 217.

———. "Indo-Hispanic Mexico." Parts 1 and 2. *Architecture* 59 (February 1929): 75–80; (March 1929): 139–44.

———. *Little Mexico.* New York: Cape and Smith, 1932. Re-published as *A Small Mexican World.* Boston: Little, Brown, 1964.

———. "Mansions of the Conquistadors." *Travel* (August 1929), 28–31.

———. "Mexican Letter." *New York Herald-Tribune Books,* March 24, 1929, 9.

———. "Mexican Letter." *New York Herald-Tribune Books,* July 28, 1929, 8.

———. "Mexican Letter." *New York Herald-Tribune Books*, November 10, 1929, 9.

———. "Mexican Letter." *New York Herald-Tribune Books*, January 26, 1930, 9.

———. "Modern Mexican Silversmithing." *Mexican Art and Life* 3 (July 1938): 1–4.

———. *More Human than Divine*. With a preface by Gordon F. Ekholm. Mexico City: Universidad Nacional Autonama de Mexico, 1960.

———. "Natchez, Mississippi." *Architectural Forum* 47 (November 1927): 425–26.

———. "On the Review of *Little Mexico* by C. G. Poore." *New York Times Book Review*, July 31, 1931, 3.

———. "Orozco." *New York Herald-Tribune Books*, April 14, 1929, 11.

———. *Pencil Drawing*. New Orleans: Pelican Book Shop, 1923.

———. *Picturesque New Orleans: Ten Drawings of the French Quarter*. With an introduction by Lyle Saxon. New Orleans: Tulane University Press, 1923.

———. "The Public Health Center, Mexico City." *Architectural Forum* 55 (November 1931): 589–94.

———. "Re-Creating a University." *New York Herald-Tribune Books*, June 2, 1929, 9.

———. "Savannah's Architectural Background." *Architectural Forum* 43 (November 1925): 273–76.

———. "The Silver City of the Clouds." *Travel* (July 1929), 22–33.

———. "Sketching in Northern Italy." *Architecture* 54 (August 1926): 236–39.

———. "Some New Discoveries in Mexican Clay." *International Studio* (February 1931): 22–23, 78, 80.

———. "Some Impressions of Mexico." Parts 1 and 2. *Architectural Forum* 47 (July 1927): 1; (August 1927): 168.

———. "Twenty Five Years of Mexican Silversmithing." *Artes de Mexico* (December 1955), 87–90.

———. "Wrought Iron Crosses from the Old Jesuit Cemetery, Grand Coteau, Louisiana." *Architecture* 53 (August 1925).

Spratling, William, and Natalie Scott. *Old Plantation Houses in Louisiana*. With an introduction by N. C. Curtis. New York: William Helburn, 1927.

Other Published Works Cited

American Federation of Arts. *Mexican Arts Catalogue of an Exhibition Organized and Circulated by the American Federation of Arts*. With a preface by

F. A. Whiting and an introduction by René d'Harnoncourt. New York: Southworth Press, 1930.

Anderson, Elizabeth, and Gerald R. Kelly. *Miss Elizabeth: A Memoir.* Boston: Little, Brown, 1969.

Anderson, Sherwood. "New Orleans, *The Double Dealer,* and the Modern Movement in America." *Double Dealer* 3 (March 1922): 125.

———. *Sherwood Anderson's Memoirs: Critical Edition.* Ed. Ray Lewis White. Chapel Hill: University of North Carolina Press, 1942.

Atl, Dr. "Mexico and the Ultra-Baroco." *Architectural Forum* 48 (February 1928): 223–24.

"Auburn Seniors to Present Portrait." *Montgomery Advertiser,* January 30, 1921.

Basso, Hamilton. "William Faulkner, Man and Writer." *Saturday Review* (July 28, 1962), 11.

Beals, Carleton. *Mexican Maze.* Philadelphia: J. B. Lippincott, 1931.

Berry, Brick. "Taxco of the Aztecs Now Greets the World." *New York Times Magazine,* April 24, 1932, 18.

Blom, Frans and Oliver La Farge. *Tribes and Temples: A Record of the Expedition to Middle America Conducted by the Tulane University of Louisiana in 1925.* 2 vols. New Orleans: Tulane University of Louisiana, 1926.

Blotner, Joseph. *Faulkner: A Biography.* New York: Random House, 1974; Vintage Books, 1991.

Brenner, Anita. *Idols Behind Altars.* New York: Harcourt, Brace, 1929.

Broughton, Panthea Reid. "Faulkner's Cubist Novels." In *A Cosmos of My Own,* ed. Doreen Fowler and Ann Abadie. Jackson: University Press of Mississippi, 1986.

Canaday, John. "Spratling's Spirit Hovers Over Touristy Taxco." *New York Times,* December 25, 1967.

Cardoza y Aragón, Luis. "Diego Rivera's Murals in Mexico and the United States." In *Diego Rivera: A Retrospective,* ed. Cynthia Newman Helms. New York: Norton, 1986.

Caso, Alfonso. "Monte Albán, Richest Archaeological Find in America." *National Geographic* (October 1932), 487–512.

Cederwall, Sandraline, and Hal Riney. *Spratling Silver.* With a preface by Barnaby Conrad. San Francisco: Chronicle Books, 1990.

Charlot, Jean. *The Mexican Mural Renaissance, 1920–1925.* New Haven: Yale University Press, 1963.

Chase, Stuart. *Mexico: A Study of Two Americas.* New York: Macmillan, 1934.

———. "On the Street of the Delights." Review of *Little Mexico,* by William Spratling. *New York Herald-Tribune Books,* February 14, 1932, 5.

Cortes, Hernan. *Five Letters, 1519–1526.* Trans. J. Bayard Morris. New York: Norton, 1928.

Covarrubias, Miguel. *Indian Art of Mexico and Central America.* New York: Knopf, 1957.

———. *The Prince of Wales and Other Famous Americans.* With a preface by Carl Van Vechten. New York: Knopf, 1925.

Cowley, Malcolm. *Exile's Return: A Literary Odyssey of the 1920s.* New York: Viking Press, 1934.

Cox, James M. *Recovering Literature's Lost Ground: Essays in American Autobiography.* Baton Rouge: Louisiana State University Press, 1989.

Cox, Richard. *Caroline Durieux: Lithographs of the Thirties and Forties.* Baton Rouge: Louisiana State University Press, 1977.

Crane, Hart. *The Letters of Hart Crane.* Ed. Brom Weber. New York: Hermitage House, 1952.

Curtis, N. C. *New Orleans: Its Old Houses, Shops, and Public Buildings.* Philadelphia: J. B. Lippincott, 1933.

Davis, Mary L., and Greta Pack. *Mexican Jewelry.* Austin: University of Texas Press, 1963.

Delpar, Helen. *The Enormous Vogue of Things Mexican: Cultural Relations Between the United States and Mexico, 1920–1935.* Tuscaloosa: University of Alabama Press, 1992.

D'Harnoncourt, René. "The Exposition of Mexican Art." *International Studio* (October 1930), 50–51.

Duncan, Alastair. *Art Deco.* London: Thames and Hudson, 1988.

Duncan, Robert David. "William Spratling's Mexican World." *Texas Quarterly* 9 (Spring 1966): 97–104.

Encisco, Jorge. *Designs from Pre-Columbian Mexico.* New York: Dover, 1971.

Faulkner, William. *Mosquitoes.* New York: Boni and Liveright, 1927.

———. *New Orleans Sketches.* Ed. Carvel Collins. London: Sidgwick and Jackson, 1958.

———. *Selected Letters of William Faulkner.* Ed. Joseph Blotner. New York: Random House, 1977.

———. *Thinking of Home: William Faulkner's Letters to His Mother and Father 1918–1925.* Ed. James G. Watson. New York: Norton, 1992.

"Fiesta at Taxco," Foreign News. *Time,* July 7, 1941, 16.

Fine, Edward J., Debra Fine, and Lilli Sentz. "The Importance of Spratling," *Archives of Neurology* 51 (January 1994): 82–86.

Garrison, W. E. "Little Mexico." Review of *Little Mexico,* by William Spratling. *Christian Century* (July 6, 1932), 864.

Goldman, Shirfa M. *Contemporary Mexican Painting in a Time of Change.* Austin: University of Texas Press, 1977.

Gruber, Carol S. *Mars and Minerva: World War I and the Uses of Higher Learning in America*. Baton Rouge: Louisiana State University Press, 1975.

"He's Teaching Eskimos in Mexico." *Times-Picayune States Magazine,* June 5, 1949, 5–6.

Holcombe, Adele M. *John Sell Cotman*. London: British Museum Publications, 1978.

Jamison, Kay Redfield. *Touched with Fire: Manic-Depressive Illness and the Artistic Temperament*. New York: Free Press, 1993.

Kennedy, Richard S., ed. *Literary New Orleans: Essays and Meditations*. Baton Rouge: Louisiana State University Press, 1992.

Kenney, Catherine M. *Thurber's Anatomy of Confusion*. Camden, Conn.: Archon Books, 1984.

Kilham, Walter. "Mexican Renaissance." Parts 1 and 2. *Architectural Forum* 40 (November 1922); 41 (January 1923).

Knoblock, K. T. "Artist Finds Gil Trying to Awake Pride of Nation." *New Orleans Sunday Times-Picayune,* October 14, 1928, 30.

Lawrence, D. H. *Mornings in Mexico*. With an introduction by Richard Aldington. London, Eng.: William Heinemann, 1927.

"A Legacy of Laughter." *Time,* June 20, 1960, 62.

"Little Mexico." Review of *Little Mexico,* by William Spratling. *Saturday Review of Literature* (May 28, 1932), 760–61.

"The Loan Exhibition of Mexican Arts." *Bulletin of the Metropolitan Museum of Art,* October 1930, 210–16.

The Man from New Orleans. Film. Warner Brothers, 1948.

McEvoy, J. P. " 'Silver Bill,' Practical Good Neighbor." *Reader's Digest* (September 1945), 19–22.

McKean, Hugh F. *The "Lost" Treasures of Louis Comfort Tiffany*. New York: Doubleday, 1980.

McNickle, D'Arcy. *Indian Man: A Life of Oliver La Farge*. Bloomington: Indiana University Press, 1971.

"Memorial Rites Set for Writer." *New Orleans Times-Picayune,* December 15, 1957, 3.

"Mexican Artist Features Exhibit." *New Orleans Times-Picayune,* October 14, 1928, 21.

Meyer, Michael, and William Sherman. *The Course of Mexican History,* 5th ed. New York: Oxford University Press, 1995.

Milestones. *Time,* August 18, 1967, 70.

"Miss Scott Final Rites in Mexico." *New Orleans Item,* November 19, 1957, 1.

Montgomery, Robert E. *The Visionary D.H. Lawrence: Beyond Philosophy and Art*. Cambridge, Eng.: Cambridge University Press, 1994.

Morel, Vera. "Sketches by Local Artists Attract Many to Art Club." *New Orleans Morning Tribune,* October 19, 1927.

Morrill, Penny C., and Carole A. Berk. *Mexican Silver.* Atglen, Pa.: Schiffer Publishing, 1994.

Morrow, Elizabeth. *Casa Mañana.* With drawings by William Spratling. Croton Falls, N.Y.: Spiral Press, 1932.

———. *The Mexican Years.* New York: Spiral Press, 1953.

Nicolson, Harold. *Dwight Morrow.* New York: Harcourt, Brace, 1935.

Nieto, Lucia Garcia-Noriega. "Mexican Silver and the Taxco Style." Trans. by Ahmed Simeon. *Journal of Decorative and Popular Arts* (Fall 1988): 42–53.

Norton, Henry Kittredge. "What's the Matter with Mexico?" Parts 1 and 2. *World's Work* 56 (May–October): 528–38, 616–25; 57 (November–December): 47–56. New York: Doubleday, Doran, 1928.

Oeschner, Frederick. "New Orleans Man Wins Wide Notice." *New Orleans Morning Tribune,* October 16, 1927, 2.

"Our Southern Neighbors." *Nation* 119 (August 27, 1924): 204.

Percy, Walker. "New Orleans Mon Amour." *Harper's Magazine,* September 1968, 86, 88.

Phillips, Howard, *et al.* "The Many Sides of William Spratling." *Mexico D.F.,* August 20, 1967, 1–2.

Pitts, Stella. "The Quarter in the Twenties." *New Orleans Times-Picayune, Dixie,* November 26, 1972, 44.

"Planes Scour Ocean Area for Craft of Ex-Orleanian." *New Orleans Times-Picayune,* December 30, 1952.

Poore, C. G. "A Corner of the Mexican Maze." Review of *Little Mexico,* by William Spratling. *New York Times Book Review,* July 31, 1932, 3.

Powys, Llewelyn. "Half-Truths." *Dial,* April 1925, 330–32.

Rajnai, Miklós, ed. *John Sell Cotman, 1782–1842.* Ithaca: Cornell University Press, 1982.

Reed, Alma M. *The Mexican Muralists.* New York: Crown Publishers, 1960.

Reif, Rita. "A Genius of Mexican Jewelry." *New York Times,* June 2, 1985, Sec. 2, 31.

Rivera, Diego. *The Frescoes of Diego Rivera.* Ed. Jere Abbott. New York: Published for the Museum of Modern Art by the Plandome Press, 1933.

Rivera, Diego, with Gladys March. *My Art, My Life: An Autobiography.* New York: Citadel Press, 1960.

Rochfort, Desmond. *Mexican Muralists.* London: Laurence King, 1993.

———. *The Murals of Diego Rivera.* London: Journeyman Press, 1987.

Rohter, Larry. "In Mexico, Spratling Means Silver." *New York Times,* December 17, 1987, C14.

Ross, Patricia Fent. *Made in Mexico.* New York: Knopf, 1952.

Saxon, Lyle. "What's Doing." *New Orleans Times-Picayune,* October 25, 1925.

———. *Fabulous New Orleans.* New York: Appleton-Century, 1928.

Schee, Kim. "A Hollywood Scenarist Looks at Taxco's William Spratling." *Mexico Magazine,* October 1938, 6–9.

Simpson, Lesley Byrd. *Many Mexicos.* New York: G. P. Putnam's Sons, 1941.

Simpson, Lewis P. *The Fable of the Southern Writer.* Baton Rouge: Louisiana State University Press, 1993.

Stromberg, Gobi. "The Marketing and Production of Innovation: The Taxco Silver Industry." Ph.D. dissertation, University of California, Berkeley, 1976.

Tannenbaum, Frank. *Peace by Revolution: An Interpretation of Mexico.* New York: Columbia University Press, 1933.

"Thach Portrait Is Added to Archives." *Montgomery Advertiser,* June 22, 1921.

Thompson, T. P. "The Renaissance of the Vieux Carré." *Double Dealer* 3 (February 1922): 85–87, 89.

Toor, Frances. "Mexico Through Frightened Eyes." *Mexican Folkways* 2 (August–September 1926): 45–6.

———. "The Children Artists in the Mexican Revolution." *Mexican Folkways* 4 (January–March 1928): 6–23.

———. *A Treasury of Mexican Folkways.* New York: Crown Publishers, 1947.

———. *Frances Toor's New Guide to Mexico.* New York: Crown Publishers, 1948.

———. *Mexican Popular Arts.* Mexico City: Frances Toor Studios, 1939.

"Tourists Follow Artists to Nature's Hideouts." *Literary Digest,* December 15, 1934, 24.

Toussaint, Manuel. *Tasco, su historia, sus monumentos, características actuales y posibilidades turísticas.* Mexico City: Publicaciones de la Secretaria de Hacienda, 1931.

Townsend, Kim. *Sherwood Anderson.* Boston: Houghton Mifflin, 1987.

Troy, Nancy J. *Modernism and the Decorative Arts in France.* New Haven: Yale University Press, 1991.

"Un Viajero Alucinado en Mexico." *Jueves de Excelsior* 27 (September 1928): n.p.

Unterecker, John. *Voyager: A Life of Hart Crane.* New York: Farrar, Straus and Giroux, 1969.

"Valued Addition to Library at Auburn Noted by Biggin." *Montgomery Advertiser,* November 13, 1937.

White, Ray Lewis. *The Achievement of Sherwood Anderson: Essays in Criticism.* Chapel Hill: University of North Carolina Press, 1966.

William Spratling. Mexico City: Centro Cultural Arte Contemporaneo, 1987.

Williams, Adriana. *Covarrubias.* Austin: University of Texas Press, 1994.

Wilson, Edmund. *The Twenties: From Notebooks and Diaries of the Period*. Ed. Leon Edel. New York: Farrar, Straus and Giroux, 1975.

Wolfe, Bertram D. *The Fabulous Life of Diego Rivera*. New York: Stein and Day, 1963.

Wyatt-Brown, Bertram. "The Desperate Imagination: Writers and Melancholy in the Modern American South." In *Southern Writers and Their Worlds*, ed. Christopher Morris and Steven G. Reinhardt. College Station: Texas A&M University Press, 1996.

Index

Werlein, Elizabeth, 126
Weston, Edward, 114
Weyhe, Ernest, 173, 176
Weyhe Gallery, 128, 146, 147, 159, 162, 170, 171, 173, 175, 207, 228, 235
Woodward, Ellsworth, 78
"World of William Spratling, The," 290, 297
World War I, 17, 19, 24–25
World War II, 4, 250, 267, 268, 271, 277, 294

World's Work, 84, 124, 125
Wright, Frank Lloyd, 253

Zigrosser, Carl, 128, 129, 146, 147, 155, 157–58, 159, 161, 162, 166, 168, 170, 171, 172, 175, 176, 177, 210, 211, 212, 213, 227, 228, 232, 235, 250